How to Make Your Child a Reader for Life

How to Make Your Child a Reader for Life

Paul Kropp

Broadway Books
New York

BROADWAY

Designed by Donna Sinisgalli.

With thanks to those authors, publishers, and copyright owners for their kind permission to use extended quotations from copyrighted works:

From *Our Daughter Learns to Read and Write* by Marcia Baghban, © 1984 The International Reading Association. Reprinted by permission of the author and the International Reading Association.

From *Read for Your Life* by Joseph Gold, © 1990 Joseph Gold. Reprinted by permission of the author and Fitzhenry & Whiteside Limited.

From *Rock n' Roll and Reading, Part 2: The Next Chapter (1991)*. Reprinted by permission of the Toronto Public Library and CITY-TV/The New Music.

From *The Orphan Boy* by Tololwa Mollel and Paul Morin, text © 1990 Tololwa M. Mollel. Reprinted by permission of Oxford University Press Canada.

From *Wordstruck* by Robert MacNeil, © 1989 Neely Productions Ltd. Reprinted by permission of Viking Penguin USA.

Library of Congress Cataloging-in-Publication Data
Kropp, Paul.
How to make your child a reader for life / Paul Kropp.
—1st Broadway Books trade pbk. ed.
p. cm.
Rev. ed. of: Raising a reader. © 1996.
Includes bibliographical references and index.
1. Reading—Parent participation. 2. Children—Books and reading. 3. Teenagers—Books and reading. I. Kropp, Paul. Raising a reader.
LB1050.2 K76 2000
649'.58—dc21   00-020115
ISBN 0-385-47913-1

00 01 02 03 04 10 9 8 7 6 5 4 3 2 1

A c k n o w l e d g m e n t s

The author would like to thank the many people involved in writing and researching this book: my children and stepchildren—Jason, Justin, Alex, Ken, and Emma—for at-home and outside research; the various families I taped while they read to their children, especially the Bradshaws, Brandons, and Jardines; all the people who wrote or phoned with ideas; Elizabeth Muir, who advised on infant reading, Lori Rog, on phonemics, and Myra Johnson, on the reluctant reader; the many parents, teachers, and librarians who looked over chapters and reading lists, including Pat Hancock, Bryan Prince, Dr. Bob Arnold, Joyce McCorquodale, Chris Rhodes, Janie Jardine, Pat Deffett; Dawn Schutz; and Gwen Kistner and her colleagues at the Amherst Public Library. A special nod to Renate Brandon, who kept me writing for a broad audience; Paul Brandon, who ripped up my first drafts; Shelly Tanaka, who helped me polish up the subsequent ones; Frances Jones, who edited an earlier version of this book; and Jennifer Griffin, who made this current book possible.

Contents

Introduction

My search for reading solutions began thirty years ago on the first day I arrived to teach at an old-fashioned boys' vocational high school. I hadn't been offered this particular teaching assignment because of my years at Columbia studying seventeenth-century poetry, or because I happened to love the works of Shakespeare. I had been sent to Parkview School because I'm over six feet tall and once took wrestling as part of university phys ed.

My assignment was to teach "reading" to teenage boys who either couldn't or wouldn't read much of anything. It meant that I spent two days a week reading a story and answering questions on the blackboard, one day with a noisy filmstrip machine that projected stories line by line on a screen, and two days with a few moldy novels of the *Silas Marner* variety.

I was struggling through one of those novels with "the guys"—actually young men who ranged in age from thirteen to twenty—when a student I'll call Randy approached me after class. Randy was the smallest person in his group, a slouching boy with large freckles and thick glasses. He always spoke in a whisper.

"Excuse me, sir," he began. "I'm having a little trouble reading the book."

"Oh?"

"Actually, I'm having a lot of trouble," Randy admitted.

"Well, I know it's a bit difficult," I said.

"The truth is, sir, I can't read it at all."

I raised one eyebrow and leaned back in my chair. "Maybe I could give you some extra help after school."

"No, no. That's not what I mean. I mean, *none* of us can read the book, sir."

"None of you?"

"Except Don and Froggy, and they don't really want to read it. The rest of us just can't. The guys asked me to tell you."

"Oh," I said.

"The guys wondered if you could maybe find something else."

"Like what?"

"Like movies, maybe. The teacher before you showed a lot of movies."

It didn't seem to me that movies or videos were the solution to the reading problems of Randy or Froggy or anyone else in that class. What they needed were some books that they *could* read and would *want* to read, books that just didn't exist at the time.

So I set out to write them myself. I began by researching everything I could find about reading, reading difficulty, vocabulary development, and areas of student interest. And I kept checking back with Randy's class.

"It says here," I told them, "that students at your age level are interested in baseball and horses."

The guys looked at each other and shook their heads.

"So what are you interested in?" I asked.

They laughed. "Sex, sir. We're interested in sex!"

When I finally finished my first book for reluctant readers, the guys were disappointed that there wasn't much sex. But there was a lot of action, and there were teenage characters they could understand. What's more, I'd used all the research into reading difficulty to make sure that each page of the book was easy enough for Randy and the others to read on their own.

Since then, besides writing a number of young-adult novels for ordinary teenagers, I've written and edited some fifty books for kids who don't much like to read. In the process, the kids themselves have taught me a great deal about reading and writing, and about the kinds of books that work for them.

Back when I was a graduate student, I used to think that reading problems were restricted to a small fraction of the population. I was under the wonderfully naive impression that most children and adults could read well enough to get by. I thought that almost everyone knew the pleasure of sitting down to read a good book.

But I was wrong. What I've learned over the last thirty years is that literacy is a problem for many of today's young people. The problem is not limited to students like Randy and Froggy but extends to many, many kids who aren't reading well—or aren't reading much. Though most young children are learning the rudiments of reading in primary school, many of them stop developing as readers in grades four and five. Another group stops bothering to read in grades eight and nine. Among our top students, many have failed to develop the range of sophisticated reading skills they'll need in college and later in life. Worst of all, too many young people today are growing up with attitudes that will always keep them apart from books and the joy that reading can be.

Perhaps that's why you, a parent, feel anxious about your own child's reading. When I travel around the country to talk about reading, parents keep coming up to ask the same difficult questions:

- "How can I get my child to be a reader?"
- "My son doesn't like to read anything. How can I get him started?"
- "Are phonics the same as phonemics?"
- "How can I work with my daughter's teacher to get her reading?"
- "What book would you suggest for my nephew? He's four and . . ."

I finally decided to answer all these questions and many others in one book—this one. My hope is that you can use these solutions, from the basic three Rs in Chapter 1 to the ideas and suggestions throughout the rest of the book, to help your child become a reader for life.

HOW TO READ THIS BOOK

You don't have to read every page of this book to get the information you need for your child. I do hope that parents will tackle the material in the first four chapters because the basic principles are important. After that, you'll likely prefer to go right to the chapter that deals with your child's age group. Chapters 12, 13, and 14 handle special problems—the bored reader, the reluctant reader, and the gifted reader—and will be of particular interest to some parents. The last chapter deals with the future of reading in an age of computers and the Internet.

In each chapter for a particular age group, I have suggested various books and included a "must-have" list at the end. In creating these lists, I tried to select just a few hundred excellent titles so you can make specific requests of your bookstore or library.

The "must-have" lists recommend fifty books worth buying, begging, or borrowing for keeps. These are books of proven appeal, written in many different styles, ranging from picture books to fiction to poetry. Of course, I hope that your child will read many other books as well. In the United States, it should be possible for every child to have access to a great variety of books—gifts from relatives, books borrowed from libraries or friends, books on loan from schools or next-door neighbors or picked up for ten cents at a lawn sale. But I feel that every child deserves a special bookshelf of truly excellent books to read and reread, perhaps to love. These "must-have" lists contain my choices for that bookshelf.

I have developed all these lists based on suggestions from parents, kids, teachers, librarians, and booksellers around the country, yet ultimately the choices are personal. If you find a new title that should be included in the next edition, drop me a note. Better yet, have your son or daughter write the letter, since reading and writing are flip sides of the literacy coin.

The boxes contain other bits and pieces of information— statistics, summaries of research, addresses and advice that might be helpful to you. In special boxes marked "Parent to Parent" I've reprinted suggestions I've received from parents like you. Some of these came in during radio phone-in shows; some are from parents I met at conferences—all are valuable ideas based on the experience of real families.

The goal of all this is to help you raise your child to become a reader for life. As a parent, you are essential in making sure that books and the sheer joy of reading are part of your child's experience. No one can encourage reading nearly as well as you can. No other skill you teach or gift you give will ever be quite as important.

How to Make Your Child a Reader for Life

Why *You* Are Essential

If you stop to consider what's involved in learning to read, it should come as no surprise that your child will need your help to become a reader for life.

Between the ages of two and five, your child will have to learn that print and language connect, that books provide both stories and information, that there are twenty-six letters in the alphabet that come in big and small sizes, straight and curly versions and make over fifty different sounds.

Between the ages of four and nine, your child will have to master dozens of phonics rules and word-attack strategies, learn to recognize 3,000 words with just a glance, and develop a comfortable reading speed approaching 100 words a minute. He will have to learn to combine words on the page with a half-dozen squiggles called punctuation into something—a voice or image in his mind—that gives back meaning.

And that's just the beginning. Between the ages of nine and fifteen, your child will have to double that reading speed, expand his recognition vocabulary to 100,000 words, learn to skim over some sections of print and to slow down to study others, all while simultaneously questioning the text and appreciating the author's artistry. The famous American novelist John Steinbeck summed up the task of learning to read as "the greatest single effort that the human mind undertakes, and he must do it as a child."

But your child cannot do it alone. To become a real reader, your child needs you. No matter how good your child's school may be, all children still need a parent who will

- read to them;
- help them with phonemics and phonics and the struggles of early reading;
- listen to their reading when they're young;
- talk to them about their reading when they're older;
- organize a quiet time so reading can happen;
- buy or borrow books and other reading material;
- serve as a model of adult reading and interest in books.

Without you, your child is unlikely to develop the attitudes that make reading easy and fun. Without you, your child can fall into that fourth-grade reading slump that affects a third of our children. Without you, your child may well lose interest in reading at age twelve or thirteen, just when he's capable of crossing over to adult books. Without you, your child is unlikely to become a reader for life.

Unfortunately, learning to read is not an easy task. It isn't like learning to walk, for instance, because the specific instinct for reading isn't part of our genetic makeup. Nor is learning to read like learning to bat a ball or play the piano. If our children show little talent for baseball or music, we know that life offers many other outlets for their energy and creativity. But if our children don't learn to read, they are virtually crippled as they attempt to deal with modern life.

At one time, of course, the skill of reading was required by only a limited portion of the population. Medieval kings and queens had letters and manuscripts read to them. Medieval peasants lived in a world of spoken language and had little reason to read for themselves. Right up until the nineteenth century, fewer than one person in ten—even in Western countries—was able to read. When Charles Dickens's great novels first appeared in the 1830s, they weren't snapped up by masses of Englishmen and women eager for the latest best-seller. They were bought in installments, like magazines, by families and groups of friends who might have only one "reader" among them. It was the job of the reader to read the book out loud to the rest of the family, or to the friends at work, or at the pub.

Throughout most of history, reading has been done out loud. Novels were read to family groups gathered around the hearth; poetry was performed with musical accompaniment after a feast; married couples read to each other before going to bed. Reading—because it took place out loud—was a social event.

It still should be. Most families today know that reading books out loud is very important for young children. According to one study, almost two-thirds of all families with young children say they regularly find time to read aloud. These families are reported to spend an average of twenty-two minutes a day reading, or listening to their children read, or talking about what's read.

Sadly, the same study reveals that family time spent reading together declines rapidly as children get older. Apparently, only a tiny fraction of families read out loud together for more than a few years in their child's life. Parents are too busy. Or they're too tired. Or it's easier to turn on the television or pop in a

Two Thousand Years of Reading Aloud

For most of recorded history, reading aloud has been the norm and reading silently has been regarded as an unusual procedure.

St. Augustine marveled that his colleague, St. Ambrose, could read while "his voice and tongue were at rest." Even St. Benedict, setting his rule for monks, did not require silent reading but that each monk should "do so in such a way as not to disturb anyone else."

Reading aloud was a source of such entertainment that Pliny the Younger (b. A.D. 62) is said to have read his own works to houseguests for two days straight. Reports do not indicate if the guests returned for another visit.

video. And the kid can read for himself, anyway, can't he? And what are schools for if they don't make the kids read? And . . . and . . . There are so many excuses—as many excuses as there are teenagers who can't be bothered to read.

This is a terrible shame. Reading out loud holds so many joys for both parents and children that I see no reason to call it quits just because children have mastered enough of the basics to begin reading themselves.

How long should you and your child keep reading together? Frankly, I don't think families should *ever* stop reading together. The educated elite have always read aloud to each other and used reading as a focal point for discussion and imagination. Only in our time have we turned reading into a solitary activity.

Reading out loud isn't nearly as difficult or time-consuming as it might seem. A short story can be read aloud in about thirty minutes. A magazine or newspaper article frequently takes less time. Even an adult novel, read twenty minutes a day, often can be finished in two or three weeks.

Many books are now available on tape, read by their authors or by professional actors with wonderful verve and flair. I know a single father who drives with his children from New York to a cottage upstate every other Friday night in the summer months. The trip takes about three hours—just enough time to listen to a tape of Charles Dickens's *David Copperfield* or Anne Rice's *Interview with the Vampire* or Sue Grafton's *G Is for Gumshoe*, which he borrows from the public library. It is almost the same as reading used to be a century ago, except that the tape deck has become the "reader." And just as at any social reading throughout history, the "reader" will be asked to repeat sections (the rewind button) or to stop (pause button) while the family asks questions about the plot or shares an idea that the story has prompted.

If you think of reading as sharing, you can see how important the social aspect must be. Reading lets us access our collective experience, to harvest the skills and wisdom of all humanity. And reading brings joy—the sheer fun of stepping into other lives, other universes—of getting caught up in a world of imagination.

THE BASICS

Your child will not become a reader overnight, or in sixty days with a phonics-based CD-ROM program, or because I can offer you a handful of gimmicks to make it happen. Your child will become a reader with your loving involvement and your

---

The Three Rs

1. Read with your child every day.
2. Reach into your wallet to buy books, magazines, and other reading material for your child and yourself.
3. Rule the media. Put a reasonable limit on television, video, computer time, and video games so there will be time for reading in your child's life.

---

commitment to a process that stretches from infancy to the teenage years and beyond. Here are three basic rules to get you started:

1. Read with your child every day.

You and your child deserve a regular reading time, fifteen to thirty minutes long, every day. Don't begin with a plan to read every other day, or twice a week, or whenever you happen to feel like it. You are going to miss days even with the best of intentions. Your commitment should be for every day so that the books you read will have some continuity. You know that if you put a novel down for a week, you'll likely have a hard time picking up the threads of the story. It is just as difficult for your child. Reading time should become a habit for you, something that is expected by your child, an activity you both can anticipate with pleasure.

Where you read doesn't matter—in your child's bedroom, on a reading chair, in the living room. When you read doesn't matter—after school, after dinner, before bed. How well you read doesn't matter. All of us, as parents, are the best readers for our own children.

What does matter is that you read *with* your child, not just *to* your child. Reading time is not simply time to open a book and read out loud. It's time to open a book to share reading and ideas. As parents, I think we do this almost instinctively. When I tape-recorded mothers and fathers reading aloud for this book, many apologized to me for talking to their children so much during their daily reading time. It was as if they had done something wrong instead of doing exactly what oral reading is all about.

Since reading is a social experience, it should always be accompanied by cuddling, talking, joking, and asking and answering questions. Especially for older children, some of the most valuable reading experiences are *not* reading; they come with the talk that is prompted by the book.

Much reading research in the 1990s has shown that phonemic awareness—a sense of the alphabet letters and the sounds they make—is crucial for early reading development. What better or more natural way to develop phonemic awareness than by reading together. While I don't think parents should regularly do reading lessons with their kids, there's much to be said for sounding out words together or asking your child to read simple words in a story. So long as you remember that long-term reading achievement comes from attitude and enjoyment, then a little time spent skill building will fit in easily.

The first reading for most children comes from memory. You'll have read one book so often that your child knows the book by heart. Your child will then want to "read" it to you, because your nightly reading will have shown just how important reading is. Later, as your child learns to recognize more words and perhaps sounds out a word or two, the memorized text will be more read than remembered. And later still, on nights when Mom is too tired or Dad wants to quit before the end of the chapter, your child will want to read on—out loud—to you.

Just be careful you don't respond to this success by getting lax about the daily reading. There are many important reasons

What About Families Who *Can't* Read Together?

With all the talk about the importance of reading with our children, families who *can't* read together often are forgotten. There are tens of millions of such families in the United States where the parents do not speak English at home or have low literacy skills themselves. What can we suggest for these families?

- *Tell stories.* Recent research indicates that simply telling stories out loud develops literacy in children as effectively as reading together. What's more, the storytelling can be in any language, and there will still be a strong impact on the children's ability to read in English. Any kind of story will do—family histories, folktales, made-up stories—so long as the storytelling is done regularly and in a loving environment.
- *Read together in your own language.* Families whose first language is not English do not have to struggle through English children's books; they should read in their own language. It is the *practice* of reading and listening that is important, not the language.

for you to keep reading out loud with your child as long as you possibly can.

When your child enters first grade, he can understand roughly 6,000 spoken words but can read only 100 or so. Both of these numbers continue to grow through elementary school, until, sometime around eighth grade, your child's listening and reading vocabularies will become equal. All through these years, your child needs your help to understand the meanings of new, more difficult words, sentences, and ideas. He needs a parent to look up what a "mandible" is or explain why there's no triceratops at the zoo. He needs you to laugh with him at a D. M. Pinkwater novel as much as he needed you to help sound out the handful of words in P. D. Eastman's *Are You My Mother?* As a parent, you should keep reading—or at least being there for the reading and the talk—as long as your child will let you. Why would you cut short such a delightful family time any sooner?

Sometimes family reading can yield results that are quite astounding. I knew a family who read regularly with all four of

Children's Reading: The News Isn't Good

From the first National Assessment of Educational Progress report:

- Percentage of fourth graders who read daily for pleasure: 45.7
- Percentage of twelfth graders who read daily for pleasure: 24.4
- Percentage of fourth graders who use the library once a week: 59
- Percentage of twelfth graders who use the library once a week: 10.2

Among eighth-grade students: 71 percent watch three or more hours of television a day; 27 percent read daily for pleasure.

their children. The first three children were very bright. They quickly became readers themselves, and went on to college and professional careers. The family's last child—I'll call her Dana— was diagnosed as developmentally delayed and spent much of her life in special schools and special classes. Nonetheless, the family kept reading with Dana, knowing that books would en- rich her life. Dana's mother says, "We treated her just like the other children, even though the doctors told us that our daugh- ter was limited and we couldn't expect very much from her."

I taught Dana in a regular tenth-grade class in which we were studying *Of Mice and Men* by John Steinbeck. After read- ing the first chapter of the novel out loud, I asked the kids to continue on their own since my throat was sore. There were the usual grumbles of protest, but it was Dana who raised her hand. "I'll read chapter two, sir." And she did, with fluency and distinc- tive character voices and wonderful animation, all with no help from me.

After four years, Dana went out on a co-op program to work at a library where her bright smile and fluent reading brought delight to everyone. Today she still works as a library helper and still loves to read. Dana has done far better, in fact, than many of her "normal" classmates. And her achievements, I think, are a tribute both to her and to her family, and to the fact that they never stopped reading out loud together.

2. Reach into your wallet to buy books, magazines, and other reading material for your child and yourself.

Children should have their own books on a special bookshelf someplace in the home. Books from the library and school are wonderful, and books borrowed from friends are important, but nothing can replace books of one's own.

Why? Because the books your child owns are the ones that you'll read to him over and over again. And the books that are read to your child over and over again at ages two and three become the first books your child will read for himself at ages four and five. These are the books he will keep going back to, reading and rereading, sometimes long after you would think they'd been outgrown. One study says that some of the books on your child's bookshelf will be read as many as 300 times before he begins to lose interest in them. This kind of repeated rereading is essential for building reading skills, but it can happen only when children have their own books.

I wish every family could afford to buy a book a month for their children. Children need a wide range of books in order to find the ones they'll read over and over again—and it's hard to predict which books those will be. When our first child was two,

---

Parent to Parent Egg and a Book

"I've raised three children and all three are now readers. I suppose they always saw their father and me with our noses in a book, but we made sure we did more than that. Books were always part of our children's lives. At Christmas and birthdays, whatever the other presents, there was always a book. Even at Easter, when other kids might get piles of chocolates in the Easter baskets, my kids got chocolates, an Easter egg, and a book."

—Elizabeth Crangle

my wife and I wanted Jason to enjoy E. B. White's *Charlotte's Web* or one of the other gorgeous books he'd received from his grandparents. But the book Jason really loved was an inexpensive, easy-to-read book called *Hand, Hand, Fingers, Thumb* by Al Perkins. *Charlotte's Web* was a wonderful read for my wife and me, but *Hand, Hand, Fingers, Thumb* had rhythm, rhyme, and action written into the story. I ended up reading the book to Jason so many times that today, almost thirty years later, I can still recite most of the book from memory. It's no wonder that *Hand, Hand, Fingers, Thumb* became the first book Jason "read" for himself at age four.

The point I'm making is that it is very hard for us, as parents, to guess which books will be our child's favorites. I can suggest, as I do later on, that Lois Ehlert's *Nuts to You!* or Katherine Paterson's *Bridge to Terabithia* might well become a favorite. But only your child can make that choice.

If you try to add a book a month to your child's bookshelf, each new book will be another chance to find one that might become a favorite. If not, at least you and your child have had an opportunity to read something new together.

Buying books for your child need not be terribly expensive. Libraries frequently offer books no longer in circulation for less than a dollar each. Secondhand bookstores sometimes have an excellent range of children's books from fifty cents for a paperback novel to five dollars for a gorgeous picture book. Lawn sales are good sources for cast-off books with prices that may start at a dollar a title in the morning, but often come down to pennies by the end of the day.

For young families without much income, grandparents and other relatives are a wonderful source of books. When I was a graduate student living on a few thousand dollars a year, we couldn't afford to buy beautiful picture books for our sons. But

Such a Pity

When Benjamin Franklin, the famous inventor and publisher, was serving as the American ambassador to France, he often impressed French intellectuals with the wisdom of his remarks. At one dinner, the question was raised, "What human condition deserves the most pity?" Each of the guests responded, but the answer that is still remembered is Benjamin Franklin's: "A lonesome man on a rainy day who does not know how to read."

my parents could, and Aunt Carol could, and sometimes friends would pass on a book that their kids no longer read. If you put the word out that you'd like to receive books for your child, then birthdays and Christmas and Hanukkah will bring many new titles for your child's bookshelf.

Still, the most exciting way to acquire books is a trip to the bookstore. It gives your child a chance to choose his own brand-spanking-new books with that wonderful feel only new books have. Your child will pick books just as you and I do—just as any reader does—by the cover, or by the back-cover blurb, or by what friends recommend. Yet real-life choices always have to be tempered by real-life limitations. It's your money that's being spent, even if it's only on an inexpensive Golden Book or a re-maindered picture book on sale for $2.99. It's quite fair for you not to fork out for another Animorphs novel, or to suggest that Lois Lowry's *The Giver* really is a better book than whatever Saturday-morning-cartoon spin-off might be on display. Because reading is a social experience, both you and your child should have a say in what's purchased and what's read. Just remember that the act of choosing a book, like the act of reading, is empowering for your child. Try to support that choice as much as you reasonably can.

One family I know always buys two books for their ten-year-old son when they go to the bookstore. One is chosen entirely by the child, another is chosen together with the parents. The family sets a price limit on each book that might be lower than what they could spend on just one title, but the method gives an important message. It's vitally important that you listen to your child and try to respect the books he loves; but it's just as important that you enjoy what you buy and read together. There are some 30,000 children's books in print and another 4,500 appearing every year. Don't lose the joy of reading by spending too much time or money on books that give you, the parent, no pleasure. There are many more that will bring delight to both you and your child.

And while you're at the bookstore, why not buy a book or two for yourself? You're not just a parent, you're a model. If you read, your child is likely to read. If you surround yourself with books and magazines, so will your child. According to research, most readers come from families with a wide assortment of books, magazines, and newspapers around the house. You don't have to be rich to make your home "print rich." This kind of rich is an attitude toward books—an attitude that says books are worth reading.

Some years ago, I taught at a school that encouraged teachers to visit the families of students. I remember going into a dismal apartment building where the single father of my best student lived. The father's apartment wasn't in much better condition than the building, with yellowed paint and cracked linoleum floors. But John's father had made the place "print rich," with books, newspapers, pamphlets, catalogs, church flyers, coffeetable books, car-repair manuals—more print than I had at my house. And John was a reader.

I also visited the home of a teenage boy whose reading skills never got beyond *Scuffy the Tugboat*. Ron's parents kept a tidy home and were at a loss to understand why their son didn't read. "We have books," they said, pointing to a single shelf of encyclopedias, *Reader's Digest* condensed books, and a half-dozen yellowed paperbacks. There was no other printed material in the house. When asked, Ron's parents told me they never read magazines or newspapers. I guessed from their bookshelf that they didn't read books either. Yet the mother was convinced Ron's illiteracy was caused by some brain damage no doctor could detect.

The point is this: You'll never make your child a reader for life merely by saying that reading is important. You have to show him. Even if you're not a reader or if you've fallen out of the habit of reading, you'll find pleasure in reading with your child. Let that be a basis for making your home "print rich"—buying some books, borrowing many others, and reading with your child every day.

3. Rule the media. Put a reasonable limit on television, video, computer time, and video games so there will be time for reading in your child's life.

By eighth grade, average American children will have spent 12,000 hours in front of the television set. They will have seen 300,000 commercials and more than 8,000 murders on the small screen. They will have watched everything from cartoons to R-rated and sometimes X-rated movies. They will have spent more hours watching television than in school—more hours

How Much TV Is Too Much?

Many studies show that reading time declines as TV watching goes up—and some show declining reading skills as a result. But pinpointing just how much TV is too much becomes harder. According to Susan Neuman of the University of Lowell in Massachusetts, there is little statistical difference in children's reading skills whether they watch two or three hours of TV a day. But beyond four hours a day, "the effects were negative and increasingly deleterious."

being a passive observer than they will spend on anything else in life except sleeping.

Too many hours.

A growing body of research indicates that a child who watches more than three hours of television a day will suffer problems in reading, at school, and in social development.

A long-term study by Caroline Snow of Harvard University reinforces this. Dr. Snow writes about the importance of family in the reading achievement of children. She demonstrates again what researchers have long known—that families who have books around the house tend to have children who read. She also found that the educational expectations set by the mother are very important in motivating a child to be a reader.

But Dr. Snow's most striking finding was about television. Her study determined that the most important factor affecting reading that is under the direct control of a parent is "rules on watching television." Students from families who set rules on television watching made significantly greater progress in developing both reading and general literacy than families without rules.

The research is clear—too much television can interfere with the intellectual development of children. Unfortunately, the research can't tell you exactly how much TV is too much. Nor can it tell you exactly what rules to apply to the television viewing for *your* child, in *your* family, where *you* live.

Nonetheless, I would suggest that three hours of television a day is probably more than enough for any child. The virtue of the three-hours-a-day rule of thumb is its simplicity. Research is unclear on the effect of less TV watching; it is very clear that more than three hours a day is not good for your children.

Of course, you'll have to talk to your children about how that three hours a day will be applied. May they watch no TV one day and six hours the next? Does a PBS special count? Are videos part of the total? The rules you set should work for you, your partner, and your children. Like any parental rules, they should be firm without being etched in stone. But there must be rules. Your child *will not* become a better student after another hour of Nintendo, or *Baywatch*, or the latest blood-and-gore video. Your child *will* do better in school if there's some quiet time at home—to read, to write a story, to dream.

One of the most wonderful suggestions I received for this book came from a teacher named Regis O'Conner. In raising his four children, he and his wife set aside the hour after supper, from seven to eight o'clock, as a quiet time. "The TV went off, there was no music, no radio, no stereo, no distractions. The rules were the same for us and for the kids. We could do one of three things—read, draw, or do homework. When the hour was up, the TV could go back on, or the kids could play a record or do whatever they wanted, but frequently we would keep on

---

Kids and Television

- Number of hours of television per week watched by children aged six to eleven: 10.9
- Number of hours of television per week watched by children aged twelve to seventeen: 12.75
- Additional hours spent playing video games: 2.0
- Number of murders a child will have seen on television before the end of elementary school: 8,000
- Rank of television watching in encouraging violent behavior among children, according to teacher surveys: #1

---

reading, or drawing or just thinking." The O'Conner family members are scattered now in various professions and locations across North America, but all the children became avid readers.

Setting rules on television—creating a time for reading to happen—will not be easy. Your children will feel no hesitation in telling you about Billy next door who watches cartoons with breakfast and movies while he's going to sleep. Your older children may offer very compelling arguments about the intellectual importance of *The Simpsons* and the reputed excellence of tonight's made-for-TV docudrama. You'll be told that "all the kids" have a Nintendo or some such device, and that your children will be social outcasts if they don't have one too. In fact, there is a tremendous industry—from television to movies and toys—that profits at the expense of your child's real development.

You have to stand up in the midst of all that and say no. No, the TV won't be on after 9:30 P.M. No, one hour of a video game is enough. No, there is more to life than another Arnold Schwarzenegger movie.

By doing that, you'll make sure there's time for reading in your child's life. If you make sure there are books available to fill that time, and you offer your own involvement to help read those books, you can virtually ensure that your child will become a reader for life.

Learning to Read—
Throughout Life

One of the most wonderful aspects of being a parent is joining in the process by which your child becomes a reader. In modern life, reading has become so tied into children's growth that each stage in learning to read offers a window on that stage of childhood.

When your infant holds up a storybook and begins to babble as if she were reading, she's experimenting with stories and the idea of a book. When your child begins decoding those first few words in a favorite book, she's trying to gain mastery over print and the whole world of language. Later, as your child gains confidence and fluency in reading, her bookshelf will mirror her exploration of the world outside your home. Then, in her teenage years, your child will offer critical commentary on everything from J. R. R. Tolkien to her history textbook, just as she often looks critically at herself, at you, and at the world she's moving into.

Obviously, learning to read doesn't happen at a single time in your child's life. Learning to read is a process, developed in stages, and your role as a parent is somewhat different at each stage.

In this chapter, I'd like to lay some groundwork by explaining why almost every child wants to learn how to read. Then I'll look at the usual stages in reading development, so you can understand how reading grows and changes for your child. I'll describe briefly how reading is taught in school and how you can support this work at home. Then I'll focus on the two danger times for young readers—fourth grade and ninth grade—so you can be aware of steps you can take to keep your child reading right into adulthood.

WHY YOUR CHILD
WANTS TO READ

Given the chance, almost every child wants to learn to read. You can see the desire in infants studying picture books, in second graders trying to figure out difficult words, in the fact that more than 90 percent of our children have mastered the basics of reading by the end of third grade. For so many children to read so well, so early, the motivation must be strong.

If you understand why your child wants to be a reader, you can help her along the way. And you can avoid some of the pitfalls and gimmicks on the market that won't help your child in the long run.

Here are five reasons why your child wants to learn to read:

- Reading helps a child make sense of the world she lives in.
- Reading is a vital social skill for everything from school to video games.
- Reading is fun.
- Reading is a wonderful way to spend time with you.

- Reading must be a very grown-up activity, because Mom and Dad are always doing it.

From your child's perspective, the world is a pretty confusing place. In the first few years of life, she must try to make sense of the end products of several thousand years of civilization—everything from the proper use of a spoon to how to work the computer. There is no better tool to help in this task than reading. My own children learned every city located along our local commuter line by reading the maps on the train. This was long before they officially knew phonics or could even read a whole sentence. Once your child understands that the word *Oakville* means "We'd better get ready to get off the train," she'll understand that reading gives us control over our lives.

The Harvard Study

Caroline Snow and her associates at Harvard University did a long-term study on home factors affecting literacy. Here are the factors that encourage childhood reading, ranked in order of their effect:

1. Home "literacy" environment: books, newspapers, attitudes
2. Mother's educational expectations of the child
3. Mother's own education
4. Parent-child interaction

The father's expectations and background apparently had no effect on reading, but they were important in promoting the child's development of writing skills.

Your child also will see that reading is a vital social skill. There is enormous peer pressure to read all the signs and symbols of modern life. One of the big motivating factors in my own reading development was the game of Monopoly. My older sister and her friends made it clear that I wasn't going to be able to play Monopoly with them until I could read the property deeds myself. No wonder my early reading vocabulary was full of such words as *Pacific* and *Boardwalk*.

Reading is also great fun. Your child will find delight in the challenge of figuring out a tough word, or reading a difficult story aloud, just as you might enjoy tackling a crossword puzzle. Any success at early reading tasks will bolster your child's sense of self-esteem as well as give her mastery over the world around her.

Finally, I cannot emphasize enough your own importance as a motivator for reading. Your attitude toward reading—expressed in what you do more than in what you say—is vital in motivating your child to be a reader. If you take the time to read with your child every day, then the physical act of reading will always be associated in her mind with warmth, safety, and love. If you surround yourself with books, magazines, and newspapers, and make time to read yourself, then your child will see reading as something adults do. According to statistics, your attitude toward reading is the strongest predictor of whether your child will be a reader or not. That's why you are so important all along the way.

Because the forces that motivate reading are so strong and so important in a child's life, parents shouldn't have to add artificial incentives or gimmicks. No child will learn to read because you tell her that someday she'll be able to appreciate Shakespeare. No child will be motivated for long by the promise of an A on a report card or a free slice of pizza for finishing a book. No child will be much interested in reading books that have nothing to do with

Parent to Parent Making Books

"My mother and I made books even before I knew how to read. These would be pictures-only books, carefully drawn and colored by me, then sewn together with my mother. Eventually I got the pictures to tell a story. Then reading just seemed to follow naturally."

—Wenda Watt

her own life, even if you pay her a quarter a title to do so. All these rewards—these gimmicks—are external to the reading. They don't connect with the social aspects of reading or with children's basic curiosity about books and life. The real motivation for reading always must be found in reading itself—and in the books, magazines, and stories that go with that. You can encourage this best by being part of your child's reading and by modeling reading for her. These acts are what create readers for life.

STAGE ONE:
THE IDEA OF READING

The first stage in learning to read is to understand that there is meaning in the words and pictures on a page. This stage frequently begins in infancy, even before your child's first birthday. She'll have sat on your lap and heard you talk through so many picture books that she understands the *idea* of a book even before she can say the word. When your child sees a stop sign, you'll read the word *stop* and then explain what it means and why you have to do it. The explanation may not make much sense to your two-year-old, but the connection between a printed word (and the red octagonal sign) and an action (stopping the car) demonstrates that words are out there for a reason. Your child begins learning very early that words and books bring meaning to a complex world.

STAGE TWO:
LEARNING TO LISTEN

The second stage in becoming a reader, for most children, is called "phonemic awareness" by teachers and reading specialists. While the phrase is a bit awkward, it simply means that children have to become aware of the letters in our alphabet and the variety of sounds they make. The latest research from California and Texas suggests that phonemic awareness is an essential skill base for further reading development, especially for disadvantaged families.

Other reading specialists wonder whether kids need to learn phonemes *first*, or whether other reading activities are just as important.

We can sidestep the debate by conceding that kids certainly need to figure out different letters and their sounds sooner or later if they are to become proficient readers. This isn't as easy as it seems. Many of the letters in our alphabet sound very similar, and it can be difficult for kids to hear the difference between the final consonants in *bid* and *bit*.

Some children, of course, figure out letter-sound correspondences just by reading along with you, or by generalizing from the handful of words they know. Others benefit from some specific practice—reading picture books aloud to emphasize the initial letter, doing a workbook with Mom or Dad, even watching *Sesame Street*. Without question, children who know most of the letters and their sounds are better off in first grade than children who are still struggling with those concepts.

STAGE THREE:
CRACKING THE CODE

When your child begins reading by herself, sometime between the ages of four and six, her progress will be made in fits and starts. There will be a word or two, a sentence or two, lots of mistakes and gradual correction. Your child won't begin reading with the rules of phonics; she'll begin with words: *stop, Mom, Daddy, Rugrats*. Our printed language is a code. Once your child understands that it's possible to decode these strange marks on the page, she'll naturally want to try to read them.

New Zealand educator Sylvia Ashton Warner used children's curiosity about their own world to help Maori children begin reading. She wrote out lists of words that pertained to her students' lives, from *mumps* to *helicopter*, words that worked far better than any purchased reading programs. You can use the same method to write out lists of words that pertain to your child's life—*Auntie Sylvia, Ralph the dog, Nintendo*. Or you could write *milk* on the milk container, or stick some magnetic letters on the fridge, starting with your child's name. As a parent, you can make words and reading fun for preschoolers.

The only serious mistakes you could make are to turn reading into work or to expect too much from your child. A number of preschool reading drill programs are on the market. These range from simple flashcards to fairly-slick computer programs like *Reader Rabbit*. Sometimes, for some children, they actually work. But I wonder what the hurry is. Your child is going to

---

One-third of 500,000 = 31?

There are almost half a million words in our English language—the largest language on earth, incidentally—but a third of all our writing is made up of only thirty-one words. Here they are, in order of descending frequency:

a, of, and, that, he, the, I, to, in, was, it, all, had, said, as, have, so, at, him, they, be, his, we, but, not, with, are, on, you, for, one.

---

learn to read—at her own pace, in her own way—without having to listen to an audiotape on phonic blending just before bedtime. Far better to associate reading with books, discovery, fun, and your love than to turn it into a childhood task done to earn parental approval.

If you read regularly with your child, the movement from simple word recognition to more complex reading will happen quite naturally. Sometimes it occurs so swiftly as to seem almost miraculous. One day your child seems to be struggling along, reading a word here, a word there. Two or three weeks later, she's zipping through a familiar book, reading to you with obvious joy and pride.

Likely we will never understand all the factors that make this first reading breakthrough happen, nor can we be sure just how it will take place for your child. For some children, reading simply clicks. Suddenly the child can recognize many words and seems to have created some internal rules for how our language works. What's more, the recognition of words and sentences becomes generalized so the *hop* in *Hop on Pop* can appear in any book, or a number of different typefaces, and still be recognized. Often this all happens at home, well before your child attends school.

For other children, the progress is less dramatic. More words are gradually recognized, reading speed slowly increases, longer words are sounded out or guessed at more successfully. It probably makes little long-term difference whether your child's reading seems to click or develops more slowly. There is no real evidence that a child who makes a breakthrough into reading at age three or four ultimately reads any better than a child who progresses more slowly from age four to seven. Far more important is your support for your child's reading, however and whenever she begins.

STAGE FOUR:
LEARNING AT SCHOOL

Chances are that when your child enters kindergarten, she will already read far more than children did thirty years ago. She probably can identify a very personal assortment of words, or read a few favorite books, or sound out and blend together some of the words she's seen on *Sesame Street*. The job of your child's school is to take these beginning skills and develop them so she can read much more widely.

How your child's school tackles this challenge depends on the teacher, the books used, and the approach that underlies the teaching.

When I grew up in the 1950s, the primers given to children were heavily based on phonics. Phonics is a system for decoding words based on what their phonic bits sound like (*sn* . . . "sna" . . . long *a* . . . "ay" . . . *k* . . . "kuh" . . . silent *e* mak_e_s the *a* long) and how they blend together ("snake"). Phonics works quite well in languages such as German where words almost invariably "sound out" quite easily. Phonics was first developed for reading German by a man named Valentin Ickelsamer back in 1534. In English, unfortunately, only about 65 percent of our words can be decoded easily by using the phonics approach. The others are exceptions, or need additional information from context. Nor is phonics a particularly easy system. One series of readers presents 240 phonics bits for young children to master. Other series have offered as many as 120 different rules for blending the phonic bits together, though only 8 of those rules work all the time. Even though phonics is helpful in tackling unfamiliar words—and, later on, for spelling—the whole system can be enough to boggle any young mind.

The big competing technique used to be "look-say," or "whole-word recognition." In this approach, children are helped to identify many hundreds of words without any formal training in phonics. From this, most children develop rules in their own minds that help them attack unfamiliar words. While students schooled in phonics seem to do better in reading unfamiliar words out loud, students taught by the look-say method seem to do better in understanding the meaning behind what they read.

Another popular approach these days is neither phonics nor look-say but "whole language." The whole-language approach to reading places its focus on stories and the child's response to them. "Whole language" means that reading, writing, and thinking are all integrated into lessons based on a piece of children's literature. A skilled teacher can do a unit on outer space and have a whole class reading words such as *Jupiter* and *mission control* long before the old phonics-based primers would even reach the J words. When done well, the whole-language approach can be wonderfully exciting; when done poorly, at least it doesn't do much damage.

Phonic Bits

Learning to read with phonics requires the student to master the sound of a number of phonic bits. Here's a sampling:

- Consonants: initial consonants such as the *b* in *blend*; final consonants such as *r* in *computer*.
- Vowels: long vowels such as the *i* in *like*; short vowels such as the *o* in *short*.
- Digraphs: special two-letter combinations such as *ch, wh, ck, ng, qu, wr*.
- Blends: letter combinations that must be blended together, such as *pl, fr, str, nk, br*.
- Diphthongs: vowel combinations such as *ay, ea, oo, oi, ay*.
- Phonograms: special combinations such as *ide, ame, ook, ight, tion*.

In the past, some schools were guilty of quite disastrous experiments in the teaching of reading. In the 1950s some schools in Britain got hooked on a system called Initial Teaching Alphabet, in which all the early stories were written in a special forty-four-letter phonetic alphabet. The system worked fine until the kids had to read real English. In the early 1960s, Chicago schools virtually banned phonics from their schools—until standardized reading tests showed a terrible drop in skills. Even today, the Distar reading system, popular in parts of Florida and many other jurisdictions, turns teachers into automatons and requires students to read nonsense texts, all in the guise of effective instruction.

The simple truth remains this: The best reading program is a mix—some phonics, some whole language, some vocabulary development, some word-attack practice, and lots of reading together. Far more important than the *theory* behind the program is the amount of *time* your child's school spends on reading—and the competence of the teacher in the classroom.

STAGE FIVE: GROWING COMPETENCE

By the end of third grade, and often long before, your child will have mastered enough of the basics to handle many different kinds of reading material. The act of decoding the page will come so quickly and so easily that some parents might feel the process of learning to read is complete.

Don't be fooled by early success. Reading is not just decoding words on a page. It is not just reading a passage and answering the questions. It is not just a trick your child has to do to get from third to fourth grade.

Reading is dreaming. Reading is entering a world of imagination shared between reader and author. Reading is getting beyond the words to the story or the meaning underneath.

Read with me the opening words of Tololwa Mollel's *The Orphan Boy:*

As he had done every night of his life, the old man gazed deep into the heavens. He had spent so much time scanning the night sky that he knew every star it held. He loved the stars as if they were his children. He always felt less lonely when the sky was clear and the stars formed a glowing canopy over the plains.

Tonight, he noticed, one of the stars was missing.

Resources: The Public Library

Any public library will have thousands of books for your child—and much more.

• Story hours. Little kids love to be read to, and librarians are trained to do it well.
• Films, author visits, and other events. Your public library is also a community center.
• Video and audiotapes. The video collection frequently has classics you won't find at the video store. Books on audiotape come with the books for kids; separately for adults.
• Fun and games. Many libraries now check out games ranging from Scrabble to Lego.
• Literacy programs. Some public libraries offer reading programs for adults with weak reading skills. If not, they'll know where to send you.
• On-line computers. Doing research? Some library research services are tied into the Internet.
• Advice. In this book, I've suggested some 300 books worth reading. A good librarian can recommend thousands more—and share her enthusiasm for the books.

Even without Paul Morin's illustrations, the text of this wonderful children's book transports us from where we are— this author at the word processor, you in your chair—to the night world outside. We move from life within ourselves, from the simple workmanlike prose of this nonfiction book, to words that have a special magic. The night sky *holds* its stars in a *glowing canopy.* The old man, who must often feel lonely just as we all do, feels reassured by the stars. Until one is missing—and with his, our hearts skip a beat.

Reading the words is really only a tool for entering into the dreams, ideas, and feelings behind them. Just as in playing the piano, the student must get beyond the keys and notes to play the music, so when reading a book, your child must get beyond the code of words to reach the author's images or concepts or experience.

By fourth grade, most children will have mastered enough of the mechanics of reading—sight vocabulary, quick sounding out, fluent reading speed—that these are no longer the prime concern. The task now, both in school and at home, is to broaden and deepen the reading. The trick is to do this while keeping the excitement of books and the joy of reading.

Your child now will have enough mastery of reading to use books for her own ends. She'll use books to fix her bike, or get caught up in a Harry Potter novel, or find a joke to tell her friends. At the same time, your child's recognition vocabulary will multiply from the 3,000 easy words most third-grade students have mastered to the 70,000 to 100,000 word recognition vocabulary a high school student needs. So long as reading is encouraged, this growth will take place on its own.

STAGE SIX:
CRITICAL JUDGMENT

The last step in developing young readers doesn't usually occur until adolescence. At this time, your child should learn that there are different ways to read: skimming (speed-reading),

Parent to Parent Starting Late

"I didn't read a book—an entire book—until I was twelve years old. Then I won a book in a newspaper contest, the Junior Press Club. I guess I was so thrilled at winning a book that I decided to read it all the way through. I tried it, and I liked it.

"For me, part of the joy of reading to my children is that it gives me a chance to read all those books I missed as a kid. I guess I'm still catching up."

—Bryan Prince

studying, and reading for enjoyment. She should learn to position herself toward the text—to be skeptical, or to be involved, or to read for her own purposes. In short, your child should learn to read as an adult does.

Children in elementary school usually read just one way—at a single speed, with a single uncritical attitude and a single kind of enthusiasm. They will zip through every book at 150 to 250 words per minute, scarcely taking the time to think about what the author's purpose was, or if they agree or disagree with the text, or why they are reading at all.

But the reading of teenagers should become much more self-aware than that. Before approaching a text, your child should have her own purpose in mind. This novel will be for enjoyment, that poem will be looked at for technique, that newspaper editorial will be read for its political bias. Successful readers then choose from an array of reading styles to suit their purposes.

The job of the high school is to help your teenage child

develop all these skills. In a good high school, every subject from English to history to physical education should teach your child important skills in reading and thinking.

As a parent, you can support these more sophisticated skills by talking about your child's reading. Your child might not be aware that virtually every newspaper has a political slant. But you can talk about it. Your teenager may think that Stephen King is a better writer than John Irving. You should talk about such critical judgments. Your daughter might be incredibly cynical about TV commercials, but quite gullible when reading a magazine interview with a rock star. Your experience in the larger world can help make sense of what your teenager is reading—and give you a chance to connect to her world.

The joy of reading with our children doesn't stop as they, and we, get older; it simply changes. At this last stage, you won't be reading out loud much, you'll be talking about what's read. Ironically, this was also the first stage, back with those wordless picture books when your child was an infant. Your family reading will have come full circle.

The Danger Times for Reading

Unfortunately, not every child will move successfully through all the stages of learning to read. There are pitfalls along the way that can hinder your child's reading development in a serious way. According to the latest research, parents should pay careful attention at the three biggest danger times: when your child is entering kindergarten, around fourth grade, and when she's about to enter high school.

The first danger time occurs before any kind of formal reading instruction has begun—and it involves listening more than reading. When your child is about to enter kindergarten and begin to learn letter sounds, it's vitally important that she can hear the fine differences between sounds that are the basis for our language. A child who cannot hear the difference between a *b* and a *t*, or an *m* and an *n*, will be seriously handicapped in understanding reading basics.

This is why talking, conversation, and storytelling are so important around the house. These activities build the listening skills that lead to aural discrimination. A child who doesn't have this background will have trouble tackling the letter sounds with which virtually all reading instruction begins.

It is unlikely that any parents reading this book would have deprived their children of language experiences in the early years, but this problem is not limited to disadvantaged families. Children whose parents are frequently away and who are left in the care of a taciturn or non-English-speaking nanny may not get as much experience hearing our language as other children. Twins who spend a great deal of time in infancy speaking mostly to each other frequently develop a special "twin speak" that doesn't help them when speaking or listening to adults and teachers.

Finally, an increasing number of children seem to be suffering from hearing problems at an early age. Parents should remember that it is much harder to teach a deaf child to read than it is to teach a blind child, because sound is the basis of our reading code. Deafness, of course, is only the most extreme hearing problem and it may be the easiest to diagnose. There are many gradations and variations in hearing difficulties. Some can be helped by hearing aids, others require special efforts to improve aural discrimination or to learn lip reading as an adjunct to hearing. In terms of reading, a child who hears muffled or distorted sounds might have almost as many problems as a child who hears nothing at all.

If you have any reason to suspect that your child might have hearing problems—whether it's an inability to hear around the house or a history of ear infections—be certain to have your family doctor arrange for a visit to an audiologist. The diagnostic equipment available there will help you determine if there is a problem and what can be done about it.

After that, you can relax for a while. Of course you'll want to follow the three Rs and enjoy watching your child's early reading development, but there's no reason to worry much about reading progress for most kids until fourth grade. This is when a quarter to a third of all children begin losing interest in reading.

The problem is not one of reading skills, which most

Words and More Words . . .

- Total number of words in English: 500,000 (excludes scientific and technical terms)
- Number of words in German: 175,000; in French: 125,000
- English words recognized by the average American adult: 125,000
- Words used in the works of Shakespeare: 30,000
- Words used in three hours of prime-time TV: 7,000
- Words recognized orally by a child entering school: 6,000
- Words ordinarily read "by sight" at the end of third grade: 3,000

---

children have mastered in the primary years. The problem—which affects more boys than girls—seems to be one of continuing interest.

Why? Researchers haven't given us an answer yet, but teachers have ventured some guesses. By fourth grade, most children are quite competent at reading for themselves—so parents stop reading with them. Without parental reinforcement, the *value* of reading goes down in the child's eyes. And reading progress can be stalled. What's more, children in fourth and fifth grades have just enough independence to hang out with friends and to play without adult supervision. Unless some time for reading is preserved, it can be lost in the frantic pace of visiting friends, watching TV, playing tag, practicing ballet, and doing math homework.

Some researchers have suggested that the root of the problem goes deeper. They feel that the conversation in some families does not support either the advanced vocabulary or the

Turning Off the TV

Too much television has become a real problem for some portions of the population. Albert Shanker, the late president of the American Federation of Teachers, noted with dismay that one of every four nine-year-olds in a 1990 study spent six or more hours a day, seven days a week, watching TV. "That's more than most adults spend at work and certainly more than these kids spent in school," he pointed out.

One solution? Leave it to American ingenuity. For a little over $100, you can buy a black box to connect to your TV that rations how much television your child can watch. Some use credit cards to provide different limits for different children; others use a four-digit number code. It's a kind of electronic parenting, like getting the Fisher Price tape recorder to read to your child at night.

I've got a better idea: real parenting. Someone has to set limits on your child's TV viewing—and that someone should be you.

more sophisticated thinking skills required by readers after fourth grade. Some children have literally never heard the words or ideas they are being asked to read in books. As a result, reading becomes more and more frustrating.

And then there's school—a number of educators are admitting that their own reading programs lose emphasis in fourth grade. When "reading" turns to "language arts," the emphasis often shifts to writing—as if the job of teaching reading were somehow complete. It's not.

The message for parents is clear. You must continue to

encourage reading at home through the crucial fourth-fifth-sixth-grade period or your child may not develop the sophisticated reading skills she needs. The readers who check out at fourth grade are barely reading at a sixth-grade level when they enter high school. They won't be ready to face the sophisticated reading demands of secondary school, where textbooks that require college-level skills are often used.

The third major danger time is around ninth grade. That is when teachers have noted a marked decline in the amount of time many students spend reading for pleasure. The decline frequently begins in seventh or eighth grade and continues through the junior year of high school. By that time, only 20 percent of high school students continue to read avidly for themselves. Some 55 percent will do little more than the minimal outside reading required for school. And a quarter of our teenagers will hardly bother to read at all.

There are many explanations for this teenage fallow period. Certainly there are many competing demands on adolescents' free time. Teenagers' attention can become centered on themselves, their social life, or the consumer products pitched at them in the media. Books can seem irrelevant—aimed at either children or adults—failing to deal with teenage concerns. And the rebellious attitude of some teenagers can be aimed not just at parents and schools but at books and reading.

Yet, despite all this, your child can continue to be a reader throughout the teenage years—and certainly will be better off for doing so. You can keep talking about your teenager's reading, keep helping her to add to her library, keep enough rules on the household so that TV and the stereo don't take over her free time. In Chapters 10 and 12, I'll offer a number of other suggestions to help you keep your child reading despite adolescent angst and distraction.

THE IMPORTANCE OF FAMILY

Although the teaching of reading has been left very much to the schools since the eighteenth century, the development of *readers* really depends on what happens at home. Our schools would do a more effective job in encouraging reading if they kept this simple fact in mind. You'll certainly do a more effective job as a parent if you pay attention to some of the dynamics in your own family.

Throughout this book, I'll be talking about ways to encourage and support your child's reading. Much of this—like the three Rs—will be quite obvious to most parents. What is not obvious is the way in which family dynamics can undermine even the best of intentions. Let me give an example that came up after I had given a talk to a group of parents about children's reading. A woman approached me, explained that she was a school librarian, and began to talk about her son, the problem reader in the family. She said, "I certainly agree with everything you said about nightly reading and books in the house and limiting TV—and I did all that for both my children. It worked fine for my daughter, who reads all the time now, but my son just

Father May Know Best

According to some researchers, fathers are better at helping their children to read because they're less patient than mothers. When a child comes across an unfamiliar word, mothers tend to make the child sound it out. Fathers are more likely to tell the child the word or tell him to skip it and carry on. Dad's approach keeps the story moving.

isn't a reader. Getting him to open a book is like pulling teeth. What can I do?"

I went through a set of questions about the son's abilities and the school program, trying to figure out what had gone wrong, but the problem wasn't there. I stumbled on the real issue with this question: "Does your husband ever read together with your son?"

The woman gave me a surprised look. "My husband? My husband doesn't have time to read—he's a man."

Despite years of teacher training, the woman just couldn't see how the hidden family attitude—reading something only women do—was crippling her son's reading progress. Nor was there much I could suggest beyond urging her to get her husband involved in daily reading.

The hidden messages in families are much more powerful than those that are verbalized because they express more deeply held values. Children learn more from your whispers, your choice of family heroes, and your example than they do from what you preach. This is not meant to pile blame on you as a parent—certainly there is enough of that going around—but it does suggest the importance of the family in establishing values and behavior. If you don't like the way your kids seem to be growing up, ask outsiders what they think could be happening. Sometimes family friends or more distant relatives are better able to see what's going on in our families than we are ourselves.

The most common problem for children in families who are readers is what I call the second-child syndrome. I've heard the story again and again: "My wife and I both read, our eldest child is a great reader, the two youngest children enjoy reading—but our second child just isn't interested." The problem second child—very often a son rather than a daughter—seems to be a nonreader because of the ways families work. Your first child always receives a great deal of attention. You're concerned about her development, thrilled at her walking, talking, reading. And your first child frequently rewards all this attention with spectacular achievements. But the second child, regardless of your best efforts to treat the kids equally, always gets a different kind of parenting. He is never the center; he must always share you; he frequently must compete for attention; and he has parents who are less anxious to prove themselves. The result, as all the studies on birth order indicate, is a very different pattern of development for the second child.

If your first child has staked out reading as *her* area of

How Well Does a Person Have to Read?

The difficulty of reading a particular piece of writing can be estimated by calculating the average sentence length, syllable count, and number of difficult words in a few sample passages. This gives a good estimate of the grade level of ability a reader would need to comfortably handle the material. Some examples:

- *Scientific American:* graduate school
- *Democracy in America* by Alexis de Tocqueville (Henry Reeve translation): college
- *San Francisco Chronicle* (news): grade 12–college
- *The Handmaid's Tale,* a novel by Margaret Atwood: grade 9–10
- *USA Today* (financial news): grade 7–9
- Ann Landers advice column: grade 6
- advertisement for a facial moisturizer: grade 5

competence, don't be surprised if your second child decides to put his energies into soccer or math or video games. Chances are, your first child will have developed her reading ability very quickly and your second child will plod along at a more normal rate. He will *seem* to be reading poorly, but more in comparison to your first child than to other children his age. And he may well choose not to compete with the first child in an area where she is clearly so far ahead.

The solution to this is simple: Make reading special and different for your second child. He should have his *own* books; he should have his *own* reading time. His achievement should never be compared to that of his older sister, nor should his obviously accomplished sister be put in a position to lord her competence over him. That means *you* should be the one to do nightly reading; *you* should be the one to ask him to read cereal boxes, recipes, video-game instructions, and whatever else comes into his life. It might be convenient to say "Oh, let Janey read it," but that will only undermine your second child's attitude and competence. Give your second child the chance to become a real reader in his own right, and likely he will reward you by doing so.

In larger families, the question of having older children read to younger ones often comes up. There's obviously nothing wrong with having a teenage sister—or a baby-sitter—read with a kindergarten child who's just beginning to sound out words. An older sibling can't substitute for your interest and involvement as a parent, but she certainly can help out when your hands are full. Just be careful that the older child's ability to read doesn't get in the way of the younger child's development. Older children, especially teenagers, frequently lack the patience to encourage their younger brother or sister to read independently. If the older child and the younger one are too close in

***Parent to Parent* Problems Also Start at Home**

"In the late 1960s, I had to examine honestly how our home life was affecting our three children. My son Robert had failed kindergarten twice. Yes, twice! The reason for Robert's problems was not too much TV or any learning disability. It was the explosive situation in which he lived, caused by our unhappy marriage.

"After I left with all three children, Robert progressed rapidly and was working at an average grade-three level by the time he was in third grade. Things continued to improve. Today he has two degrees and works as a systems analyst for a major bank. I think his progress has a lot to do with the fact that I was honest enough to see what was wrong with my child's home situation.

"A home where parents fight or argue isn't conducive for a child learning to read. Now that almost half our marriages end in divorce, many children face unhappy social situations in their own homes. A child can't read if he is fearful, apprehensive, or uncertain about what will happen next."

—Name withheld

age, or busily engaged in sibling rivalry, then reading can be part of a battleground or an activity where the younger child's developing abilities are put down. Far better to put family reading off for a day until you can give your younger child the attention she deserves.

At various times in your family life, you may find that your children's reading is a symptom not of the program at school but of what is happening at home and in their lives. As I will point out several times later on in this book, few children will learn to read or keep reading in a home that is under stress from marital, financial, or emotional problems. If you and your spouse are going through a divorce, you can expect your child's schoolwork and her reading to decline for six months to a year. If there is a death within the family or close to the family, you can expect consequences that last for several years. If your child is going through a rebellious period, you can expect that her attitude toward reading will be affected, marked either by a rejection of books or a retreat into them.

None of these is really a reading problem, but all of them deserve your attention. An observant parent will find that reading is an indicator of much that is happening in the family and within the child. You should pay attention to this, just as you would to your child's physical health, and seek outside help if you need it.

Chapter 4

Parents and the School

Your child's school is certainly your most important partner in encouraging your child to become a reader for life. The teachers at that school will develop lessons with phonics exercises, word-attack practice, and "whole-language" books in the early grades. They'll push for vocabulary development and comprehension skills to match the more sophisticated reading of the middle grades. And the teachers will do their best to keep your child reading and thinking about literature in senior elementary grades and high school. Most teachers will try to meet your child's individual needs while also trying to meet demands from the state, the local school board, the principal, and twenty-five other children who *all* have pressing needs—from wanting to feed the gerbils to surviving a messy divorce at home.

Amazingly, the teachers will do a pretty good job in the midst of all this.

But learning to read—and learning to love reading—requires more than just teachers who do a pretty good job. Reading is so important that our children need excellent instruction in reading and writing fundamentals. They need schools that spur creativity and a sense of excitement about reading. They

---

Characteristics of Effective Schools

Research into what makes an effective school has identified seven key factors for schools that deliver real gains for students and garner strong parent satisfaction ratings. In ordinary language, here's what the success factors are:

- The principal and teachers put a strong emphasis on high-quality teaching.
- Teachers, administrators, and parents share a clear purpose for the school.
- High expectations are set for all students to be successful.
- The environment is safe and students are calm and orderly.
- Adequate time is spent on academic tasks so all students can learn.
- Student progress is monitored closely and feedback is given to both students and parents.
- Parents and school staff communicate and work together.

---

need school libraries with great books in great condition. They need state departments of education and school boards that set reading as a top priority and give it the time, the books, and the money that it requires. And they need administrators who are clever enough to find federal funds that can boost the reading programs at your child's school.

AN EXCELLENT SCHOOL
READING PROGRAM

An excellent school reading program involves commitment, energy, and imagination. It is linked to every subject area, but especially to writing, speaking, and dramatic arts. It is eclectic. An excellent reading program isn't limited to phonics, or direct instruction, or whole-language philosophy; it draws from all these approaches. An excellent reading program is always organized and structured to make sure that both reading and reading instruction are taking place. But it makes reading fun, not just work. It makes decoding words and responding to books a creative endeavor, not drudgery.

In Chapters 5 to 14, I'll discuss excellent programs at specific grade levels and for special situations. But first let me suggest three ideas to promote reading for an entire school.

• No school-based approach to encourage reading works better than SEAR (Stop Everything and Read), sometimes called SQUIRT (Sustained, Quiet, Uninterrupted Reading Time) or USSR (Universal, Silent, Structured Reading). In this approach, everybody from kindergartners to custodians takes time out from classes and work to read for fifteen minutes a day. Not only does this provide time for reading, it gives children models of adults who read and get excited about books.

• No single place at school is more important in developing reading than the school library. The library must always be open, staffed, inviting, and full of books. Computers are a handy reference tool in a library, but they will never turn your child into a reader.

• No program works better for helping weak readers than a buddy system in which senior students read with junior ones and adult volunteers work with students who are having the most trouble in reading.

The teachers at an excellent school know that these programs and the attitudes they represent are as important as any particular technique used in any given classroom. And they're not expensive. Unlike computers or new textbooks or driver-education classrooms, a strong school reading program needs only a little taxpayer money. What's required is a commitment of time and organization—and the recognition that literacy must be the first goal of our schools.

THE PARENTS' ROLE

The way you deal with your child's school and your child's teachers will depend on the kind of job they are already doing. If the school and teacher are excellent, you can content yourself with being a quiet partner in boosting your child's reading. But if the school or teacher is less than excellent, your position must be more aggressive—sometimes even adversarial—to get the kind of education your child deserves.

Here are thumbnail portraits of three schools and three teachers as you and I would see them on a visit. They are, incidentally, three real schools and three composite teachers from the hundreds I've visited over the past few years. One of them probably will resemble the school your child attends or the teacher he has this year.

School A

School A is a small elementary school with 300 students, drawing half its kids from farms and half from a nearby subdivision. It's 9:45 A.M. Walk inside the doors and the principal's office is to the right. But the principal isn't in his office, he's off looking at posters in the kindergarten classroom. The library down the hall isn't elaborate—just two connected classrooms—but the place is full of kids working on projects. There are books everywhere and comfortable couches to sit and read. And there are staff—a full-time librarian, a part-time library/media technician, and two parent volunteers.

Walk down the halls and you'll see photographs of kids everywhere, as if every student in the school has won some kind

---

Educational Buzzwords in Reading

- Basal readers: Books of gradually increasing difficulty based on increasingly complex phonic rules, such as the famous Dick and Jane series.
- Whole language: A philosophy of teaching reading using children's literature instead of basal readers, with an attempt to integrate reading, language, and writing.
- Phonics: The traditional means of teaching reading by sounding out unfamiliar words.
- Direct instruction: Reading programs that script how teachers should teach.
- Chapter 1 (or Title 1) reading teacher: A federally funded teacher who assists classroom teachers on reading strategies and interventions.

of award. You have to step around kids as you walk because so many of them are working on the floors, or measuring locker heights, or otherwise using the hallway as if it were an extension of the classroom.

Walk into room 224 and you'll find it noisy. Teacher A has arranged the students in groups of three or four. All of them are

---

An Excellent School Reading Program

Here are some things an excellent school reading program does:

- It sets aside time for reading every day.
- It involves the whole school in reading, including teachers, administrators, students, and custodians.
- It makes effective use of the school library.
- It has novels and magazines in every classroom to augment the library.
- At the primary level, it uses a number of teaching approaches: phonics, reading aloud, whole language.
- It uses reading and writing as part of every subject from math to geography.
- It has resource teachers to help students who are having trouble reading.
- It uses parent volunteers, teachers' aides, and older students as reading buddies to help junior readers.
- It encourages kids to respond to their reading through drama, or art, or writing, not simply to answer set questions or fill out workbook sheets.

A Lousy School Reading Program

Your child's school needs help when . . .

- The school library has only a handful of books or is closed.
- Reading instruction is done only through phonics or look-say, or without any structure.
- Reading is done only one period a day, and it's work.
- The principal or teacher says, "Personally, I don't have time to read."
- Your child comes home every day with no homework, no book to read, and no excitement about school.
- You ask your child, "What are you reading in school these days?" and she says, "Nothing." When you say, "Come on, you must be reading something," she repeats, "Nothing" and means it.

---

working on an art and drama project connected to an author's visit later in the week. On the walls are the kids' own novels, carefully bound with wallpaper covers and a very professional about-the-author page, including the information that Jenny Ferrara, age eleven, has two cats, Muffy and Smith.

Teacher A, dressed in jeans and boots for an afternoon field trip to a nearby conservation area, hasn't noticed you because she's too busy with one of the groups. But everyone notices a bell that sounds at 10:00. It's reading time. The groups disband. Students grab books or magazines from their desks, then slump against the walls or into chairs and begin to read. It's quiet. The teacher is reading too, her boots propped up on a file cabinet. Out in the hall, the custodian is reading a Thomas Harris novel.

Fifteen minutes later, it's back to regular lessons, even though half the kids groan when they have to put their books away.

School B

School B is a sprawling junior high school with an enrollment pushing 1,000. The school draws its students from six elementary schools, some as far as forty miles away. There is a string of portable classrooms on part of the school yard.

It's 11:30 A.M.—almost lunch—and there's a lot of noise pouring from classrooms into the halls, even though no one is in sight. The halls themselves are undecorated, walls of lockers stretching out their full length. There is dust on the trophies in the display cabinet.

Walk down the hall and peek into the library. It's a good-size room with probably 3,000 books—hardcovers from the time the school was built and racks of newer paperbacks. There are two computers, one of which is out of order, and a number of tables and study carrels, some of them occupied. The librarian is busy trying to convince an eighth-grade teacher that perhaps she should use a new book by Jerry Spinelli instead of doing *Shane* for the fifteenth year.

Keep walking down the hall and turn into classroom 113. The desks are in neat rows, though the kids are sprawled all over. The kids in this seventh-grade class are watching Teacher B as he passes out the comprehension questions on a short story called "The Monkey's Paw" by W. W. Jacobs. Most of the kids have read the story, except for two at the back of the room who never read anything. Teacher B explains that he used to try more elaborate lessons with the kids—dramatizing stories, interviewing characters in books, even shooting videos instead of doing written book reports. But now he's emphasizing writing, because there's a new statewide initiative and the principal expects the kids' expensive cardboard portfolios to be filled by the end of the year.

Teacher B reminds the students that they have a book report due next week, though most of them haven't started reading a book yet. There just doesn't seem to be time, Teacher B will tell you, to get through the curriculum, do all the paperwork, and still read books.

School C

School C serves a farming area. It's a small school with only 250 students in a reasonably new and clean building.

It's 2:30 P.M. when you walk into the school. The classroom doors are closed and there are no kids in the halls. There's a sign that orders you to report to the office, but the principal is busy disciplining a kid, and the secretary is too busy to notice you.

Instead of waiting, you head down the hall, past the library with its handful of books. The teacher-librarian comes in every other day now, due to budget cutbacks, but there's a parent volunteer at her desk. If you look through the collection, you won't find many books for the seventh- and eighth-grade kids because the teacher-librarian likes to avoid controversy. She heard about the trouble a local high school had with the swear words in John Steinbeck's *Of Mice and Men*, so you won't find even a *damn* in any of the books in her library.

Walk into the fifth-grade classroom of Teacher C, and everything is very orderly. You could hear a pin drop as the kids work, warily eyeing the teacher who sits at her desk at the front of the room. The students are looking up vocabulary words in dictionaries to complete definitions demanded by their spelling text.

When the students do "reading" at 9:15 A.M. tomorrow, the story will be from a textbook with questions at the end of the selection.

Reading in Teacher C's classroom is frequently out loud, even though a third of the kids get nervous and make a lot of mistakes when they're called upon. The good readers are forbidden to laugh at the weak readers, but the kids still know. Most of the weak readers will tell you that they hate reading, but that may just mean they're embarrassed to read out loud.

Teacher C doesn't feel there is much she can do about the

Dysteachia: What to Look For

Not every child who has a problem in school is a problem child; sometimes he just has a poor teacher. Educator Arn Bowers' term for this is "dysteachia." Here are some signs:

- The homework is busywork, copied from a teacher's resource book, or nonexistent.
- Marking is done late (a reasonable turnaround time is two days) or not at all.
- Record keeping is spotty or "lost."
- The class is frequently out of control, or many kids end up being sent to the office.
- Even "good" students are yelled at or given repeated detentions.
- The teacher is "sick" often and takes days off, leaving the kids with substitute teachers.
- There is lots of attention to form ("name, date, title") but no attention to learning.

attitude of some of the kids. With thirty-two children in the classroom, she sometimes feels buried under the grading load. And the school district isn't providing any help, because the once-a-week reading specialists were cut with the last budget crunch.

Teacher C hasn't heard of reading buddies, or quiet reading time, and doesn't much like this whole-language idea. She believes in good old oral reading from the approved textbook. She likes vocabulary study with dictionaries and grammar sheets from a workbook because that's what worked for her. Maybe it would still work, if the kids weren't so "difficult" these days.

Virtually all of America's 130,000 schools fall into the range I've just described. In a few schools, the level of experimentation, excitement, and cooperation will impress you within minutes. In a great many others, the school is good enough and teachers are trying, but something is missing—staff morale, money for books and equipment, or a dynamic principal. Sadly, there are still thousands of schools where rigid administrations or lackluster teachers have eliminated any excitement or joy that children have the right to expect. As a visitor, these schools appall me because they deaden the joy of learning for our children.

OBSERVE YOUR CHILD'S SCHOOL AND CLASSROOM

The first step in working with your child's school is to observe, much as I have done in the visits just described. Too many parents worry that they don't belong in the school, or they feel awkward talking to teachers or stepping into the halls. But your taxes built the school and pay teacher salaries—and you've entrusted your own child to their care. Surely, *you*, even more than I, have the right to know what's going on at your child's school.

So nose around. Drop in to chat with the principal—you don't really need an appointment, though it's wise to call ahead. Say that you're interested in the school reading program. A good principal will be pleased to talk about what her school is doing. On your way out, check out the hall displays, look around the library, chat with the custodian or the secretary at the front desk. You'll get an immediate impression about the "feel" of the school.

Then use the school's parents' night to find out about your child's teacher and classroom. The first parents' night is usually sometime before Halloween. This initial visit is more important than your sales meeting or poker night or anything else you might prefer to do. Always go to the first meet-the-teacher night. It's vital for your child and his teacher to know you support his education. And it's important for you to know what's going on.

Look around the classroom. Is it bright, lively, full of displays of the kids' work? Is there a classroom library? Is there a computer, science equipment, a reading corner? Is your child's work organized into a folder or on display?

Then talk to the teacher. What books are used for the reading program? How often does the class go to the school library? Are there reading buddies, drama exercises, projects coming up, field trips planned? How much homework does the teacher expect? How much outside reading? Is there anything you can do to help on field trip days or as a volunteer?

Always keep your ears open to that third great source of information—your child. When you ask, "What did you do at school today?" try to get past the immediate "Nothing" to find out what really happened. What is your child reading? How does he feel about his teacher? How does he talk about school—with excitement or with boredom? Often the tone of kids talking about their school and their teacher will tell you more than the words they use. Be sure to *listen*.

Then use this book. Check the box on page 52 to see how many components of a top-level reading program are present in your school. Check in the later chapters for information on what a school should be doing in the specific grades for your child. Once you've made a reasonably solid judgment on how good your child's school is, you'll be ready to decide what to do next.

IF YOU'RE LUCKY: AN "A" SCHOOL, AN "A" TEACHER

In my travels, I've run across dozens of "A" schools, from small schools in farming communities to sprawling, multicultural inner-city schools, from wealthy private schools to dirt-poor alternative schools. There is no single system that produces a fine school. Instead, it takes some combination of a dynamic principal, committed teachers, community support, and good luck. If your child is in an "A" school, with an "A" teacher, your job is to support and encourage what's going on. Here are some ways to do that:

• Praise the teacher. A note of thanks or appreciation often makes a difficult job worthwhile. Some years ago I chaired an organization for student debating that involved twenty-four schools and 300 kids. This bit of volunteer work used up some twenty hours a month of my time, and after two years and one particularly exhausting tournament, I was ready to call it quits. But that night I got a call from a parent who said nothing more than thanks for organizing such an opportunity for his son. It made my evening and kept me in the chair for another year.

• Volunteer your time. An excellent school always makes use of volunteers. That means you. If your days are relatively free, why not tutor reading, or help in the library, or take the kindergarten kids to the zoo? Even if you work every day, the school can still use your help. Join the PTA or the principal's advisory group. Make yourself available for career day or concert night. Let the school and your child's teacher know that you can be counted on.

• If you work for a large corporation, see if it will consider an Adopt-a-School Program that could donate money for books or time at lunch for you to go read at the local school. Chances are that other parents at work will be glad to support this program as well.

• Pay attention to your child's schoolwork. Even excellent schools and teachers can't do their job unless you do yours. In many years of teaching, I've encountered only a handful of families who interfered too much in their children's education, but I knew thousands who paid virtually no attention to what was going on in school. If you are reading nightly with your child, you will naturally talk about what is being read at school. Keep on asking questions. The older a child gets, the more you'll have to push for answers. Is there a science fair? What project does your daughter have in mind for geography? Does your son want to try some of the mental math problems on you? Your interest in schoolwork, like your involvement in reading, gives importance to what happens in school.

• Protect your school. There are many forces that endanger all our schools—from budget-cutting trustees to self-righteous

Seven Easy Ways to Stay Involved

- Read the newsletter, monthly calendar, notes from the teacher.
- Go to parents' night, open house, the school musical.
- Join the PTA or parent advisory council.
- Chaperone a dance, supervise a school trip, and the like.
- Send notes to your child's teacher—or call her to keep in contact.
- Talk to your child about what he did in school.
- Eyeball your child's homework before it gets turned in.

zealots who would purge libraries of such "dangerous" books as J. D. Salinger's *Catcher in the Rye*. Your school may need your help just to protect what it already has.

DEALING WITH "B" SCHOOLS AND "B" TEACHERS

The "B" school and "B" teacher are not excellent but not clearly deficient either. They simply lack the energy, imagination, and commitment that would lead to real excellence.

You can make up for some of this by effective parenting at home. If you support your child's reading with the three Rs, chances are your child will develop excellent reading skills and learn to love reading on his own. But you'll find it harder to develop home programs to support a weak geography or math teacher. When your child gets older, you'll find it very difficult to help much in calculus or physics. That's why you have to use

Federal Money Can Help

While education is mainly a state responsibility, the federal government provides billions of dollars each year to support special programs and to help at-risk students. This Title 1 funding provides for:

- Teacher aides. Often they are parents who work with reluctant readers on a one-to-one basis in consultation with the classroom teacher.
- Consultants and testing. Specialist teachers advise classroom teachers on strategies, work with the most difficult students, or regularly test student progress.
- Equipment and books. Computers can help with classroom writing, big books encourage whole-language reading.

Eligibility for federal money depends on teachers finding that a student is "at risk" of problems in learning. If over 75 percent of the students are deemed at risk, as may be the case in some inner-city schools, the whole school gets extra funding; otherwise the money is designated for individual students, programs, or classrooms.

some of your energy to press for better education at school. Here are some ways to do that:

- Use the ideas in this book to promote a strong school reading program. There are no particularly radical ideas here, so a comment such as "I was reading a book that says every school should have a silent reading time" ought to get at least a few heads nodding in agreement, especially as this costs nothing to implement. In my experience, most "B" schools want to be better; they just haven't figured out how yet.

• Organize with other parents. As an individual or couple, you don't have much clout. As part of the principal's advisory group, or the music parents' association, or the PTA, you speak with greater authority. Good principals are always seeking out input from parents on everything from report card design to attendance procedures. As part of an organization, your voice will be heard.

Parent organizations often serve another useful function: raising cash for special projects. While I hate to see parents' energies devoted entirely to fund-raising—after all, that's what our school taxes are for—sometimes a little extra money will buy those frills that make school an exciting place to learn.

• Seek out the excellent teachers. Every ordinary school has some quite extraordinary teachers. In high school, with some careful course choices and a little quiet nudging, your child often can arrange for classes with the very best teachers. Many elementary schools have two or three teachers at each grade level. If you can determine from friends and neighbors which teacher is superior, try to get your child into her class by speaking carefully with the principal.

Always back up those excellent teachers when they come up with an exciting initiative for the school. Sometimes a handful of dynamic staff members can make a school soar despite a lackluster principal.

BAD NEWS:
THE "C" SCHOOL AND
"C" TEACHER

These are the most discouraging schools to deal with. The administration and staff are closed off and unfriendly. The school or classroom atmosphere is rigid, boring, or disorganized almost to the point of chaos. Your child suddenly doesn't want to go to school, or wakes up late again and again, or develops mysterious ailments that seem to go away as soon as you say "Okay, you can stay home today."

The solutions here come down to three:

• First, you can take your kids out of school and do what you can as a "home schooler." This route takes a tremendous commitment of time and energy and is rarely possible beyond elementary school. Formal application must be made to your state department of education. Course outlines are kept on file and official guidelines must be followed. No wonder only a tiny fraction of American children are home-schooled.

• Second, you can try to move your family or your child. Schools and school budgets vary tremendously from state to state, county to county. Parents sometimes find it necessary to move the whole household just to find a good school for their children.

If your child has ended up in a poor school and your efforts to work with the principal and teachers have failed, it might well be best to move your child to a different school. Many urban school systems permit school-to-school moves for any valid reason, from "I want my son to take Spanish" to "My daughter is unhappy here." A supportive teacher can tell you what kind of reason is likely to work with your school system.

An Essential Parent Tool: The File Folder

If your child has ended up with a truly incompetent or mediocre teacher, or in a dreadful school, then you have to take action to change the situation. Your first tool is a file folder. Here's what to keep in it:

- Notes sent by the teacher/school
- Copies of notes you send to the teacher/school
- Notes on conversations with the teacher/school
- Notes on particular events at school that you've heard about from your child
- Your observations on your child's behavior or learning
- Quotations from your child or other children about the teacher/school
- Copies of marked tests, homework, handouts
- Report cards

Remember to date all the material. You will never have to use all this as you might in a legal case, but it is vital to be able to refer to specific incidents or specific meetings on a given date. This gives you credibility.

Many school districts now have "magnet schools" with specialized programs that may be superior to those in your neighborhood school. Check to see if there are magnet schools in your area and what admissions requirements your child will face.

- Third, you can put pressure on an inadequate school or

teacher to improve. That's what the rest of this chapter is all about.

HOW TO SPEAK WITH YOUR CHILD'S TEACHER

If the problems you observe are at the classroom level, the place to start is with the classroom teacher. Two or three times a year, you'll be invited into the school to speak with your child's teacher. This doesn't mean you may not visit any other time—twice a month if you want to—but twice a year you'll be invited to do so. Always attend. Your child's education is worth the effort.

Be charming but firm. You never want to be in the position of making the teacher feel defensive—that doesn't make for change. Try to understand the teacher's side: "Yes, it must be difficult with thirty children in the class. . . . I can understand how irritable my son can get." Even excellent teachers can have personal problems, or especially difficult classes, or an administration that doesn't support what they would like to do.

But always have your own agenda. You have already made your observations. Before you go in for the interview, you should have a good idea what's needed and you should have concrete suggestions. You want a reading program with a wide range of books. Maybe you want some stimulating classroom discussion and activities, not just answering questions on page such-and-such. Maybe you want writing tied to reading, and spelling from what the kids are reading, and some creative writing in the classroom. Whatever you'd like to have happen, make your expectations clear. Don't let the teacher suggest that problems in instruction are the result of bad or stupid kids. More often classroom problems have to do with lifeless teaching.

Don't be afraid to offer ideas. Your daughter's teacher may not have thought about reading buddies, or visiting the public library once a month, or sending books home to be read with the parent. Since you know about these ideas, suggest them.

Follow through. It is impossible to emphasize enough the importance of follow-through. Your last comment to a teacher should always be "I'll phone you in two weeks to see how all this is coming along." Then do it. The teacher should return your call. If not, call again and call the principal: "I haven't been able to get in touch with Mrs. Martin. Maybe you could help."

A file folder can be your most important tool in dealing with a difficult teacher or principal. Keep a record of your visits, your calls, and what was said. The date and a few notes are all you need. If push does come to shove, it's far better to tell the principal that you spoke with Mrs. Martin on September 23, October 4, 9, and 15, than to mumble, "Well, I talked to her a couple of times."

Five Questions for Parents' Night

Q: What books or textbooks do you use in language arts?
   May I look through one?
Q: What homework should my child expect? Do you have
   a regular homework schedule?
Q: How often does the class visit the library to get books?
   Can my child bring these books home?
Q: Do you have any special activities going on this year?
   A young authors' workshop? A special drama
   performance? Field trips?
Q: How may I help?

Parents are always afraid that any aggressiveness they show toward a teacher will be taken out on their child. In my experience, that's rarely the case. Usually your child will get kid-glove treatment because you have shown so much interest. Even better, you may be able to make real changes in what happens in your child's classroom.

WHEN PUSH COMES TO SHOVE

The keys to making lasting changes in your child's school or classroom are persistence and organization. I have seen at least two persistent parents, bothered by what was happening in their local schools, go from pestering their boards and being labeled as "wackos" to become a school trustee in one case and a member of the state legislature in the other. It is amazing how power makes that "wacko" label just disappear.

You can be just as successful. What you need is a calm, persistent approach, a way to organize yourself and other parents, and some knowledge of how power works in the schools.

Teachers are at the low end of the power scale. They have some control over how they teach but little say over what they teach, or the books they use, or the size of their classes, or the tone of their schools. Teachers who teach poorly can be helped or prodded by their principals. Only very new teachers can be fired easily for incompetence. Teachers close to retirement might be safe even from forced transfer. Nonetheless, you have every right to demand up-to-date and effective instruction from a professional who makes $30,000 to $60,000 a year.

Principals have differing levels of power, depending on their school board and the community where they teach. In the old days, a principal could dismiss a teacher for failing to shine his shoes. These days teachers' unions and federations make that impossible. But principals still have substantial powers in their schools: They distribute money, approve field trips, transfer staff, and do much to set the tone and keep up the morale in their school. Effective principals may plead powerlessness, but the good ones find ways to get the staff they want and push forward the programs they believe in. If you can get the principal on your side, much can be done to change what happens in your child's school.

Consultants, supervisors, and superintendents have been promoted from classrooms and schools to oversee whole subject areas or groups of schools. They have power based on elaborate flowcharts at your school board or district. Superintendents are drawn from the ranks of principals either for educational leadership or "fire-fighting" skills. You can assume the educational leaders will be on your side; just watch out that you don't get hosed by the superintendent assigned to handle parental brush-fires. None of these individuals has much power in your son's classroom, but a phone call to the right one can put pressure on a foot-dragging principal.

School districts usually are controlled by elected officials called trustees. It is at this level that local budgets are set and program emphasis is determined. If libraries are underfunded while football teams ride around in chauffeured limos, then your local school board has its values backward. Work to turf out the offending trustees by electing people who support serious education.

A good school trustee can be quite helpful in adding muscle to your dealings with a school principal. While the trustees' role is technically advisory, their voices still carry a fair amount of weight. If push comes to shove, try to get one or more trustees on your side.

Your state department of education is the place where the power really sits—but is rarely used. The department sets goals, doles out money, and sometimes creates programs in the schools. If your school decides it wants to add 100 books to its library, that's three bake sales for the PTA and it's still only books for one school. If your state department of education decides that kids should be reading more—that school libraries are essential in every school—then one piece of legislation will send millions of dollars moving in that direction. Remember: The money spent building a mile of two-lane highway would pro-

---

The Power Chart

School power starts at the top (state level) and trickles down. As a parent, you have to start at the bottom and pester your way up.

- Your state department of education
- Your local elected board of education trustees
- Superintendents of your school board or division
- Subject supervisors/consultants/directors—especially in English, reading, and libraries
- The principal of your child's school
- The teacher of your child's class
- Teacher aides
- You
- Your child

There is also a national Department of Education in Washington, but that serves mostly an advisory role.

vide more than 125,000 paperback books for the school libraries in your state. Keep that in mind when you vote.

Parents should understand the levers of power in school systems just in case they have to use them. It's unlikely your child
will be in a terrible school, or have three poor teachers in a row.
But you can't afford to stand by if you feel the school or teachers
are unsatisfactory. In this book, I've suggested ways for you to
encourage and support your child's reading, but it is not your
job to *teach* reading. That's the school's job. You should be able
to rely on the school to do that teaching in an organized, effective, and exciting way. Don't settle for less.

Getting Started:
Infancy to Age Three

Your two-year-old sits on your lap, pointing at pictures in a book that she looks at again and again, calling out the names of the animals, telling you what's going to happen on the next page. This is a wonderful part of being a parent, but is it reading?

Of course it is. For too many years we have had a very narrow view of reading, one that confuses the lifelong process of learning to read with the simple decoding we learn around age six and seven.

We now know that the toddler who experiences language and stories through books is the child who will find it easy to read for herself later on. The child who doesn't hear our language, who isn't told stories, and who doesn't have the opportunity to look at books in childhood will be at a disadvantage for the rest of her life.

So "infant reading" must begin early. We will never fully know how much an infant sees, or hears, or understands. We suspect that babies can focus only at close distances, and that they hear higher-pitched voices better than lower ones, and that they are busy constructing in their minds the universe that surrounds them. We know they need closeness and cuddling and love.

What better way to meet all these needs than by "infant reading" to a baby as young as three weeks old?

I've been using the expression "infant reading" instead of "reading" because the activity we do with infants bears as much resemblance to later reading as T-ball does to the World Series. Of course, T-ball is good for kids and will likely be the start for our next generation of baseball players. Just so, early infant reading develops an attitude toward books and print that is vitally important for reading later on.

Infant reading doesn't have that much to do with the actual words on the page; it has more to do with playing and talking, singing and laughing, observing and exploring, tickling and having fun together. For tiny infants, there are special books with waterproof vinyl pages that can be propped up on the changing table, left in the crib, or even set to float in the bathtub. While you can't very well sit down and read with your infant for long periods of time as you would with an older child, you still can encourage infant reading by making sure there are books in your child's crib or playpen or out on the floor. When your baby looks at a book out of curiosity, you can use that interest to talk about the pictures, to read the simple text, or to have fun by singing, clapping, or making funny sounds.

Infants look at books with bursts of intense concentration. That's when you should do infant reading with your baby. The best books for infants have big, simple shapes that your baby will scrutinize for a few minutes while you read or talk or explain. Then the baby will turn away, because this early experience of reading is a very intense one.

For four chapters now, I've been talking about reading as an

Board Books for Babies

If you read to your baby, your baby will want to read to herself—or at least pretend to. Here are some board books that will take rough treatment.

Janet and Allan Ahlberg, *Peekaboo* (Viking). A book to accompany that wonderful baby game.

Dick Bruna, *Miffy* (Price Stern) and many other titles. Bruna's simple, brightly colored illustrations were all the rage a few years ago. Babies still love them.

Eric Hill, *Where's Spot* (Putnam) and many others. That puppy Spot gets into trouble in book after book. Reinforced construction helps the book last.

Peggy Parish, *I Can—Can You?* (Greenwillow). Ten laminated pages about important things: toes and fingers.

Washable cloth books (Random House) including Norman Gorbaty's *Baby Animals Say Hello* and other titles. Chewable. But be sure to keep them clean.

attitude more than a set of skills. Attitudes start early. The one-year-old who wants to eat her cloth book about bears is busy exploring the world of print. Eating for a baby is part of her process of understanding the world. To understand the idea of "book," she must eat it, tear it, crunch it, and ignore it—all at the same time she learns that a book is something to be encountered visually. Obviously, some first books will be damaged as they're touched and manipulated by your child. Just keep the expensive illustrated hardcover books out of the playpen. They're for you and your baby to read together at other times in order for books to become part of your relationship with each other.

GETTING INTO STORIES

Sometime between eighteen and thirty months, a baby's language skills develop dramatically. Just as crawling turns to walking, so babbling turns to talking. At this stage, infant reading becomes much closer to ordinary reading. Current research says that your child is busy at this point creating stories in her own mind—to understand herself, the spot of sunlight on the floor, her teddy bear. This is the time when books become much more than shapes and sounds for her. They begin to convey both language and story.

The key for this change lies in favorite books. In dealing with young children, I cannot overemphasize the importance of letting children select their favorites from a large number of books. Then read those favorite books together with your child again and again.

Marcia Baghban, the author of *Our Daughter Learns to Read and Write*, offers a remarkable study of the way her daughter, Gita, picked up language skills from birth to age three. As part of her graduate work at Indiana University, she tape-recorded many of their times reading together. Here's a transcript that shows the kind of reading Gita was doing at twenty-four months:

MOM: How about your book about Winnie-the-Pooh? Do you think you can read this yourself?
GITA: No. Mommy. You. You.

MOM: O.K. Let's try this book. Who's this book about?

GITA: Winnie Pooh.

MOM: Right. (reads) *Winnie-the-Pooh lives in a house in the forest. Here is Pooh Bear—*

GITA: Pooh Bear.

MOM: *—with his friend Christopher Robin. They are reading a funny story.*

GITA: Story.

MOM: Um hum (reading) *Shy Piglet is afraid of his own shadow. There's nothing Pooh likes better than eating honey with Piglet.* (to Gita) Where's the honey?

GITA: (Points to honey pot.) Honey.

MOM: Who's this?

GITA: Tiger.

MOM: Right. (reading) *Tigger is Pooh's bouncy friend. And Owl is Pooh's knowing friend. He explains things to Pooh.*

GITA: E-ore. E-ore.

MOM: Right. (reading) *Eeyore is a gloomy friend.* (to Gita) He's a donkey, see?

GITA: Donkey.

MOM: (reading) *Now Eeyore is happy. He's glad to see Winnie-the-Pooh. Winnie-the-Pooh is happy to see Eeyore.*

GITA: Winnie Pooh happy. Susie happy. Lassie happy. Mommy happy. Baba happy.

Looking at this conversation carefully, you can see how the favorite book brings about the entire exchange. Gita is responding to a story and characters she already knows. Sometimes she is predicting the next picture or section in the book. Sometimes she is echoing her mother's words. Sometimes she is using the model of the story to understand her own world and to express her own experience.

Reading Aloud—Any Questions?

Researchers in Houston, Texas, tape-recorded 147 hours of parents reading with young children aged three to five. They found that girls in their sample tended to ask more questions than boys, but all children were curious about pictures, the story, and word meaning—in that order.

How many questions? On average, the children asked one question every 2.26 minutes.

Of course, young children also enjoy new and different books, but it is in repeated reading of favorite books that real gains are made in understanding stories and language. After twenty readings of *Each Peach Pear Plum* by Janet and Allan Ahlberg or *The Cat in the Hat* by Dr. Seuss or *Owl Moon* by Jane Yolen or whatever book she loves, you'll desperately want to move on to another book. But your child will still be taking in the language, the pictures, the ideas, and the experience of reading that favorite book. For her sake, keep reading it.

One of the wonderful things about good children's books is that they are often so interesting to adults. Something in us responds, as we read, to the kinds of stories that children also love. Timeless stories ranging from *Three Little Pigs* to Robert Munsch's *Love You Forever* will find a resonant chord that makes reading fun for us too.

It is our interest and attention that makes reading such a wonderful experience for young children. If you count the words in Marcia Baghban's reading to her daughter, you'll find that only half of what's spoken is actually reading. The other half is explaining, asking, identifying, and exploring. These

Reading in Day Care

Almost half the young children in the United States will spend some time in day care—and some of that time should be spent reading. Here's what to expect in a good reading program:

- A book area for children in every room
- Daily reading and storytelling time in small groups or "circles"
- Trips to the library for books, films, puppet shows
- Sing-along time with song sheets; read-along time with audiotapes
- Quiet time with a special book and a volunteer to help reading
- Exploration through books of theme units, from dinosaurs to clowns to family problems

aren't activities that just go along with reading—they are *part* of reading. If you take too much time with the text and ignore all the rest, then the process of reading will be dry and lifeless. Reading time should always be full of talk and play, even if that has little obvious connection to the story.

To maintain your own interest—and expand your child's experience with books—it's also important to keep trying to enlarge the field of what's read. Book clubs for young children are an especially good source, since a new book or two appears on your doorstep each month. A weekly trip to the bookstore or library is even better because your range of choice is wider and it turns book selection into a special event. Grandparents and other relatives can be encouraged to give books or bring library books when they come to visit. There's always the chance that one of the new books will become a favorite. In fact, the better the book, the far more likely it is to become a favorite.

Many young children enter day care quite early on. A good

Easy on the Budget

A good children's book can be quite expensive, though never as much as a pair of jeans or a good dinner out. Some publishers offer bargain-basement prices on books for young children.

• Golden Books. These are mass produced in several sizes with titles and designs that go back fifty years or more. Some have become classics. All are less than two dollars. My favorites:

> *The Little Red Caboose*
> *Little Toot*
> *Animal Daddies and My Daddy*
> *Dumbo* (and other Disney favorites)

• HarperCollins "I Can Read" Series. These are slightly more expensive titles, but each is still less than four dollars. The series features some of the best writers for beginning readers in a sturdy paperback format.
• Random House "Step Into Reading" books. Not as prestigious as the HarperCollins line, but still well produced and at the same price.

day care program should offer much more than just baby-sitting. Part of the daily activities should be reading books. When you are evaluating day care options, look around the home or day care center for the bookshelf and ask questions about how much time is spent reading. Excellent day care is always an extension of your own parenting—and it should include lots of time reading together with the children.

HOW TO TELL A GOOD PICTURE BOOK

While your child will always pick her own favorite books for herself, you and other relatives probably will select the books that are available to her. These guidelines, based on the experience of parents, preschool teachers, and librarians, will help you choose good books to buy or bring home from the library.

• The illustrations should be rich enough and detailed enough that you can find extra material to talk about. Some of Mercer Mayer's books have no text at all, so the story becomes what you and your daughter talk about together. The illustrations in Maurice Sendak's *In the Night Kitchen* are so complex and detailed that they would support several stories besides the one in the text.

• The book should be appropriate not just for the child's current age but also for the next year or two. For instance, Dr. Seuss's *Green Eggs and Ham* appeals to babies for its rhythm and rhyme, to three- and four-year-olds because Ham-I-Am is an extension of their own rebelliousness, and to early readers because it's simple enough that they can read it themselves.

• The printed text should be short—a sentence or two per

Books by Mail

If there are no bookstores in your area, a good way to get new books for your child is to sign up for a children's book club. All offer great opening deals, then send one or two books a month (at the normal list price) to your mailbox.

- Children's Book-of-the-Month Club
  Camp Hill, PA 17011
- Doubleday Children's Book Club
  Box 6342
  Indianapolis, IN 46209
- Grolier Books Club
  Box 1772
  Danbury, CT 06816
- Parents Magazine Read Aloud Book Club
  P.O. Box 10264
  Des Moines, IA 50336
- Weekly Reader Book Club
  P.O. Box 16613
  Columbus, OH 43216

page—but not so short that the pages will be flipped through without discussion. In a picture book, the illustrations are as important as the text. (Often they are created by separate individuals.) In Allen Say's *Grandfather's Journey* the text is very short; in *The Balloon Tree* by Phoebe Gilman the text takes up half a page and is probably at the upper limit of how much your young child will accept before wanting a page turn.

- The text should be predictable, through rhythm, rhyme,

or logic, to make it easy for your child to "read" for herself. The early book-babble of babies is mostly based on memorized sounds, many of which are not even understood. Rhyming books such as *One Fish, Two Fish, Red Fish, Blue Fish* by Dr. Seuss or books with repeated lines such as *Frederick* by Leo Lionni are easy to memorize and easy for your child to respond to or to recite as you read.

• The story should engage both you and your child. Since reading is sharing, parents will want a book that has some interest for them as well as their child. The emotional beauty of *Whose Mouse Are You?* by Robert Kraus appeals to any adult; the magical text of Margaret Wise Brown's *Goodnight Moon* or the spunky preschoolers in Robert Munsch's books appeal to the kid in all of us.

• Nonetheless, the book should be for and about children. In Peggy Parish's *I Can—Can You?* the appeal of seeing all those babies in illustrations is primarily for other babies. Your child will want to read about other children her own age or slightly older, so she can see herself in the characters of the story.

• The story should suggest some of the great themes— struggle, growth, love, loss—so the book will be useful in the process of growing up. Bruno Bettelheim makes an impressive case in his book *The Uses of Enchantment* that early reading has an important psychological function which requires that it touch honestly on the major tasks and traumas of life. While Grimm's *Fairy Tales* obviously fill the bill, the same might also be said of Robert Munsch's *Thomas' Snowsuit* and its focus on anger and frustration, or P. D. Eastman's *Are You My Mother?* with its tale of loss and search for comfort. A great children's book is never just silly or sweet. It speaks deeply to both parent and child.

• The book should be made well enough to withstand

tough use. Heavy board or cloth pages are best for the playpen, and many children's classics are now available in this format. Sewn bindings withstand repeated readings. Most cheap paperbacks have what is called a "perfect" binding, which is nothing more than glue. They simply fall apart, fast. The pages of a sewn book are stitched together with thread before the cover is glued on. These are the books that last.

- One caution to book-buying parents: Don't buy pop-up books for babies. More and more books are appearing in pop-up format these days, but these books fall apart very quickly given the heavy handling they receive.

GROWING VOCABULARY AND UNDERSTANDING

One amazing fact about children is how much reading they can do at a very early age. In North America, a great many children can recognize the word *McDonald's* with the golden arches as early as twenty-four months. By age three, many children have a very practical sight vocabulary of two dozen words or so: *Big Mac, Wal-Mart, Cheerios, Stop, Dairy Queen.* As a parent, you may not even be aware that your child is already reading, but she is. The first reading always is based on the words that make sense of the child's world.

The problem with phonics for early readers is that the young mind isn't much interested in theoretical constructions such as *choo-boo-too.* While any number of programs exist to teach phonics to young children, the long-term benefit is questionable. You can do phonic drills by the crib, or buy kits that use phonic parts to make snakes or circles, but these exercises are

Five Gorgeous Illustrated Books

Eric Carle, *The Very Hungry Caterpillar* (Philomel) and other books. Carle's modern, painterly illustrations are matched here by a cute gimmick.

Helen Cooper, *The House Cat* (Scholastic). Positively luminous illustrations make cats seem even more magical than they really are.

The Boy Who Held Back the Sea, illustrated by Thomas Locker (Dial). Very realistic, Whistler-like illustrations tell this traditional story.

Maurice Sendak, *In the Night Kitchen* (HarperCollins). A magical, dreamlike story with realistic, anatomically-correct drawings.

Brian Wildsmith, *Python's Party* (Oxford). British whimsy with clever, colorful illustrations.

not likely to have much meaning for your child. And there's always the chance that overzealous instruction will backfire and interfere with your child's love of reading. I suggest you let any formal phonics instruction wait until your child enters school and has a vocabulary and experience base large enough that it will be useful to her.

All you really have to do to start your child reading is read with her.* When your child is ready to read for herself—and that

---

*Some experts say that for 80 percent of children, simple immersion in reading and books will lead to real, independent reading by school age.

*Five Classics That Have Stood
the Test of Time*

Laurent De Brunhoff, *Babar* (Random House). The characters are dated, but the simple stories and art still appeal.

A. A. Milne, *Winnie-the-Pooh* (Dell). A delight, both in the original and the Disney-ized versions.

H. A. Rey, *Curious George* (Houghton Mifflin). The childish monkey is annoying to parents but works for kids. The originals are much better than the made-for-TV cartoon versions.

Dr. Seuss, *Green Eggs and Ham* (Random House). Easy-to-read text and a naughty beast have made this book a winner for many years.

Mother Goose. These wonderful tales have been done up beautifully by Brian Wildsmith, Raymond Briggs, and many other illustrators in a variety of editions.

will happen at a number of different times in a number of different ways—she'll take over the reading from you. She'll repeat some of your words in that favorite book, then proudly declare that she'll read the next page, or the next word in a line, all by herself. Of course it's as much memory and guesswork as decoding, but it's still reading—just as that first toddling step really is walking. As a parent, you can support and encourage that first step and that first reading, but you can't force them to happen.

What's essential in building your child's reading is your in-volvement. Early reading is always social. No three-year-old, or five-year-old for that matter, wants to read to herself. Her read-ing, when it comes, will be out loud—just as your reading, with her, was out loud through the years of early childhood. You have to be there to hear the reading when it happens.

These days, many books for young children are available on audiotape and can be popped into a child's tape recorder. There's nothing wrong with your child's doing this after you've read the book a few times. Just remember that no tape recorder or videotape can ever substitute for you, your time, and your love.

READING TOGETHER— AND VARIATIONS

The reading demands of a three-year-old can be quite substan-tial. While a younger child frequently will be satisfied with a book or two at various times of the day, a three-year-old who says, "Daddy, read to me," often will be prepared to sit for an hour or more and read twenty or thirty books. This kind of marathon might be far more than Daddy had in mind.

So mix it up. Reading a book is only one kind of reading ac-tivity. Why not try a few others?

- Draw a picture and make up a story about it.
- Make up a story with your child as the central character.
- Read the newspaper together, especially the comics or children's page.
- Play with letters on the fridge or your child's blackboard.
- Read a magazine like *Owl* or *Stone Soup*.

Stuff to Encourage Reading

Reading is more than books. Make sure your preschooler has some of the following:

- magnetic fridge letters
- felt board and letters
- easel, pad, and markers
- alphabet placemat
- chalkboard

Don't forget the gimmick books: cut-outs, paste-ins, coloring books. They're fun for tiny hands and can help develop both language and a sense of story.

- Write a letter to Grandma, or the Easter bunny, or the *Lego News*.
- Look through a catalog or photo album together.
- Tell a story about your own life as a child.

Reading, listening, and language skills all develop together. The more your child reads and hears, the more sophisticated her talking and imagining will become. The great advantage of reading, of course, is that she'll have a chance to hear words that don't come up in ordinary conversation. We have more than 500,000 words in the English language, yet we rarely use more than 15,000 in everyday speech. One researcher videotaped three hours of television and found that only 7,000 different words were used in all that time. Neither talk nor television, then, is sufficient to build your child's vocabulary.

Reading, on the other hand, opens a door to language for your child that would otherwise remain closed. It allows her to hear longer sentences, more carefully structured and beautifully balanced than those of everyday speech.

What's more, reading creates windows on parts of the world and experiences that your child will never get to know otherwise. When my children were young, they loved *Babar and the Moustache Man*. They'd never been to Paris or Africa, never seen a subway, or held a flute, or seen a king. But thanks to the Laurent de Brunhoff classic, all these became part of their early lives.

Books expand language and experience in ways that are obvious, like my Babar example, and ways that are subtle. When your child reads *Franklin in the Dark* by Paulette Bourgeois, she won't learn much about turtles, but she'll find her own fear of the dark validated by seeing it in print. The human-looking animals in picture books are there for a reason: often it's more comforting to recognize our fears in those of a frightened turtle than it is to admit them out loud. Books not only expand the outer world for your child, they articulate the feelings of her inner world as well.

YOUR CHILD'S BOOKSHELF— AND STILL MORE BOOKS

By the time your child is three, her bookshelf will probably have twenty or thirty books on it. Some you'll have bought, some will be gifts, some you'll get as hand-me-downs or by trading with other parents. These books are vitally important—but your child will still want to look at and read many more. That's where the public library can help.

Some of America's Top Author/Illustrators for Preschoolers

Jan and Allan Ahlberg. It's Allen who comes up with the ideas and Janet who does the watercolors with so many layers of meaning. Among their best: *Jeremiah in the Dark Woods*.

Chris Van Allsburg has twice won the prestigious Caldecott Award for his highly realistic illustrations and warm-hearted stories. Van Allsburg studied sculpture before he took up illustration; now he works in oils and watercolors.

Mercer Mayer. Born in Arkansas, Mayer now lives in Connecticut where he creates dogs, porcupines, frogs, and spiders that are often more human and more humorous than any real critters.

Richard Scarry was born in Boston but now lives in Switzerland, thanks to the royalties from over 150 books. Critics find Scarry's simple animals, such as Lowly Worm, a bit cutesy, but kids love them.

Maurice Sendak became famous with "Rosie" and infamous with *In the Night Kitchen*. His illustrations combine whimsy and magic; his genius has led him to design sets for the Metropolitan Opera.

If you read for just twenty minutes a day, you and your young child will go through over one hundred books each month. Some of these will be favorite books, read over and over again, but many will be on loan from the local library. Your library will likely have most of the titles recommended in this book and thousands of others as well: storybooks; fairy tales; nonfiction books; animal books; books with audiotapes; joke books; photo-illustrated books; poetry books; books about love, death, and anger; books about babies and going to school and divorce; books about . . . Well, you get the idea.

When our children were young, my wife and I used the library to bring in a dozen new children's books every week; then we ordered from a bookstore the titles that caught the boys' interest. Since a big illustrated book can cost twenty dollars, the "library-first, bookstore-second" approach gave us a chance to buy books that were sure favorites, because we'd already tested out their appeal when they were on loan from the library. What's more, the selection of children's books in most libraries is much wider than that of even the best bookstore. With thousands of new children's books published every year, few bookstores can stock even a fraction of what's current. And backlist titles— books that came out last year or the year before—can disappear far too quickly from bookstore shelves. Your library will still have these books and many other titles from a collection that might stretch back over decades. Your child can enjoy them all.

READING IS SPECIAL

When reading together, most parents like to hold young children on their laps. Even Alex, my squirmiest son, would sit reasonably still on my lap when he was being read to. Grandparents and baby-sitters may prefer to have children sit beside them, but snuggling close. Some parents read to their children in bed. My own father had a special reading chair, wide enough for my brother and me to sit together on his lap. At day care centers, reading often takes place in small groups, with kids sitting on mats or pillows. The physical arrangements for reading are relatively unimportant. What matters is that there is time for reading.

A few parents like to read in the morning, but this is becoming more difficult for busy, two-income families. My favorite reading time is after school, when I'm relaxed but still have some energy. My parents liked to read right after supper, because they were too sleepy at bedtime. But the favorite reading time of all, of course, is just before bed.

Make sure that reading time is a special time. Older children might be able to read with the TV on or with headphones blasting rock music into their ears, but young children cannot. Reading time should be a quiet time, a settling time. The TV goes off, your voice begins the story, and the dream begins.

Reading doesn't happen "out there," like the experience of television; the experience of reading is inside us. When your

What About Teletubbies?

Publishers have been doing book spin-offs of TV series ever since the 1950s. The books are never really bad, but none of the old Howdy Doody books ever became a classic. Nonetheless, many little kids find real delight in reading books based on *Teletubbies* or *Sesame Street*, just as they'll enjoy the books they see on *Reading Rainbow*. And these TV spin-off books are usually quite economical.

child hears you read *The Runaway Bunny* by Margaret Wise Brown, she *becomes* the little rabbit of the story. The wonderful thing about reading is that we enter into the action—we are *in* the book. Reading always should be active and involving.

Never force a book, or keep reading if your child wants to stop. There is a difference between waiting for your child to settle down and dealing with a child who just isn't interested. Don't expect a quiet reading time to be successful right after a boisterous birthday party, or when your child is cranky and tired. Let it go. Don't try to force cuddly animal stories if your child doesn't want to listen to them. On some days, your child won't want to hear even favorite books. That's when you should both take a day off from your daily reading.

Sometimes you'll have to wait until your child is ready for certain books. My youngest child wasn't at all interested in Rupert the Bear books when he was four and at home, but he found great delight in them at the summer cottage when he was eight. The book that bores one day may well amuse the next day, or next week, or next year. In reading, as in so much else, parents must be patient.

Relax and enjoy. Young children are responsive and curious and loving when you read with them. Their books will be a joy to both you and your child. Soon enough your child will be too large to sit on your lap anymore. Make sure you have many days and many books to remember before she's off in her own chair with a book.

ELEVEN MUST-HAVE BOOKS FOR YOUR VERY YOUNG CHILD'S BOOKSHELF

Janet and Allan Ahlberg, *Each Peach Pear Plum* (Scholastic). Really a peekaboo game in a book—great for reading together with your kids.

Margaret Wise Brown, *Goodnight Moon* (HarperCollins). Simple and repetitive for adults but the best bedtime book ever for young children. Moms, especially, will also love Brown's *Runaway Bunny* (HarperCollins).

Paulette Bourgeois, *Franklin in the Dark* (Scholastic) and many other Franklin titles. Illustrations by Brenda Clark. This is the charming story of Franklin, the timid turtle, who overcomes his fear in the dark. First of the Franklin series, now on television.

P. D. Eastman, *Are You My Mother?* (Random House). A young bird falls from his nest and has to find his mother. Warm, charming, and easy to read.

Ezra Jack Keats, *The Snowy Day* (Puffin). A boy makes a snowball and keeps it in his pocket. Street-smart illustrations by an American award-winner.

Robert Kraus, *Whose Mouse Are You?* (Macmillan). Identity and family are the themes in one of the most beautiful and moving children's books ever written.

Arnold Lobel, *Fables* (HarperCollins). Short, original fables written and illustrated with Lobel's gentle wit. This is a wonderful read-aloud for both you and your child.

Mercer Mayer, *A Boy, a Dog and a Frog* (Dial). No words, but evocative drawings to tell the story and to discuss with your child.

Robert Munsch, *Thomas' Snowsuit* (Firefly). Because it really is hard to get dressed to go out and play.

Maurice Sendak, *Where the Wild Things Are* (HarperCollins). Beautiful, quirky, and adventurous. Scary for some young readers, but worth it.

Chris Van Allsburg, *The Polar Express* (Houghton Mifflin). This is probably the most beautiful Christmas story ever written and illustrated.

Chapter 6

The Beginning Reader:
Ages Four and Five

It wasn't until the research of the 1990s that we really understood how important this early reading stage was in developing
lifelong reading habits. Unlike infants and toddlers, your beginning reader isn't just listening to stories and picking up individual words. Quite simply, your four- or five-year-old is trying
hard to understand how reading works. This understanding is
crucial to further reading development in primary school, especially for children who don't have wide experience with print at
home.

The current school buzzwords around this stage in reading
development are *phonemics* or *phonological awareness*. Though
the Latin root *phon* is the same as that for phonics, phonemics is
really quite different from the old phonics programs that so
dominated our schools fifty years ago. Phonemics refers to the
smallest bits of sound (phonemes) that can be heard—usually
individual letters or what linguists called digraphs, like *sh*.
Phonological refers to the ability to hear and discern specific
sounds in our language—*m* as opposed to *n*, for instance—and
then use them to construct meaning.

While the technical definitions are complex, the basic idea is not. Phonemic awareness is really an oral language skill that seems to be very important in developing reading. Combined with basic concepts about print, the capacity to hear distinct sounds is quite essential for beginning readers. A child who often speaks with adults, who hears language spoken around the home, who listens to stories being read aloud is mastering the skill of discriminating phonemes. A child who doesn't have these experiences will be in trouble when it comes time to learn to read.

The second important part of beginning reading is for your child to understand some basic concepts about how print works in English. These concepts include:

- Words in English print go from left to right, from top to bottom (a pattern which is not true in Hebrew or Japanese or many other languages).
- Pages in a book go from front to back (again, a Western European pattern).
- The letters in our alphabet are the same, regardless of their typeface, size, or shape.
- The letters in our alphabet have a specific set of forty or more sounds.
- Connected letter sounds are used to make up words.
- The words on a page are really the same as words that people speak.

This simple understanding of print and sound correlation seems to be essential for the more sophisticated reading skills that develop later. A vast majority of children catch on to these concepts simply by listening to stories, looking at books, and talking to parents. Mom and Dad read to the kids; they see that the print on the page makes their parents say certain words—the same words—each time; and they make the connection. Many kids learn in a very offhand way how print flows on a page and over the page and connects to pictures in a book to make meaning.

But some children don't "get it" from early read-together activities. These are the kids who enter junior or senior kindergarten without a clue about the way print and words connect. For these kids to read, the very basics have to be learned first.

PHONEMICS IN KINDERGARTEN

A reading program in junior and senior kindergarten will probably have lots of reading during story time, many picture books for shared or paired reading, and labels on virtually everything in the room. As a parent, you should expect your child to be immersed in print at this crucial stage in her development.

But the latest research from California and Texas suggests that immersion isn't sufficient to give every child the grounding she needs to become a competent reader later on. While the academic debate is still raging over this, it seems that some explicit instruction—or at least some serious classroom time—should be given to the basic rudiments of reading. A good kindergarten program will do this.

The first job is to get across the idea that we speak using something called "words." While this seems pretty elementary, the idea of individual words making up thoughts and sentences is not as obvious as it seems. Consider this conversation:

MOM: Djawanna eetnow?
KID: Nah. Iwannawatch TV.

MOM: Yagonnaeetnow or yagonnawatchnow? Yadonwan-
naeet, yagonnastarv. Sowhaddayawahnndo?

KID: GuessIgoddaeet.

My point is that much of our everyday conversation is so slurred together that the sounds of individual words can easily be lost on a child. For kids who have been read to every night, who have looked at picture books, who regularly have conversations with their parents and siblings, the idea of *words* comes across early on. But even these kids often mistake syllables for words, or lump prepositional phrases together as a single word.

After this, little kids have to understand the idea of syllables so they can begin to decode larger words. There's no particular reason this has to be done perfectly. The convention that the word *syllable* splits between the *l*'s isn't important at this stage, but the fact that it has three syllables is good, solid information that will pay off later on. In kindergarten, kids can do many different exercises to break down words into syllables. They can also count or clap syllables along with their teacher. But all of this is done aurally and orally, not using print. Syllabication as a print decoding skill comes much later, around grade two or three. The idea in kindergarten is to help the kids *hear* how our language works, so when they eventually start reading, the printed words will make sense.

The final kindergarten task is to learn letter-sound correspondences such as *b* makes a "buh" sound. This task is far more important than learning the "name" of the letter, or being able to recite the alphabet from memory. In teacher language, this is called pairing up phonemes with graphemes; for the rest of us, this learning is the basis for the most basic word-attack skill: the initial letter sound.

But this seems like phonics, you say. And it does. Traditional phonics, however, was an elaborate system that took many months to teach. It was riddled with rules that only sometimes worked. And it was based on print conventions, not on the way words actually sound. Phonemic awareness, on the other hand, is primarily an effort to build aural discrimination so that kids will be able to tackle words later on using phonics and other clues that will help them get meaning from the print on a page.

In kindergarten, the teacher will spend a fair amount of class time on the concepts of "onsets" and "rimes." The idea is that any syllable can be split into its initial sound (onset) and the vowel and consonant sound (rime) that completes it. The word *sit*, for instance, has an onset of "s-" and a rime of "it." A teacher can play word games with other *s* onset words (soon, sat, Sam) and rhyming games with the "it" (pit, hit, mitt, fit).

How is this different from the old phonics books—"The man with the pan had a fan"? The difference is one of approach and meaning. The problem with much phonics instruction is that it sacrificed meaning for the requirements of a system. The result was sometimes nonsense—and who wants to read

---

Syllables are the largest and most easily recognized sound in a word.

Phonemes are the smallest units of sound that can change the meaning of a word. Often they are associated with individual letters such as *s* or combinations such as *sh*.

Onsets are the initial consonant or consonant cluster in a syllable: the *st* in "start," for example.

Rimes are the vowel and any consonants that come after it: the *art* in "start."

nonsense? (Unless it's by Dr. Seuss, who gave the most wonderful sense to nonsense.)

Another activity in kindergarten and the primary grades is to manipulate the onsets and rimes of words to come up with new words. Kids are sometimes asked to do word transformations where a word like *cap* will turn to *tap* and then to *tan* by changing a letter each time. This kind of exercise teaches kids an essential concept: While we can combine onsets and rimes any which way, only certain combinations will give a real word.

Teachers and tutors can demonstrate these ideas to kids through games, by helping them do writing with whatever spelling they can muster, and by writing down dictated stories from the kids' own speech. Of course, reading books and experiencing print in the traditional ways also does much to boost phonemic awareness. Whole-language diehards would maintain it does plenty, all by itself.

Despite all the research done in the '90s by our six federally funded reading research centers, learning how to read still remains a mystery. Children seem to learn in many different ways, following many different timetables. A varied program in junior and senior kindergarten is obviously the best approach to follow until solid research, backed up and tested on a wide range of kids, tells us exactly what to do. So far, we're not that advanced.

But one item does seem especially clear—kids learn to read better when they're excited and enthusiastic about reading. Again and again, research tells us that the quality of the teaching and the enthusiasm of children is more important in developing reading skills than any particular program of instruction. Let's hope your child's kindergarten classroom is full of many different centers and activities, presided over by a teacher who shows the children how much joy can be found on the printed page.

PHONEMICS AT HOME

Let me repeat: If you've been reading regularly with your child, if you talk together regularly over breakfast and dinner, if you model the enjoyment of reading yourself, then your child will most assuredly learn to read. You don't need to buy special reading programs advertised on TV, or pick up the latest instructional CD-ROM for your computer, or follow any program of instruction at home. Follow the three Rs in this book and your child will become a reader.

The problem that I hear again and again from parents is that they are anxious about their child's reading. She seems to lag behind the other kids at school, or lose interest when reading together at night, or not be reading as well as her older sister. Often these "reading problems" are nothing more than a combination of parental anxiety and unfair comparisons with other kids. We must always remember that children have their own timetables of development. Parents should know, too, that second and third children rarely develop their reading skills as quickly as did the first child. But there is no particular advantage, long term, in a child reading by herself early on—and there is considerable disadvantage for any family where the kids are compared to each other or to the seemingly model child next door.

Nonetheless, parents going through this book want to give their child every possible break in developing her reading. Rightly so. Just as there are activities in school that do work well in developing reading skills and some that don't, so there are good and bad activities for building your child's reading skills and attitudes at home.

Let's start with a list of what you should be doing:

- Do continue reading with your child every night. By and large, you'll be doing the reading aloud, but your child will frequently become more involved at this stage.
- Do remember that reading time is playtime: games, songs, stories, and talk are as important as the reading of words on a page.
- Do encourage phonemic skills in your reading/playtime: songs, rhymes, limericks, clapping, dancing—all offer a reading payoff.
- Do encourage word recognition and sounding out wherever you can: words on the fridge, picture dictionary books, sing-along/read-along tapes.

I'll come back to all of these ideas, but first let me offer a list of cautions:

- Don't force an organized reading program. Whether it's a set of flashcards or computer instruction, it's too early for these mostly phonics programs. And there's a real danger that pushing such a program, prematurely, will hurt your child's attitude toward reading.
- Don't turn reading time into a work-study session. You will get more long-term reading advancement from games and stories than from a rigorous study of word segmentation. And there's no point in asking a young child "comprehension" questions to see if she's paying attention. You'll know by the wiggles.

- Don't let a slightly older brother or sister take over reading. Sibling rivalry is such that a child who is four or five years older can take on quasi-adult responsibilities like nightly reading without much danger of claiming the territory for herself. But don't let your seven-year-old son start showing off his reading skills while your five-year-old daughter is still struggling with her first steps in reading. That's a recipe for disaster.

When you and your kindergarten child read together, chances are good that your child will do "pretend" reading long before she can actually decode words. Children who have been read to by parents frequently like to turn the pages of a book and tell the story themselves using the same vocal tones and language that you do.

According to one authority on early reading, there are a number of stages in this storybook retelling. Often it begins when your child simply describes the pictures on each page. Later, she may create a story based on the pictures in the book or on some remembered bits of the actual story. The third stage, a real crossover to decoding, is one where your child will create a story that is influenced by words and phrases from the actual text. The fifth stage is when your child begins struggling much more with the words on the page—remembering some, figuring others out from visual clues, sounding out some, guessing at others.

Much parental anxiety comes from the fourth stage—the one I skipped up above. In this stage, your child may suddenly refuse to try to read at all. No explanation. No excuses. Just no reading. This stage rarely lasts for more than a few weeks, and it happens for a very good reason. Suddenly your child realizes that the story is all there, on the pages, and that she can't read it all, or read it very well. The frustration causes many children to simply stop reading: "No, *you* read it, Mommy." And you should. As your child's confidence grows, she'll tackle reading again.

The read-it-again phenomenon is also a key feature of reading together with four- and five-year-olds. While you'll likely get bored reading the same handful of books night after night, your child loves the predictability of these favorite books. These are the books she'll memorize. And these are likely the first books she'll "read" all by herself.

Reading together, however, is only one activity that is helpful for children at this age. Just as important are the games and silly activities that you do together as you read. The latest research would indicate that word play, rhythm, and rhyme are very valuable for kindergartners who may still be struggling with actual reading of books. We also know that music activities and music education offer big rewards in many school areas as a child grows older. So this is definitely the time to

- sing (you don't have to be good);
- clap (along with a poem is excellent);
- dance (to music or words or both);
- recite (poems with rhythm and rhyme work very well);
- laugh (if you're not having fun, it won't be fun for your child).

This age from four to five is also a wonderful one for nursery rhymes. While psychologists may point out the developmental value of the story, reading specialists will tell you that the simple rhythms and rhymes—tested for centuries—do much to promote phonemic awareness.

Another valuable exercise, as your child's reading develops, is to begin tracing with your finger below each word as you read. This helps kids track with their eyes as they hear you read the

Five Games for Building Phonemic Awareness

1. **How many words are in your name?** The name Anthony, for instance, contains *an, ant, on* as well as the nonstandard *hon* and the abbreviation for NY. If you mix the letters up, there are dozens more.

2. **Clap the poem.** Most poetry for little kids is very rhythmic. Encourage your child to clap along as you read classics like "Willoughby, Walloby, Woo" or "Down by the Bay."

3. **I Spy.** You remember this one: "I spy, with my little eye, something that starts with B!" You might even write down whatever you "spied," just to emphasize the print-word correspondence—and to keep you from cheating.

4. **Fill in the rhyme.** You can use any form, just leave a blank for your child to fill. Limericks are great: "There once was a girl name Ruth, who had one very wobbly tooth, she stuck in her thumb, until it felt numb, and ended up looking _____ ."

5. **Wrong word!** This works especially well in a poem, when you substitute a silly wrong word in the text. Your child will giggle. Then you ask which word didn't make sense.

➔ Remember that your "reading" at this stage is really about sounds, stories, and silly play.

words. Teachers have used this for years, and it's an essential part of the highly disciplined though greatly flawed Distar reading system. You might find it useful with your child.

In kindergarten, the teacher or her aide will often make little storybooks of what your child dictates to her. This is a

valuable activity for you to do at home, too. Not only does it emphasize that spoken word–written word connection, but it gives
value to the story that your child tells you. Ask her to draw illustrations after you write the story down, then save these books
for the future. Twenty years from now, you'll have a keepsake
from childhood that will still have value when your turn-of-the-
millennium videos are decaying to carbon dust.

BOOKS FOR THE
BEGINNING READER

While the gorgeous picture books of early childhood are still
very valuable and will still have great appeal for your kindergarten almost-reader, you'll also find that new books provide
support for developing phonemic skills. Many of these bring delight for both you and your child.

In choosing fiction for reading aloud, your kindergarten
reader will want less print on the page than in the beautiful picture books you read to her earlier. She'll want illustrations that
offer as much fun as artistic beauty. The Dr. Seuss books have
worked well for fifty years, not because Theodor Geisel could
draw very well, but because he created wonderful characters, he
used rhythm and rhyme effectively, and his books are easy to
memorize and decode.

Picture books with a simple, action-oriented plot—prefer-
ably with a bit of surprise along the way—tend to work well. A
story written with lots of dialogue gives you a chance to use
your various reading voices, and gives your child a chance to join
in on sections that she's memorized or may be able to read for
herself.

My Desert Island Choices

Suppose you were marooned on a desert island with a couple of preschool kids, and you could have only two books. Which ones would you choose? My call would be for two big, hardcover titles: *The 20th Century Children's Poetry Treasury* and *The 20th Century Children's Book Treasury* (both Random House). Together they offer hundreds of selections, and the *Book Treasury* has forty-four of everyone's favorite picture books and stories complete with their illustrations.

Probably most important is a main character with whom your child can identify. Obviously this main character may be different for each child . . . but a great character is a great character regardless of gender, race, or physical appearance. Many great characters are animals, like Franklin the Turtle or Clifford the Dog, or fantasy figures like the Cat-in-the-Hat.

Another very valuable genre for your kindergarten child will be word books and picture dictionaries. Richard Scarry has dozens of these, but many other talented writers and illustrators have created them, too. While these may not be much fun for you to read aloud, your child will enjoy naming the pictures, thereby "reading" the label underneath. For many years, this was the basis for the look-say approach to reading, and it still works well for all sorts of kids. In terms of developing phonemic awareness, some sounding out of words beneath their picture will do much to give your child a sense of syllables, onsets, and rimes.

Poetry, of course, can't be beaten for rhyme and rhythm.

Little kids enjoy everything with a beat, from the song/poems of Raffi to the wonderful lyrics of Jack Prelutsky. They'll gladly fill in words that you leave out, and can easily memorize lines, stanzas, and whole poems.

These days, there are more and more excellent picture books of nonfiction—what librarians call "information books"—on everything from bicycle repair to the *Titanic*. Some children find these remarkably fascinating. Later on, you'll find that boys, especially, will turn to nonfiction while girls are happy to continue reading storybooks. The keys for buying these books are in the illustrations, a limited amount of text per page, the interests of your child, and *your* interests too. It's so important for dads to read with children that perhaps certain nonfiction books should be reserved especially for them. Certainly when my kids were young, you'd never find my wife "reading" the Sears hardware

Precocious Young Readers

Between 2 percent and 5 percent of young children begin reading early and can often read aloud sophisticated material when other kids are still struggling with sight words and blending sounds. This can seem quite impressive and lead you to think that they've mastered "reading" when all they've really got down is "decoding." Even if your five-year-old can read *Time* magazine quite fluently, it doesn't mean she can comprehend the politics or the other issues in the text. And don't be surprised if, given the choice, she'd rather read a *Franklin* picture book—it deals with issues a five-year-old can really understand.

catalog to them, but you could frequently find me doing exactly that.

Your interest is also important because that's what leads to talk about the books and the topics they present. With bright children, all you have to do to start questions rolling is to stop reading. They'll find plenty to ask you and you'll both have plenty to talk about. Excitement in reading is contagious.

Remember, finally, how important rereading is for young children. Your child will ask for her favorite books to be read again and again, and that's what you must do. These are the first books she'll memorize and pretend read and almost read and then really read. But that will only happen after you've gotten pretty bored with *Franklin Fibs* or *Polar Bear Express*. While I would never say that a parent should give in to a child's wishes all the time, one place to wisely indulge your children is in reading. You simply can't read favorite books too much.

TEN MUST-HAVE BOOKS FOR YOUR BEGINNING READER

Remember that the point of these books isn't that they can be read easily by your four- or five-year-old. These books are for you to read aloud. Use them to develop reading attitude and phonemic awareness through rhyme and word play.

Lois Ehlert, *Nuts to You!* (Harcourt) and many others by this author. Good concepts-based books for beginning readers.

Bill Grossman, *My Little Sister Ate One Hare* (Random House). A counting book that's really funny—it even has the word *underpants* in it! Shocking stuff for the preschool set.

Kady MacDonald Denton (illustrator), *A Child's Treasury of Nursery Rhymes* (Kingfisher). Traditional folk, nursery, and Mother Goose rhymes with award-winning art.

Bill Martin Jr. and John Archambault, *Chicka Chicka Boom Boom* (Simon & Schuster). A wonderful extended poem, beautifully illustrated.

Jack Prelutsky, *Read-Aloud Rhymes for the Very Young* (Knopf) (illustrated by Marc Brown). A splendid collection of all the classic rhymes.

Dr. Seuss, *There's a Wocket in My Pocket* (Random House) and forty-three others. Brilliant phonics and phonemics lessons are carried through all these wacky books.

Marilyn Tolhurst, *Somebody and the Three Blairs* (Orchard). Kids love this reversal of the classic Goldilocks tale.

Joseph Slate, *Miss Bindergarten Gets Ready for Kindergarten* (Dutton) (illustrated by Ashley Wolf). Kindergarten is a big issue when you're five, and the rhyme here is good ear training.

Richard Scarry, *The Best Word Book Ever* (Golden) and many others. Scarry's books are wonderful word encyclopedias for the young. Only cartoon-level art, but a nice way to show that words name things.

Paul Zelinsky (illustrator), *The Wheels on the Bus* (Dutton). A beautiful version of the kid-famous song, complete with interesting foldups and cutouts.

Chapter 7

The Novice Reader:
Ages Six to Eight

The big new factor in your child's life at age six is school, serious school.

Your child's teachers in the primary years will attempt to teach a great variety of skills—from reading and math to shoelace-tying—to a great variety of children. The goals in reading are to have every child master the basics by the end of third grade. These basics include recognition of the alphabet and its sounds, a quick sight vocabulary of 3,000 or more everyday words, enough word-attack skills to tackle more difficult words, and a comfortable reading speed so stories can be read silently and with some enjoyment.

Schools try to do all this with one teacher in a classroom of twenty-five kids who have an enormous range of abilities and backgrounds. That real learning takes place in such circumstances is a tribute to the natural curiosity of children and to the wonderful dedication of primary teachers.

With luck, your child will be with a good teacher in a good school. Then you're likely to see some of the following:

- Parent volunteers to help with reading, field trips, special activities, and the library
- Peer tutors—older students working with younger children in reading and mathematics
- A strong library program, with check-out privileges starting in kindergarten and a librarian who acts as a reading teacher and enthusiast
- Group learning with kids clustered in different groups—sometimes based on ability, or interest, or friendship—for a variety of learning tasks
- Labels on almost everything in class, colorful bulletin boards, pictures of the kids, awards for virtually any achievement
- And books—not just primers, but real books, worn out from reading and rereading

If you don't see much of this, then reread Chapter 4 and put pressure on your school and school board. And do it directly—not by complaining in front of your child. He'll pick up the attitude that his school and teacher are lousy, and that won't help any of you to improve the situation. For school to do its job, your child must see that formal education is important in your eyes. Ms. Jones might not be the world's best teacher, but she is the best teacher your child will ever have for first grade. Be enthusiastic. Ask questions about what happens in school. Phone or drop notes to the teacher about absences or problems at home that she should know about. Become a partner in your child's education, even if there's work to do in making it better.

LEARNING TO READ
IN SCHOOL

In the past, learning to read at home was fun and learning to read at school was formal. At home, kids would read books; at school, they'd read basal readers or primers. At home, kids would sit on your lap and ask questions as you read; at school, they'd sit in desks and sound out bunches of *B* words. At home, kids would learn to read and love reading; at school, alas, the results were spotty.

Thank goodness, things have changed. These days, most schools try to simulate the home reading environment as much as possible. The old phonics drills have largely disappeared; the Dick and Jane readers have become real books; the desk work has been replaced by a cozy reading corner. Instead of phonics and color-the-mimeographed-page, we have "children's literature" and "big books" that are printed on huge pages and can be seen at the back of the classroom. These new approaches seem to be producing the most literate group of young people in history—up to at least fourth grade.

You shouldn't be upset that the schools aren't drilling your child in phonics. There is no real evidence that formal instruction in phonics rules produces more readers than any other technique. For some children—perhaps that quarter of the student population who can apply theoretical rules to real situations—formal phonics is an effective means of learning to read. For most others, phonics is just one more tool for figuring out what the tough words are.

The current approach in schools recognizes that different children learn in different ways (the buzz phrase is a "balanced" approach to reading). For some children, reading just clicks without formal instruction. For others, phonics is essential for

Teaching Reading Since the Thirteenth Century

The first recorded reference in English to a "primer," an early book of the alphabet and simple reading, goes back to the thirteenth century. Three hundred years later, there were a number of ideas on how to instruct children in reading similar to William Kemp's (1580): "After the four and twenty letters, and the tables of the syllables . . . [the child] shall proceed to practice the same in spelling and reading other men's works."

By the eighteenth century, children would begin reading with "hornbooks." A hornbook was a book whose single page was glued to a wooden paddle and then covered with a thin sheet of transparent horn to protect it from harsh treatment. The handle of the paddle had a hole with a string running through it that would be attached to a child's waist. This way, these "books" were not supposed to get lost.

Students quickly discovered that hornbooks also made excellent bats for a kind of badminton called battledore, which shows that kids two hundred years ago were really no better than today's students.

making sense of words on the printed page. For still others, context clues or word families work better. The style with which your child learns best will help determine what kind of teaching will be most effective for him.

The whole-language philosophy in schools tries to accommodate many different styles of learning—and preserve some of the sheer joy in reading. Chances are your child will read—and have read to him—many more books than you did in the primary grades. Chances are your child will master about as many phonic rules as you did, though not in such a rigorous way. And chances are your child will enjoy reading in school much more than those kids at the back of the class did thirty years ago.

Does the whole-language philosophy work? Wonderfully—for *some* kids, especially bright middle-class children. Does it work for all kids? No, but neither does phonics. Good teachers know that whole language doesn't eliminate phonics or "direct instruction." The danger is when a weak teacher uses the phrase "whole language" as an excuse for a slipshod reading program.

READING AT HOME

Regardless of how good your child's school may be, the most important reading environment is not the classroom or the school library. The single most important reading environment is your home.

• Continue to read every day with your child. No matter how independent he may appear, he still needs your interest and your time. If your home is going through a period of stress, this quiet time together with you will be even more important. Many young children suffer through the turmoil of divorce or a parent's job insecurity. Mom and Dad may be arguing, or too preoccupied to pay attention to the kids. Children can't articulate their needs for love and care, but they do show family stress through restlessness, attention-seeking behavior in school, and limited attention span. Sometimes parents need to examine their home life seriously so their children can get the stability they need to grow. Daily reading time, whatever else might be going on, can be an important island of security for your child.

• Continue to reach into your wallet to buy many kinds of print material. Your child learns about the variety of what he can read by seeing books, magazines, newsletters, cookbooks, newspapers, family letters, clippings, postcards, cereal-box backs, and anything else with print on it lying around the house. Your child learns about the value of reading by watching you read. He must see that reading is important to you for reading to become important for him.

• Continue to make sure that your child has time to read at home. Quiet time. Time with the TV turned off. Time with you. Your child's school will devote an hour a day to reading for the 180 days of the school year. You can double that time simply by reading with your child for half an hour each day right through the calendar year.

Reading together with your child is almost always a wonderful time for both of you. But—there's always at least one "but"—moms and dads do have tendencies in reading time that can make the experience less valuable for their children. So here's a little advice:

Mom: Resist the temptation to teach. Many mothers feel that family reading time also should make up for any defects in the school reading program, so your poor child is asked to sound out word after word when he just wants to get on with the story. Ease up. Keep the reading fun.

Dad: Don't rush it. Some fathers seem to set a goal of getting through so many books or so many pages during family reading time. The result is a tendency to give short shrift to your child's questions or the talk that should come out of reading. Slow down. If you read only one page and then spend fifteen

**Eight Phonics Rules That *Do* Work
(Almost All the Time . . .)**

1. In these double-vowel combinations, the first vowel is long and the second is silent: *oa, ay, ai,* and *ee.*
2. When *y* is the final letter in a word, it sounds like *ee.*
3. When there is one *e* in a word that ends in a consonant, the *e* is short.
4. G, followed by *e, i,* or *y,* sounds soft, like *j.* Otherwise it is hard, as in *gate.*
5. When *c* and *h* are next to each other, they form a single sound as in *chair.*
6. When the letter *c* is followed by *o* or *a,* it sounds like *k;* when it is followed by *e* or *i,* it sounds like *s.*
7. A vowel coming before *r, l,* or *w* is neither long nor short.
8. When two identical consonants are side by side (as in *cc* or *ss*), only one is heard.

Some of the remaining 110 phonics rules are also valuable, but none of them works more than 75 percent of the time.

minutes having a lengthy discussion, your child's reading development will still be well served.

A good time to review rules on watching television is when your child is entering first grade. Since school will be taking up six to eight hours a day, less time is available to do everything else. To keep some balance in your child's life, explain that the television has to be kept under control. The research doesn't say that you should throw the TV away, or limit it to an hour a day—the research says set rules. I suspect every family already has rules on television viewing that they never even think about: Turn it off at midnight, keep it quiet before the parents get up, no TV at dinner. All I'm suggesting is that these rules be extended so there is some structure in your child's free time and enough quiet time for reading to happen.

These early school years are crucial to teach decision making and self-reliance. A child who has to make up his mind just which two or three hours of television to watch is also making decisions about what to do with the other hours in the day. When you say, "Two hours of TV a day is enough," you're also saying "Now decide what you want to do with the other three hours before bed." By making yourself available to help, reading will be one of those choices.

BUILDING THE BOOKSHELF

By now, your child should have more than a dozen favorite books on his bookshelf. These books haven't become obsolete just because your child is beginning to read for himself. But now he needs new and different books, with an emphasis on those he'll be able to read for himself. Although William Steig's *Spinky Sulks* is a beautiful book, its "splendiferous" language requires reading skills that are too sophisticated for beginning readers. Arthur Yorinks's *Hey, Al* or Chris Raschka's *Yo! Yes!* are more closely linked to reading skills at the first- and second-grade level. By reading daily with your child, you'll know just how good his reading skills are.

If your child is choosing his own books, he'll naturally pick books written at a level he can read. If you're doing the choosing, look for the qualities that make a book easy for beginning readers to read:

The Caldecott Award Winners

The prestigious Caldecott Award dates back to 1938. It recognizes the "best" American illustrated book for young children in any given year. The most recent winners:

1999: Jacqueline Briggs Martin, *Snowflake Bentley* (Houghton Mifflin).

1998: Paul O. Zelinsky, *Rapunzel* (Dutton).

1997: David Wisniewski, *Golem* (Clarion).

1996: Peggy Rathmann, *Officer Buckle and Gloria* (Putnam).

1995: Eve Bunting, *Smoky Night* (Harcourt Brace).

1994: Allen Say, *Grandfather's Journey* (Houghton Mifflin).

1993: Emily McCully, *Mirette on the High Wire* (Putnam).

1992: David Wiesner, *Tuesday* (Clarion).

1991: David Macaulay, *Black and White* (Houghton Mifflin).

1990: Ed Young, *Lon Po Po: A Red-Riding Hood Story from China* (Philomel).

1989: Karen Ackerman, *Song and Dance Man* (Knopf).

1988: Jane Yolen, *Owl Moon* (Philomel).

1987: Arthur Yorinks, *Hey, Al* (Farrar, Strauss).

1986: Chris Van Allsburg, *The Polar Express* (Houghton Mifflin).

- Simple vocabulary and short sentences—because beginner's recognition vocabularies are small and their reading speed is slow

- Not too much print—because it's frustrating for any reader to be stuck too long on one page
- Illustrations to give clues about the story—even if a picture isn't worth a thousand words, it might give clues about one or two tough ones
- Relatively large type—because it's easier to read
- A "predictable" text, but not so predictable it becomes boring to you or your child. A book doesn't have to sound like Dick and Jane to be easy to read.

When your child begins to read for himself, a number of things will happen all at once. The first is usually memorization. Your child will have read one favorite book over and over again until the words are memorized. Then your child will begin to connect those words to the print on the accompanying page. This mixture of recognition and remembering is often the first reading. That's the reason children can "read" favorite books with vocabulary ranging from *Alexander* to *zoological* even though those words are much more sophisticated than they could possibly recognize or sound out.

Other children will begin reading with simple words they can recognize at a glance. The single-syllable vocabulary of P. D. Eastman's *Go, Dog, Go* includes the short, commonplace words that are easiest for young children to recognize without help. You'll find other books with the same approach. If your child likes to pick out words he can recognize, then these are the books you should be reading again and again.

Some children will combine words they know with phonic rules to sound out others. This process is painfully slow at first, but it can handle the more difficult vocabulary in books like Judith Viorst's *Alexander and the Terrible, Horrible, No Good, Very Bad Day*. If your child takes well to phonics, your choice of

The Five-Finger Reading Check

When your child starts to read for himself, it's important that the books he tackles aren't too difficult for him to handle successfully. Teachers have a simple way to match kids with the reading difficulty of a book: the five-finger check.

Ask your child to read a page from a book. Everytime he stumbles or skips a word, curl up one of your fingers. If all five fingers are curled up by the end of the page, the book is too tough. Read it to him this time, and put off his own reading for later on.

books is very wide. But you must be there to help in sounding out. Unlike German or Italian, in which words almost always "sound out" quite readily, English is quite erratic. Your child will need help sounding out and blending sounds. We all read in order to pull meaning from the printed page. The danger in phonics is that even careful reading will produce nonsense. This is the time a parent must help.

The key to all beginner books is a certain predictability in the text. Books for both younger and older children can offer prose rich in poetic language and surprising turns of phrase. For younger children, this richness works because you are doing the reading; for older children, it works because they have the skills to read more difficult material. But the first books your child reads for himself should be predictable: a regular rhythm, a repeated sentence structure, or a repeated set of lines (like a refrain in poetry) to make easier the task of looking at words or sounding out what's on the page.

How to Help When Your Child Reads to You

A beginning reader often gets stuck or makes mistakes on words when trying to read out loud to you. Parents have a natural tendency to want to rush in with the difficult word, but you'll help your child more if you count to five before you jump in.

If your child is stuck on a word:

- Wait five seconds.
- Ask your child to reread the sentence and see if the word pops into place. (This is a very important word-attack skill.)
- Ask your child to try to tackle the word herself using letter clues, phonics, similar words, context clues, or whatever techniques might work. (You might even suggest the meaning of the word, but not the word itself.)
- If all that fails (everything above might take twenty seconds), tell your child the word.

If your child makes a mistake on a word:

- If the mistake makes sense and the reading continues, ignore it.
- If the mistake doesn't make sense and your child hesitates (this is a good sign, incidentally, it means your child is reading for meaning), wait five seconds.
- Ask, "Does that make sense?" Then, "Maybe we should look again at this word," and point at the word in question.
- Try rereading the sentence using a blank for the word.
- If all that fails, tell your child the word.

KEEP IT FUN

Beginning reading shouldn't be work—it should be fun. Your child has lots of time to learn to decode words on a page—and this is only one stage in that whole process. So don't load on the pressure. There is no magic timetable for learning how to read. There are no particular skills or drills that will make it happen. And nothing will turn your child off reading more than too much pressure from you. All you have to do is enjoy reading to your child. Sooner or later your child will take over the reading from you.

In Chapter 5, we looked at reading to a three-year-old. When Marcia Baghban read to young Gita, the emphasis was on the baby's responses, on participation, on remembering key words. There was no "reading" in the sense of decoding print on the page, but there was lots of real reading going on.

Now let's listen to Janie Jardine read with her seven-year-old son, John. The story is Roch Carrier's *The Hockey Sweater*, one which is still too difficult for John to read on his own.

> MOM: (reading) *The winters of my childhood were long, long seasons. We lived in three places*—see in the picture—
>
> JOHN: Yeah, it's snowing, like outside.
>
> MOM: That's true. (reading)—*the church, the school and the skating rink. But our real life was on the skating rink*—
>
> John nods. (He's a hockey player himself.)
>
> MOM: (reading) *Real battles were won on the skating rink. Real strength appeared on the skating rink. The real leaders showed themselves on the skating rink. School was sort of a punishment. Parents always want to punish their children and school is their most natural way of punishing them.*
>
> John shakes his head.

Some of America's Top Authors and Illustrators
for Beginning Readers

Arnold Lobel, who died in 1987, was known for his gentle
Frog and Toad books as well as for his award-winning
illustrations.

James Marshall was born in Texas and worked as a musician,
teacher, and painter before he became so famous with his
hippos, George and Martha. His simple, expressive line
drawings help to carry stories that have much to say about
relationships—to both children and adults.

Robert Munsch was born in Pittsburgh but had moved to
Canada when he wrote the best-selling children's book of all
time, *Love You Forever.* His thirty other books are less warm-
hearted, but all have strong kid appeal.

Jane Yolen was inspired by her own children to write books
like *Milkweed Days* and *No Bath Tonight.* This New York
City–born, Connecticut-bred author does many kinds of
writing, for both children and adults.

MOM: You don't think so?

JOHN: School's okay.

MOM: Well, maybe when this book was written schools
weren't so much fun. (reads) *However, school was also a
quiet place where we could prepare for the next hockey game
and lay out our next strategy. As for church, we found there*

the tranquillity of God. There we forgot school and dreamed *about our next hockey game.*

John smiles.

MOM: (reading) *Through our daydreams it might happen that we would recite a prayer and ask God to help us play as well as Maurice Richard*—Do you know who Maurice Richard is?

JOHN: No.

MOM: He was a famous hockey player when I was a young girl. He was born in, uh, 1925.

JOHN: Is he still alive?

MOM: I don't know. I think he is.

JOHN: Okay, read some more.

This transcript shows you exactly why your involvement with reading is so important. Not only are John's reading skills too limited to handle words like *tranquillity*, his experience is too limited to understand just why hockey player Maurice Richard should be so important to the young boy in the story. His mother can fill in these gaps and help relate the story to John's life. What's more, her reading is expanding John's universe. John is listening to a story, but he's also learning vocabulary, a bit of history, and a sense of what life was like in Canada in the 1940s.

Much of the time you and your child spend reading together will still involve *you* as the reader—even though your child can read for himself. But with easy and familiar books, your child might be more than willing to help out with some of the reading. Here's a transcript of an old family tape of me reading from Dr. Seuss's *Green Eggs and Ham* with my son Alex, who was then six years old. Alex was reading some of the pages, I was reading the others.

DAD: Can you read the sign?

ALEX: *I am Sam.* (page turn) Zoom. *I am Sam.* (page turn) *Sam I am!*

DAD: *That Sam-I-am! That Sam-I-am! I do not like that—*

ALEX: *Sam I am.* (page turn) (To Dad) No, me. (reading) *Do you like green eggs and ham?*

DAD: *I do not like them, Sam-I-am.*

ALEX (shouting) and DAD: *I do not like green eggs and ham.*

Was Alex reading or was he reciting memorized passages? I don't think it really matters. What's important is that the experience of reading is shared and it's fun.

Don't spend a lot of time correcting your child if he makes a mistake, or prodding him into reading himself if he doesn't want to. All that will fix itself over time. But you can make deals that will help the process. My middle son was a very good reader early on, but a very lazy one. He'd far rather have Dad read to him than read himself, so I ended up bargaining with him. I'd start a story, read about half, and then say, "Oh, I'm getting tired now, Justin. I think we'll have to finish it tomorrow." He'd complain, so I'd reply, "Well, my voice is tired so why don't you read a few pages and give me a rest, then I'll finish up." It worked—almost every time.

Our goal as parents is to build our child's skills so he will be able to read when we're not around. We start by reading all the words, then gradually encourage our child to read more and more on his own. With my boys, by age seven, I was simply the guy who held them on his lap and turned the pages. Ironically, when my children were older and had become very accomplished readers, I went back to my first role. I was the one who did virtually all the reading out loud. Then they'd carry on themselves, silently, long after I left the bedroom.

Part of keeping reading fun, of course, is to mix up book

Psst . . . Don't Tell the Kids, These Books Are Really for Us

Roy Gerrard, *Sir Cedric Rides Again* (FSG). A balding knight in a rhyming tale of derring-do.

Alexander Wolf and Jon Scieszka, *The True Story of the Three Little Pigs* (Viking). Told from the innocent wolf's point of view, of course. Jon Scieszka's newer book *The Stinky Cheese Man* (Viking) is truly zany.

James Marshall, *George and Martha* (Houghton Mifflin). Charming and insightful stories about the ongoing lives of two hippopotamuses. Good for your relationship and your funny bone.

Robert Munsch, *Love You Forever* (Firefly). Until Harry Potter, this was the best-selling kids' book of all time. But it makes big people cry.

Shel Silverstein, *Where the Sidewalk Ends* (HarperCollins). Wild line drawings combine with Silverstein's sardonic, neurotic humor.

reading with other kinds of language and story activities. Since kids at this age actually can read or reread simple books on their own, your role as a parent is to keep the fun rolling with some reading games. These often help to keep a child's oral reading going when they get tired or are struggling with difficult stories. Here are four of my favorites:

- **Trade a page.** It's the famous deal: "I'll read one page and you read the next." You still have to help your child when he gets stuck on a word, of course, and you'll sometimes end up reading more than one page, especially if the next one has lots of print on it. But by doing half the reading you'll keep the meaning of the book clear—and you'll give your child that wonderful chance to catch your mistakes. "Dad, there's no 'and' there!"

- **Hot dog.** While you're reading a story out loud, substitute a nonsense word every so often: "The three little pigs lived in a hot dog in the forest." Your child will correct you instantly: "No, Mommy. House!" This game also keeps your child's eyes focused on the print. Just don't keep it up forever—five or ten minutes of this is plenty.

- **Finish the page.** Just read along normally until you reach a point about three words from the end of the page; then stop. "How about you finish up? You can read those words." Most kids will enjoy doing so.

- **Put your child in the story.** Who says that *David's Bike* has to be about a kid named David if your son is named Tyler? Who says that Alexander in the Judith Viorst books has to be named Alexander if your child, Julio, wants to be in the story? Of course, if you change the gender of the central character, you'll have to keep an eye open for every "he" and "his," but kids often enjoy our reading most when we get all messed up.

Some parents are really wonderful story readers and can add exotic voices and funny sounds as they read along. Others can read like Robert Munsch, full of drama and exaggeration in the voice, sometimes s-t-r-e-t-c-h-i-n-g out words, and sometimes readingreallyfast.

And other parents are great natural storytellers, whether or

Series Books for Beginning Readers

Publishers have created a number of series that feature easy-to-read stories, organized by grade level, often done by excellent writers. While not every book in a series will be a winner, they'll all be fulfilling for your novice reader.

Scholastic Cartwheel (Scholastic)
Puffin Easy-to-Read (Penguin)
Bank Street Ready-to-Read (Simon & Schuster)
Step Into Reading (Random House)
Arthur's Chapter Books (Little, Brown)
Junie B. Jones (Random House) by Barbara Park—my pick for overall quality

not they are particularly good readers. I confess that my own reading aloud is full of errors. I pretend I'm just trying to fix up the author's work, but my kids would tell you the truth—Dad just goofs up a lot. But I do have some talent as an instant story-teller—and so might you. Bedtime stories work best when your children are made the central characters and the story itself follows a simple format. My kids' favorites were "The Haunted House," "The Pirate Ship," and "Kidnapped by a Space Monster." None of these will ever see publication, but they worked with my kids because the stories were predictable and I could ask the kids to fill in dialogue or sound effects.

DAD: "Jason was walking up the stairs to the old house . . ."
KIDS: *Pound out footsteps sound effect.*
DAD: "When suddenly the door slammed open."

The One Reading Gimmick That Works: A Flashlight

If you're worried about your child's reading, don't go out and spend hundreds of dollars on "the book/cassette kits you see advertised on TV or even twenty dollars for a CD-ROM. Buy a flashlight instead.

Flashlight reading works like this: Your child has a regular bedtime, say eight or nine o'clock, and an enforced lights-out time when he can't read in bed anymore. But somehow there's this special flashlight in his room—always with fresh batteries—and you just never notice the pale glow visible around the edge of the door.

When I speak to parents about reading, I always ask how many of them, as children, read under the covers with a flashlight. Invariably, a quarter of the audience laughs and raises their hands. No gimmick works better to keep reading going long after you leave the bedroom.

KIDS: *Slam!*
DAD: "And Jason said . . ."
JASON: "Uh . . . I'm not afraid."
DAD: "When suddenly he heard . . ."
JUSTIN: "A scream. Yaaaaah!"

You can use a tape recorder or a video camera to record these epics for posterity, but then there will be a nasty temptation to go back and do stories over again until you "get them right," as the kids would say. This could take forever.

Since your kids are already writing at school, you might well want to take some time and write down a story of theirs. While their spelling is still pretty iffy, yours will probably be good enough for the job—and then you can ask your kids to illustrate the finished product. Once again, you'll end up with a keepsake that will have real value twenty years from now.

MANY DIFFERENT BOOKS FOR THE NOVICE READER

Your primary school reader probably will enjoy many of the same children's books that you do. But if you'd like to tune in more directly to the special interests of the six-to-eight crowd, here are some suggestions:

- Humor always works. Try the Berenstains' *Inside, Outside, Upside Down*, or some simple joke books, or the poems by Jack Prelutsky.
- Animals. Kids have a fondness for animals, both real and imaginary. They even like to read about dinosaurs, though there haven't been any around for 65 million years. Arnold Lobel's *Frog and Toad All Year* and William Steig's beautifully illustrated *The Amazing Bone* tie into these interests.
- The real life of kids. Judith Viorst's *Alexander and the Terrible, Horrible, No Good, Very Bad Day* has quickly become a classic. Bob Munsch's *Thomas' Snowsuit* and *I Have to Go* are delightfully honest about the trials and tribulations of a young child's life.
- Your child's interests. If your son is playing T-ball, get a baseball book, such as Johanna Hurwitz's *Baseball Fever*, and read it together. If your daughter is wild about horses, try Walter Farley's *The Black Stallion*. Neither of these books is easy for

---

Magazines for Beginning Readers

- *Electric Company, Sesame Street,* and *Kid City.* From the creators of the television shows: colorful, playful, and slick.
- *National Geographic World* has great photography—as you'd expect—but also games, articles, and cartoons.
- *Ranger Rick* from the National Wildlife Federation. Very short articles on animals but great illustrations for projects.
- *Stone Soup.* A literary magazine for kids with a great deal of artwork for young Rembrandts.

---

young kids to read for themselves, but your child's fascination with the subject will make up the difference.

• TV tie-ins. Nothing's wrong with Sesame Street books—they're never inspired but always good enough. The same can be said for Disney books or even books that are spin-off products from a currently popular movie. No child was ever hurt by reading schlock—so long as it's not the entire literary diet.

Beginning readers—and their parents—have an amazing appetite for books. You'll go through hundreds in the space of three years: good books, lousy ones, beautiful books, plain ones, favorite books, and one-read-only books, books you'll both love and books that will make you groan.

Your child will choose books just as adults do—by the cover, by the obvious content, by what a page looks like. Sometimes their choices will become repetitive. After all, just how many Animorphs books are you prepared to read to your six-year-old? And some very valuable books—books with history or moral lessons or important ideas—won't jump off the library shelves into your child's hands. Use some parental discretion. "Sure, I'll read *Clifford the Dog* again, but then I want to try this book of African folktales." Ultimately, we can never force our children to enjoy a book, but we can make some effort to broaden their tastes.

TEN MUST-HAVE, EASY-TO-READ BOOKS FOR YOUR NOVICE READER'S BOOKSHELF

The Berenstains, *Inside, Outside, Upside Down* (Random House) and many other titles. Adorable bears and simple text makes all these books winners.

Michael Bond, *A Bear Called Paddington* (Dell). Paddington Bear has become highly commercialized over the years, but the original books are still quite wonderful for beginning readers.

Norman Bridwell, *Clifford Takes a Trip* (Scholastic) and other Clifford books. Take one large, amusing dog and some big print and you have a very popular, easy-to-read book.

Beverly Cleary, *Ramona the Pest* (Avon) and many others. Ramona has been called a "national treasure." Certainly these books for early readers are popular with both teachers and primary school kids in grades two and three.

P. D. Eastman, *Go, Dog, Go* (Random House). Simple vocabulary but an endearing story. A good starter book because the words are short and predictable.

Arnold Lobel, *Mouse Tales* (HarperCollins). The seven tales are short and easy to read but still carry a fair deal of wisdom. Charming illustrations. A great book for the kids to read to Dad.

A. A. Milne, *Winnie-the-Pooh*. A 1926 classic that comes in many versions. You'll have to help with reading the original, but many of the Disney-ized Golden Books are easy enough for your child to read on his own.

Robert Munsch, *The Paperbag Princess* (Firefly). Munsch's twist on the traditional fairy tale—with a surprisingly liberated princess—is a favorite for both parents and kids.

Dr. Seuss, *One Fish, Two Fish* or *Cat in the Hat* (Random House) and many other titles. Dr. Seuss virtually invented the easy-to-read book back in the 1940s. Many of his titles have become classics—with good reason.

Judith Viorst, *Alexander and the Terrible, Horrible, No Good, Very Bad Day* (Colliers). The title says it all. You'll have to read the text for the first few times, then the book's rhythm and repetition will let your child take over.

Chapter 8

The Middle Reader:
Ages Eight to Ten

Jennifer is in fourth grade. She reads for herself now, sometimes picture books from earlier years, sometimes short novels that she brings home from the school library. She reads silently with good speed and understanding. She reads out loud with expression and only a few problems with difficult words. She enjoys your reading to her and frequently takes over when you say you're tired. Sometimes you feel that your job is finished—that Jennifer is all set up to be a reader for life.

But it's not that easy.

Your child has only begun to build her skills in reading, and she still has a great many more to learn. She enjoys books now, but if enough distractions occur she might well turn away from books. Fourth grade is the year in which as many as a third of our children stop bothering to read. Dr. Jeanne Chall of Harvard University calls this the "fourth-grade slump," a problem that seems to affect boys more than girls, but that can happen to any child.

For the child who gets caught in fourth-grade slump, the time spent reading declines rapidly, concentration decreases, and vocabulary growth slows down. The child's reading development becomes stalled right after it's begun, like a plane whose engines cut out just as it's taking off. The effects of both are disastrous. Children who are affected by fourth-grade slump develop skills at half the rate of their peers. By eighth grade, they're reading at a sixth-grade level. When they begin high school, they just don't have the ability to handle textbooks that frequently require college-level reading skills.

This is a tragedy, but it can be prevented by parents who are still involved in their children's reading. The solution is to continue with the basics: reading out loud with your child, buying at least one new book a month, and keeping rules on television watching and other distractions.

As long as you continue with the basics, you need not panic if you see signs of a decline in reading interest. To some extent, setbacks are natural as part of any child's mental growth. Researchers suspect that before each stage of intellectual development, a child has to consolidate what she has already learned. Before moving on to first novels, a child might limit herself to familiar picture books for a period of months. Before taking over the daily reading almost entirely, she may insist that Mom read *everything*. Rather than getting upset or overly worried when your child seems to be regressing, parents have to understand that this stage could be a necessary one before the next big jump can be made. Your child's brain is somehow solidifying what it already knows so she can move on. You've got to support that process when it occurs. Yet you also have to be watchful in case a temporary slump is a sign of a more serious problem. See Chapters 12 and 13 if any setback seems to last for more than a month or two.

DAILY READING

By now your child probably has taken over a fair amount of your daily reading, but that doesn't mean you've stopped being important. By continuing to be part of family reading time, you're providing three important things:

- Your presence
- Proper pronunciation and explanations of unfamiliar words
- Improved comprehension

Your presence validates the importance of reading to your child, and it silently applauds her success. You are also beside her if she gets in trouble—when the sentence doesn't make sense, or she can't pronounce a word, or she doesn't know what a word means.

Some researchers suspect that the difference between children who glide over the fourth-grade slump and those who are stalled by it is simple—vocabulary. The books read in middle school and up require much bigger vocabularies than the basal readers and controlled-vocabulary books of the primary grades. Your child ultimately needs to be familiar with many more than the "magic 3,000" words recognized by the average nine-year-old to read confidently the 120,000 words that are recognized by a competent adult. By being with her at reading time, you're there to explain difficult words.

Through your talk about the book or story, you're also assisting in better comprehension of the print. Reading, as I've said, isn't just decoding the words on the page; it's understanding and thinking about the ideas or images behind those words. Your daughter isn't reading just because she can sound out the words in Watty Piper's *The Little Engine That Could*. She's reading when she can feel the rhythm of the prose, the strength of the little engine's struggle, and the thrill of his success. Your presence and interest help that to happen.

Let's listen to eight-year-old James Bradshaw reading with

Some Easy Books, Just for Fun

These books are all relatively easy to read for your child, and fun for you to read along.

Harry Allard and James Marshall, *The Stupids Take Off* (Houghton Mifflin) and other Stupids books. Silly but satisfying, with clever illustrations.

Jonathan Etra and Stephanie Spinner, *Aliens for Breakfast* (Random House). Aliens in the cereal, aliens at school—very funny, very rudimentary sci-fi.

Johanna Hurwitz, *Aldo Peanut Butter* (Morrow) and the other Aldo books offer a not-so-subtle humor in a not-so-difficult style.

Daniel Pinkwater, *Guys from Space* (Macmillan). Friendly aliens, a talking rock, and Pinkwater zaniness make this a winner. Easier to read than some Pinkwater books.

Dav Pilkey, *Captain Underpants and the Attack of the Talking Toilets* (Scholastic). There are a number of Captain Underpants mock-heroic epics, all of them good fun.

his mother, Diana. James is a very bright student who had just finished a Hardy Boys book as part of a school read-a-thon. This transcript records him reading *Star Trek VI: The Undiscovered Country*, which he had bought at a school book fair. The text is somewhat too difficult for him, but with Diana's help he can succeed even with this adult-level novel.

JAMES: *Admiral Cartwright rose angrily, "I must protest. To offer the Klingons a safe haa-ven . . .*

MOM: That's haven. It means a safe place.

JAMES: *A haven within Federation space is . . . suicide. Klingons would become an alien underclass. If we dis—dismantle the fleet, we'd be defenseless before an aggressive species with a . . .* what?

MOM: *Foothold.*

JAMES: Oh, it looks like foo'th'old. (reads)—*foothold on our territory. Led by an unprincipled tyrant?*

Mom nods.

"Boys'" Books and "Girls'" Books

Boys and girls do tend to read somewhat different books, beginning in middle school, when peer group pressure becomes so important. Most girls remain quite willing to read a book whose central character is a boy, perhaps because they read well enough to project themselves into any character. Boys, alas, become increasingly unwilling to read any book that has a girl as the central character. Maybe the young male sexual identity is that much more fragile.

And the reading went on. James had little difficulty reading even such bizarre words as *Klingons* and *Romulans* because he watches *Star Trek* on TV, but other words, such as *foothold*, gave him some problems. Here Diana's input was important. She could correct pronunciations as they came up and provide explanations when James needed them.

Children, like adults, will frequently skip over short, difficult sections of print to keep the story going. But they'll ask a question when a word or phrase interferes with overall meaning. I doubt that eight-year-old James could define *unprincipled tyrant*, but he was sure enough of the meaning in context to go ahead after a quick look at Mom to check pronunciation. If he was really confused by the phrase, Diana was there to offer help.

James struggled through about sixty pages of *Star Trek* before abandoning it. He could have asked Diana to continue reading it out loud to him, but he preferred to go back to reading that he could handle more easily. Middle readers will do this frequently: attempt a difficult adult book, then return to something that really suits them. Sometimes they even reread favorite picture books from early childhood. As a parent, you need to support all this reading—for the challenge, the joy, and the consolidation of reading skills.

Like many children in the middle grades, James is very proud of his reading. He will often tell his parents that he doesn't need their help. This was technically true for his last book, The Hardy Boys' *Mystery of the Samurai Sword*, which James read to me for twenty minutes and stumbled over only a single word (*jimmied*—which needed a definition). But James still needs someone to talk to about swords and scabbards and sword hilts, someone to grab a big picture book on Japan to show him a ceremonial sword, someone to ask just a few questions about how the mystery is developing.

That someone ought to be you. Children at this age also will talk to their friends, brothers, sisters, teachers, grandparents, and the school librarian—but it is your attention that gives reading such value in your child's eyes. A nine-year-old is perfectly capable of reading alone, up in her bedroom or down in the basement. But if reading loses its social context, if it becomes entirely a private experience, then it will lose much of its joy.

Your role in daily reading will have changed already by this time. When you read with your child at age seven, the reading often stopped when you left the room. Now the reading will likely continue for up to an hour after you've left. This practice leads to a certain amount of discontinuity—you end up reading half of chapter 2, and half of chapter 6, and you never do find

---

The Guest Reader

Throughout this book, I've been talking about the importance of daily reading time. The best reader, of course, is you. But "guest readers" can offer some variety for your child. Older brothers and sisters frequently serve as guest readers in families—and this benefits both them and the younger child. Grandparents are important guest readers for many families, especially if they live in the house or close by.

But guest readers need not be relatives. Family friends can be wonderful readers. If you regularly read to your child before bed, why not ask a dinner guest if he'd mind reading for five minutes while you get dessert ready. The results are often delightful—for your child and your guest. And you'll have plenty to talk about over dessert.

out how the story ends. But it also gives you a chance to ask your child to fill you in on the story that you've missed.

As your child grows, the function of your reading is focused much less on the mechanics of words and decoding, and much more on discussion of what's happening. By actually reading a page yourself, you'll be able to ask questions whose answers will give you an interesting window on your child's own opinions. Daily reading is as much about your relationship to your child as it is about reading. Don't stop just because your child is capable of sitting in her own chair and reading a book to herself.

WHAT YOUR CHILD
PROBABLY KNOWS NOW

The older children become, the more difficult it is to generalize about what they should or shouldn't know. Every child develops at her own pace. Some children read fluently and avidly at age six, others not until age nine, and I have known some who didn't get excited about reading until twelve or fifteen. For each of these chapters, I've indicated an age span to correspond to a reading stage. But these are guidelines. There are no rules on the speed at which your child will develop.

At the same time, you naturally want your child to keep up with her classmates. You want her to have the reading skills that school will require not just in language arts but also in math, geography, and history. So let me generalize a bit on the basis of what schools expect of students and what research says about children as they go into the third, fourth, and fifth grade.

- **Phonics.** By the end of third grade, most children know the basic principles of phonics (vowel sounds, consonants, diphthongs such as *ay* and *ey*, phonograms such as *ight* and *tion*) and can blend phonic pieces together to form words. Teaching of new skills in phonics slows down markedly in fourth grade and usually is tied to spelling, where phonics can be quite helpful, rather than reading, where phonics is only a tool.

• **Word attack.** Phonics is only one way to tackle a strange word; other word-attack skills are just as important. These skills include using context clues in the sentence, using picture clues from the page, making a structural analysis of the difficult words for roots, prefixes, and suffixes, and—when all else fails—using the dictionary. These skills develop from second through sixth grade.

• **Sight vocabulary and reading speed.** By the beginning of fourth grade, most children can quickly recognize most of the words that Jeanne Chall called the "magic 3,000." Once these 3,000 words can be recognized at a glance, reading speed will increase to a comfortable level for understanding the text. A reading speed of seventy words per minute (about half as fast as we normally talk) seems to be a crossover point. Children who read more slowly have to work hard at comprehension because their energy is still on decoding the words. Children who read faster find it easier to understand the meaning of the book or story.

• **Oral and silent reading** both take place at school through fourth grade; in fifth and sixth grade, the emphasis will turn to silent reading. Early silent reading will be no faster than reading out loud, and many children will "subvocalize"—move their lips even as they read silently. For successful readers, silent reading eventually becomes much faster than oral reading (225 to 400 words per minute silently as opposed to 125 to 175 words per minute out loud) and subvocalization is left behind. Early reading crutches such as subvocalizing and using a finger pointer are not bad in themselves. There are times when we, as adults, also

---

Five Scary Books for Kids Aged 8–10

Sylvia Cassedy, *Behind the Attic Wall* (Avon). Twelve-year-old Maggie is sent off to creepy Uncle Morris.

Deborah and James Howe, *Bunnicula* (Avon). A vegetarian vampire bunny? Why not!

Angela Sommer-Bodenburg, *My Friend the Vampire* (Pocket Books). A nine-year-old boy makes friends with a comic vampire.

Alvin Schwartz, *Scary Stories to Tell in the Dark* (HarperCollins). Perfect for a campfire and reading aloud.

R. L. Stine, the Goosebumps series. These are schlocky, contrived little novels that only pave the way for Christopher Pike and Stephen King later on—but some kids love them.

---

move our lips when reading or follow a text with our fingers. But, sooner or later, these artificial supports shouldn't be needed anymore. Parents sometimes can help this along with an occasional comment during family reading time. "I bet you really don't need your finger helper for this book. The lines of print are pretty far apart." Or touch your daughter's chin when she's reading silently and the subvocalization will stop. "You'll read better if you don't move your lips" is all you need to say.

• **Reading materials.** By the end of third grade, many children will have enough confidence in their own reading ability to

Five Funny Books for Kids
Aged 8 – 10

Bruce Coville, *My Teacher Is an Alien* (Pocket Books). Just what every middle-school kid suspected. Coville does great satire.

Ellen Conford, *A Job for Jenny Archer* (Little, Brown). Part of a series with a determined nine-year-old central character who never fails to captivate young readers.

Paula Danziger, *The Cat Ate My Gymsuit* (Dell) and anything else by America's funniest writer for kids. This one is about a girl who thinks she's "a blimp" but leads a student rebellion to save a popular teacher. Her latest is *P.S. Longer Letter Later.*

Barthe DeClements, *Nothing's Fair in Fifth Grade* (Penguin). Because it just isn't.

Barbara Park, *Don't Make Me Smile* (Knopf). A funny book about a boy whose parents are getting a divorce. Only Barbara Park could make it work.

pass beyond favorite books and familiar material. Your second-grade child wants to read about herself, even in the guise of Franklin the turtle. Your fourth grader is more willing to read about astronauts, even though she isn't one, or racing cars, even though she's not old enough to drive one. Your child will begin using books not just to understand the world around her but to extend that world. Books offer more than just stories. They are

Nancy Drew and the Hardy Boys

When these two book series began over sixty years ago, no one could have anticipated that they would survive quite so long. The writing is uneven, the plots go *clunk* far too often, and the dialogue is from a B-movie. The original "Carolyn Keene," whose real name is Mildred Wirt Benson, was paid just $125 each for twenty-three of the first thirty Nancy Drew books. Now there are over a hundred of these mysteries, by many authors, and the books still have an amazing appeal to many young readers.

In 1986, Simon & Schuster decided that an update was in order, so they created *The Hardy Boys Files* and *The Nancy Drew Files*. While the original books at least had some charm, these new titles marry the worst of the Hardy Boys to the worst of the Sweet Valley High genre. Best to stick to the originals. As Mildred Benson recently told the *New York Times:* "I made Nancy Drew good-looking, smart and a perfectionist. I made her a concept of the girl I'd like to be."

tools that your curious child can use to explore the whole universe.

By fourth grade, pictures will be less important than words in the books your child reads. The books themselves will be longer—"chapter books" is the school term—and reading will stretch over several sittings.

By fifth grade, many novels will have no illustrations at all, or perhaps only a few at the beginning of chapters. Your child will no longer need line drawings to appreciate Louise

Fitzhugh's *Harriet the Spy* or the Nancy Drew mysteries. But she still needs you to keep her enthusiasm going.

GOOD PROGRAMS AT SCHOOL

Your child's school should still be working to turn your child into an independent reader. Though instruction in phonics and word-attack skills is usually finished in third grade, the job of encouraging reading goes on. Good schools will use a number of techniques and approaches to consolidate basic reading skills and to promote wide, independent reading for their students.

Most Popular Writer: Ann Martin

Most parents have never heard of Ann Martin, the author behind The Baby-Sitters Club series, but she has some 82 million copies of her books (and spin-offs) in print—all directed at preteen girls. Until the recent craze for horror fiction, she was without doubt the single most popular American author for young readers.

But popularity doesn't always garner respect. The forty-year-old creator of the club suffers from considerable criticism, like this from the *New York Times:* "Her prose is efficient and grammatically correct but not memorable." Her middle-grade fans, however, respond strongly to the simple stories, familiar characters, and easy readability of the books. As one ten-year-old commented, "Her books describe life as it really is for girls of our age."

In the classroom, the teacher still should be reading out loud, just as you are, so the kids can hear the language of more sophisticated works. *Charlotte's Web, Freaky Friday*, Roald Dahl's books, and the various Ramona novels are popular with teachers for reading with the class in third and fourth grades. In fourth and fifth grades, books by authors such as Judy Blume, Paula Danziger, E. L. Konigsburg, and many other writers can be read aloud.

At other times, when the kids read on their own or in groups, the works tend to be shorter and simpler. Your child always can read more difficult books when an adult is around to help. The difference between reading with some adult help and reading independently comes to about two grade levels. If your child has an average fourth-grade reading ability, she will be more comfortable with third-grade-level books when reading on her own but can probably understand a fifth-grade-level book when someone is reading with her. The ordinary fourth grader, for instance, would have trouble reading Donald Sobol's popular *The Great Brain* books by herself because of sentence length and some difficult vocabulary. But she can enjoy the books easily when they're read to her, or when she reads along with the teacher.

Classroom teachers begin shifting their emphasis away from reading toward writing in fourth and fifth grade. This shift makes the school library and the teacher-librarian even more important in encouraging outside reading. Your child needs more than just a classroom library with its handful of books. She needs a good-size school library with several thousand titles, from simple novels to detailed nonfiction books on insects or space flight. Your child is naturally curious. The library should have books and magazines to allow her to explore the full range of her interests.

I wrote in Chapter 4 about the importance of the whole school being involved in a reading program. This involvement is especially important to prevent the fourth-grade slump. An excellent school provides for silent reading time and for reading buddies to help kids who are falling behind. An excellent school offers chances for children to use reading in plays, or dramatizations, or the morning announcements. An excellent school has book fairs and book exchanges and visits to the public library to encourage children to get books from a wide variety of sources. In some schools, I've seen labs with twenty computers at which kids not only read but write—and computers can be useful for promoting both skills. But an excellent school reading program does not require expensive electronics to be successful. It requires commitment.

In second and third grade, many schools test students for their reading and math skills. All the children in a class or a school will take two hours or more to do the California, Iowa, or one of the dozens of other achievement tests available. These tests usually have a vocabulary section and then a set of short passages with questions to measure reading comprehension. Your child will have to do the required reading, look at the choices, and mark the right answer with a pencil on a "bubble sheet" to be computer scored. A few weeks later, the results come back to the teacher or the school. The scoring will assign a "grade-level" reading ability for each student. It also shows how well your child reads in comparison with a national average or norm.

The results of such tests can serve as a school report card—just how well is your child's school doing in building reading skills? Many school boards use these standardized reading tests as a first screening to determine which students need extra help. So long as the tests are followed by individualized testing and

Computer Software for Reading

Kids can go overboard with computers and the Internet, but some computer programs on CD-ROM do offer a lot of reading practice and a boost for early writing.

Arthur's Talking Books. A CD-ROM won't replace real books, but this one sure is fun. Various ways to read and respond to Marc Brown's popular stories. Ages four to eight.

Kid Works Deluxe. A talking story-writer with a graphics program. Your child can write and illustrate her own story, then hear it read back. Ages four to eight.

Learn to Read. If you really think a computer can teach your kid to read, this is the program. Personally, I doubt it.

Mickey's ABC introduces letters and easy words, complete with Mickey Mouse's voice and some music. Ages two to five.

Reader Rabbit. If you really want a phonics program for home use, this is probably the one. It turns phonics lessons into a set of games. *Learning Center Phonics* is cheaper, and not as slick.

Reading and Me. Fine graphics and voice simulation with a dozen games for beginning readers. Ages four to seven.

Where in the World Is Carmen Sandiego? and other Carmen Sandiego titles. These excellent programs don't pretend to teach reading, they just ask for lots of it to play the game. Great graphics. Ages six to twelve.

teacher consultation, they are a good way to start identifying children with reading problems.

But testing in itself is not an answer. The results sometimes can be quite inaccurate if your child doesn't know how to pace the test, or puts the pencil marks in the wrong bubbles, or maybe just feels sick or upset on the day of the test. Even when the results are accurate, few teachers can individualize their programs enough to make much use of the information that comes back. The fact that your child might be stronger in vocabulary and weaker in comprehension, or vice versa, means little for most children in terms of what happens in the classroom or with a teachers' aide. The overall quality of the school reading program is what makes the difference.

USE BOREDOM

"Mom, I'm bored" is the common refrain of children this age. I remember throwing that whine at my own mother back in the 1950s. Children in middle school are wonderfully energetic and easily bored. In fact, the brighter the child, the more often she'll complain. This is natural.

So is the proper reply: "So find yourself something to do," as you continue reading or cooking or writing a report.

Don't rush out to rent a video, or buy a new computer game, or even pull out a book for your child. Boredom can be remarkably productive—when your child learns to deal with it. And your child will learn to deal with it only if given a chance to do so. If you intervene too much, you will short-circuit your child's own imagination and resources.

The media and the toy manufacturers all want your child to live a frantic life. They want her to be a consumer, a viewer, a kid constantly searching for new products to fill the void of boredom. If you allow it, these high-profit forces will raise your child for you. They will produce an adult who cannot relax, who can't find peace within herself so she seeks to buy it at the local tavern, at the drugstore, or at Macy's.

This is no legacy for your child. You must take control, ironically, by being laissez-faire. That wonderful French phrase literally translates as "leave to do," but I prefer the translation "free to be." Your child needs quiet time simply *to be*, to be herself or engage her fantasies, to read and think, or just to be bored. To provide this freedom in our society, you must take action—turn off the TV, put away the videos, unplug the video games, turn off the stereo.

Your child will amaze you. She'll read, or draw, or write her own book. She'll play fantasy games with neighborhood kids. She'll design her own Halloween costume, or turn scraps of wood into an airplane, or learn to make shadow pictures on the wall. But only if she has the freedom to be bored for a while first.

WHAT TO READ

The best phrase I've heard to describe the reading habits of children in third through fifth grade is "erratic independence." At this age, your child's reading will run from picture books to *Time* magazine, often with no discernible pattern. And that's fine.

One new influence on your child's reading is her friends. If "all the kids" are reading Francesca Lia Block or R. L. Stine, your child will too. If "all the kids" have been hooked on some series, such as Goosebumps or Animorphs or the Saddle Club books, then your child will want to read some too.

250 Years of Books for Children

The first English book for children appeared in 1744, assembled by publisher John Newbery—who also sold school textbooks and patent medicines. The popularity of *A Little Pretty Pocket Book* led to the growth of publishing for children through the rest of the eighteenth century. Some critics consider these early volumes to be more propaganda than literature since their real goal was to help parents in the religious and moral upbringing of their children.

The idea of producing entertaining children's books has always been at war with printing books that are supposed to be instructive or inspiring. The great children's books that we recall from the nineteenth century, such as *Treasure Island* and *Coral Island*, actually were written for adults to be read with the entire family. It wasn't until the end of that century that children's book writers finally conceded that entertainment might be slightly more important than instruction. Some present-day teachers and librarians still aren't so sure about this.

Just don't spend all *your* time satisfying your child's peer group. You, too, should enjoy what you read with your child. The books she reads now are longer, so she won't be going through 300 a year anymore. Try to make sure the ones you read together are worth the effort. A book like Daniel Manus Pinkwater's *The Snarkout Boys and the Avocado of Death* offers delights for you and your child both. But don't waste too much of your family reading time on the likes of Animorphs or The Baby-Sitters Club, unless your child is really determined to do

Book Reviews of Kids' Books

Parents who want to get ahold of the best new books for their children will have to rely on a knowledgeable bookseller, teacher, or librarian—or read reviews themselves. While some of the big daily papers have regular children's book reviewers, most newspapers tend to give kids' books a quick once-over a few weeks before Christmas. For more detailed reviews, check:

- *Booklist.* This journal of the American Library Association reviews most new children's books—and offers insightful articles on trends in the field.
- *Horn Book.* The distinguished, sometimes scholarly, magazine for people interested in children's literature.
- *Parent's Choice.* This tabloid reviews books, TV shows, and videos for children from a parent's perspective. Honest and straightforward (Box 185, Waban, MA 02168).
- *School Library Journal.* The title reveals the real audience. *SLJ* offers concise, honest reviews of most new children's books.

so. There are many books that appeal to children in the middle grades without pandering to them.

This age is often an excellent time to begin exploring more nonfiction. If your child is developing a special interest in baseball or ballet or bugs, you'll find nonfiction, or "information," books at the library on all these topics. By zeroing in on your child's interests, you can show her that books offer far more than just stories.

How you read with your child depends really on what you

choose to read together. Chances are your child will need some help starting off Louise Fitzhugh's *Harriet the Spy* to deal with some of the vocabulary and to get her involved in the story. On the other hand, most nine-year-olds can sail through Beverly Cleary's *Henry Huggins* with little help from a parent. You should still be there—to listen to the reading and to talk about the book—but your child will likely do most of the actual reading herself. This is not the time to walk away from your child and her books; it's time to begin defining a new role that will involve you in a different way—listening more than reading aloud. As your child gets older and more independent, books will become some of the common ground you both have for conversation. Start staking out that territory now, and stay involved in your child's reading for life.

I've listed some of the best books for young readers in the sidebars to this chapter. Your local bookstore brings in new books all the time. Your public library and your child's school library will have hundreds more, new and old. Enjoy reading as many as you can. Together.

TEN MUST-HAVE BOOKS FOR YOUR MIDDLE READER'S BOOKSHELF

Judy Blume, *Tales of a Fourth Grade Nothing* (Dell). Full of nine-year-old angst and the problems of an annoying two-year-old brother named Fudge, but warm, funny, and entertaining. A modern classic.

Frances Hodgson Burnett, *The Secret Garden* (Harper). For many young girls, especially, this is among the most memorable books ever written. A young orphan, sent to her guardian's house in Yorkshire, England, begins to bloom personally as the secret garden comes into flower.

Betsy Byars, *Summer of the Swans* (Puffin). A fourteen-year-old girl deals with her own problems and finds her lost retarded younger brother—all in a single day. A powerful story for fifth and sixth graders.

Beverly Cleary. If your child has read *Ramona* (Avon) in school, try the slightly harder *Henry Huggins* (Avon), or the harder still *Dear Mr. Henshaw* (Dell Yearling) about divorce and adjusting to a new school.

Roald Dahl, *Charlie and the Chocolate Factory* (Penguin). The bizarre story of Charlie and Willie Wonka by the British writer became a cute movie with Gene Wilder. You can use the film to spur reading of the book.

Daniel Manus Pinkwater, *The Snarkout Boys and the Avocado of Death* (NAL). A zany mystery-adventure, amusing for both adult and child. There are also many other excellent Pinkwater novels at various levels of reading difficulty.

Mary Rodgers, *Freaky Friday* (HarperCollins). Imagine a young girl becoming her mother. Funny, well written, and insightful. The movie is also cute.

Donald J. Sobol, *Encyclopedia Brown* (Bantam). Over a dozen books in this series of simple mysteries solved by a young detective named Leroy "Encyclopedia" Brown.

Mildred Taylor, *Roll of Thunder, Hear My Cry* (Puffin). The author drew this lovely story about a poor black Mississippi family from her own experience. The sequel is *Let the Circle Be Unbroken*.

E. B. White, *Charlotte's Web* (HarperCollins). Charlotte the Spider and Wilbur the Pig have become justly famous in this wonderful, warm story. By third or fourth grade, your child should be ready for the original—so long as she has your help. Also try E. B. White's other children's classics, *Trumpet of the Swan* and *Stuart Little*.

The Proficient Reader:
Ages Eight to Twelve

This should be a golden age for your child as a reader—a time when he'll read widely on his own yet still need your approval and still value what you have to say. If your child is a fluent reader by now, he will want to read everything, and likely will. He'll move from Bruce Coville's *My Teacher Is an Alien* to comic books to Tolkien's *The Lord of the Rings* with absolutely no sense that one is much different in quality from another. He'll read at breakfast and in bed, on the bus and in the car, and sometimes for an hour or more with a flashlight after you say "Lights out."

Of course, there is no chronological age when your child becomes a proficient reader. It's a matter of skill and attitude. When he's mastered the basics and brought his silent reading speed up to around 200 words a minute, when his recognition vocabulary is verging on adult levels and he truly enjoys reading, then your child is a proficient reader. This stage can come any time between the ages of seven and thirteen.

Unfortunately, some children never reach proficiency or are delayed trying to get there. The causes are many—from the fourth-grade slump, to boredom, to distraction, to physical problems, to emotional turmoil in the family. If your child seems to be having trouble reaching the stage of proficiency that allows easy reading for enjoyment, I suggest you skip to Chapters 12 and 13 to try to understand the problem. The remainder of this chapter talks about the parents' role for children who already read quite well.

YOUR NEW ROLE

When your child has become a proficient reader, he no longer needs your help to tackle the tough words or to explain those bits of history or foreign culture that were stumbling blocks in the past. He'll be reading so many books so quickly that the details get lost in the speed of it all. Your child will likely be satisfied with a superficial sense of the plot or the ideas in a book. He'll figure out difficult vocabulary from context and probably not care much how the word might be pronounced. When your child stops long enough to ask you what a word means, you may both have to look it up.

But you still have a vital role in his reading. Your child still needs to talk about books he's read. You can still use his reading to begin more general talks about life, the universe, and the one or two other things in between. And you are still important in shaping and expanding your child's reading experience.

The three Rs remain vital, even if your child seems to be a very accomplished reader. The best way to avoid the boredom and disinterest that afflicts so many teenagers in ninth grade is to keep on with the basics right through elementary school: Read with your child every day; reach into your wallet to buy a wide selection of books and magazines for your child; rule the television and other media distractions so there's time for reading to happen.

Your family reading will have changed by now. Your child will be reading for up to an hour after you leave the bedroom, and maybe another hour during the day. By ninth grade, the real readers will read well over ten hours a week. So when you drop into the bedroom, the page or two you read together won't have much connection to the page or two you read the night before.

Read the page anyway. Reading the page aloud slows down the pace of your child's reading so he can ask questions, or get the meaning of that word he skipped over, or enjoy the flavor of the prose. Reading the page aloud gives you the chance to ask an important question before you begin: "What happened in the story since the last time we read?" This gives your child a chance to explain what's going on (an important skill in itself), or to say why he changed books ("Aw, Mom, it got so boring"), or to draw you into the reading ("Let me read you this funny part back on page, uh, I'll find it").

Some children at this age will begin to protest: "Dad, I can read better than you now." Or they'll pretend independence: "I don't need to be read to anymore. That's for kids." Or they'll find the idea of sitting down with you to read for half an hour just "gross." I suggest that you not give in too easily to these protests. Try to make a deal that keeps family reading time going. Here are some answers you might try:

- "Right, you are an excellent reader. So why don't you read to me for fifteen minutes?"
- "Let me read just a couple of pages so I can see what the book's about."
- "Okay, why don't I just look through the book for a minute and then we can talk about it?"
- "How about I read the narration and you read the dialogue. It'll be fun."

- "Okay, so let me read you just a page from this novel your mom and I are reading."

As your child approaches the teenage years, his reading will necessarily become more private. When my kids started reading Ruth Bell's *Changing Bodies, Changing Lives*, they didn't want me reading aloud the descriptive sections on sex or making out. But we could continue our reading together by opening a novel or a comic book that was a bit less emotionally charged.

The fallback position, of course, is to stop the reading and simply talk about a book. Talking is not as good as reading out loud together, but it is better than making reading a private and lonely experience. Statisticians tell us that the average parent engages in real conversation with a teenage child for less than four minutes a week. By sitting down with your son or daughter to talk about what they're reading, you'll triple that time with hardly any work at all.

WHAT'S HAPPENING AT SCHOOL

In the senior elementary grades, "reading" turns into "English" or "language arts." This doesn't mean that reading has stopped, only that the emphasis has changed to writing and responding. Your child's class might all be reading *The Diary of Anne Frank* or *Jacob Have I Loved*, but the reading will mostly be silent and often will occur at home. Time in school will be spent discussing the characters, or the turns of plot, or trying to understand concepts such as theme and irony.

Assuming your child is a reader, he'll have to put his energy into the writing part of language arts. Senior elementary

The Newbery Awards

These American awards for the "best" children's books go back to 1922. Here are some selections from the winners' list:

2000: Christopher Paul Curtis, *Bud, Not Buddy* (Delacorte).

1999: Louis Sachar, *Holes* (Frances Foster).

1998: Karen Hesse, *Out of the Dust* (Scholastic).

1997: E. L. Konigsburg, *The View from Saturday* (Jean Karl/Atheneum).

1996: Karen Cushman, *The Midwife's Apprentice* (Clarion).

1995: Sharon Creech, *Walk Two Moons* (HarperCollins).

1994: Lois Lowry, *The Giver* (Houghton Mifflin).

1993: Cynthia Rylant, *Missing May* (Jackson/Orchard).

1992: Phyllis Reynolds Naylor, *Shiloh* (Atheneum).

1991: Jerry Spinelli, *Maniac Magee* (Little, Brown).

1986: Patricia MacLachlan, *Sarah, Plain and Tall* (HarperCollins).

1981: Katherine Paterson, *Jacob Have I Loved* (HarperCollins).

1978: Katherine Paterson, *Bridge to Terabithia* (HarperCollins).

1977: Mildred Taylor, *Roll of Thunder, Hear My Cry* (Penguin).

1971: Betsy Byars, *Summer of the Swans* (Puffin).

1970: W. H. Armstrong, *Sounder* (HarperCollins).

1963: Madeleine L'Engle, *A Wrinkle in Time* (Dell).

1961: Scott O'Dell, *Island of the Blue Dolphins* (Dell).

students move quickly from single paragraphs to longer reports and presentations. The books they read are really material for a writing program that can range from reader-response journals (a diary for recording your child's ideas after each chapter) to book reports.

A good senior elementary English program also will offer any number of other means of responding to books—making videos, doing dramatizations, recording radio plays, interviewing the characters, perhaps even interviewing you. The only limit is the imagination of your child's teacher (if your child is still in a single classroom) or teachers (if the school is on a rotary system where kids move to different rooms for different subjects). An excellent school will offer all sorts of outreach programs—from trips to the local theater, to public library visits, to school musicals, to being a reading buddy for a younger student.

Your child's school should expect and support a certain amount of reading at home—at least a book a month. How your child reports back on that reading is up to the teacher, but you should check up on those expectations on parents' night. Your child also will be getting nightly homework, which should amount to at least an hour a night by eighth grade. Some of this will be in geography, history, math, and health, but much will be writing for language arts.

The key for supporting student work through the senior elementary and early high school grades is simple: the kitchen table.

The Harry Potter Craze

British writers seem to produce a kid book phenomenon on a regular basis. After World War II there was William Golding's *Lord of the Flies*, ignored in Britain, but made famous in the United States. The Brits have also given us the C. S. Lewis Narnia books and Sue Townsend's wonderful Adrian Mole series that was so popular in the early 1990s.

The latest British phenomenon is Harry Potter, an eleven-year-old apprentice wizard, created by J. K. Rowling. The story begins with *Harry Potter and the Sorcerer's Stone* (Scholastic) and will continue over seven more books as Harry grows through adolescence. The books are winners: engaging characters, a great fantasy adventure, whimsical writing. They're often enjoyed by parents as much as by kids aged eight to twelve.

I imagine you're looking strangely at the page now, wondering if there's been some strange typographical error. Let me repeat: The key to helping your child through school from age ten to age sixteen is the kitchen table (or its equivalent). Homework—reports, math problems, French verbs, essay questions—should be done at the kitchen table or some other central location in the house. Homework should be worked on someplace where you or another adult will be nearby.

Teachers stumbled across the "kitchen table" phenomenon when they went looking for explanations of student achievement. In recent years, many immigrant children have been outperforming American-born children in virtually every subject area, even in English at senior grades. Teachers wondered why.

Six Heartbreakers

For senior elementary kids who don't mind a good cry:

Natalie Babbitt, *Eyes of the Amaryllis* (Sunburst). Geneva Reade's grandmother has been trying to get a message from the sea for thirty years.

Betsy Byars, *Summer of the Swans* (Penguin). An earnest fourteen-year-old on the day her retarded brother gets lost.

Norma Fox Mazer and Harry Mazer, *Heartbeat* (Bantam). Love, death, and complex relationships in a novel by two of our top authors for young people.

Katherine Paterson, *Bridge to Terabithia* (HarperCollins). Offers a tale of friendship, courage, and long suffering. Her *Jacob Have I Loved* (HarperCollins) is fast becoming a classic.

Cynthia Voigt, *Homecoming* (Atheneum). An independent thirteen-year-old saves her family after their mother deserts them.

Obviously, parents couldn't be doing the work for their kids; the parents themselves often had a hard time with our language. Social and family attitudes account for some of the difference, but hardly all of it. What observation showed was this: The immigrant children were doing their homework with their family physically in the room. They weren't told, "Go to the bedroom

Six Page - Turners

For senior elementary kids who want a gripping story:

John Bellairs, *The House with a Clock in Its Walls* (Dell) and many other titles. Spooky and ghoulish but always fun.

Bruce Coville, *My Teacher Is an Alien* (Minstrel). Just what we always suspected. First of a series of similar mock-horror books.

Gary Paulsen, *Dogsong* (Simon & Schuster). A chilling adventure up north, complete with dog teams. *Hatchet* is even grittier.

Christopher Pike, *Slumber Party* (Scholastic). This book started the middle-school horror craze. Later novels are more complex in terms of plot.

Willo Davis Roberts, *Nightmare* (Atheneum). A cross-country chase with lots of tension and action.

R. L. Stine, *Go Eat Worms* (Avon) and many others in the Fear Street series. While no one ever dies in Stine's Goosebumps books, the high school mortality rate in these Fear Street books is incredible.

and do your homework." They were expected to sit at the kitchen table, or dining room table, or counter in the store, and get on with their work. This accomplished two things: It provided an adult to show interest, supervise work, and help if help was needed; and it said that schoolwork was important to the whole family.

I am not suggesting that parents should stick their noses into homework, any more than they should stick their noses into their children's reading at this stage. But I would suggest that you try to create an environment that supports and gives importance to schoolwork. And that you find a way to make homework a social experience, just like reading.

In my house, when I was growing up in the 1950s, homework was done in the dining room with a vigor that left permanent scratches in my mother's cherrywood dining room table. To this day, I prefer to work close to other people. My office is located on the second floor, just over the kitchen, where I can hear everyone else even as I type this page. My stepdaughter, Emma, still prefers to do her university work at our dining room table, even though she has her own room and her own computer. For both of us, there is something comforting about taking on a big project with other, supportive people around. I suggest that every family give it a try.

GUIDING YOUR CHILD'S READING

A portion of your child's reading in the senior elementary grades will be for school and might well be serious literature, books that require reasonable thought and carefully written out responses. But your child also should be reading much more, both in school and at home. He should be going through books, magazines, short stories, poetry, essays, the great classics—and junk.

Yes, I'm in favor of junk reading. Every reader I know reads junk: cheap mysteries, *Cosmopolitan*, Harlequin romances, true-crime stories, *The National Enquirer*. Once we've become proficient readers, we'll read everything. I can't stand in line at the supermarket without picking up those newspapers with headlines such as "My child had two heads—but I loved her anyway."

Your children should be allowed their fair share of junk reading too. No child was ever helped to become a reader for life by being force-fed the Bible, or New Age pamphlets, or Immanuel Kant. No child was ever hurt by reading a half-dozen R. L. Stine horror stories.

But I have seen children hurt—intellectually and emotionally—by a steady diet of junk that stretched over a number of years. In my creative writing class, I can tell the girls who have read too many Harlequins by their breathless prose and impossible characters. Even worse, I can see them dreaming about the young doctor with whom they'll fall in love on their vacation in Fiji. The real world, I'm afraid, rarely works like that.

Your job, as the parent of a proficient reader, is to encourage variety. For a boy who's reading his seventh fantasy novel, it's quite fair to say "I don't want to hear any more of that tonight. Let's start this book by Jerry Spinelli." Sure, there may be complaints, but you've made your point. Reading time is shared time; it's disposition is up to you too.

A wonderful aspect of the senior elementary school reader is suggestibility. At this age, unlike the teen reader, children still respond to our likes and dislikes. As parents, using our judgment and the ideas from this book, we can promote the reading of good books and discourage a steady diet of junk.

Try these techniques:

- "Okay, you can take out only three books on your library card. How about one Choose Your Own Adventure and this

Junior Sci-Fi and Fantasy

In seventh and eighth grades some kids get hooked on this genre. Try these titles for starters:

Ann McCaffrey, *Dragonsong* (Bantam) and many other novels in this fantasy saga draw young readers into a heroic world of castles, dragons, and adventure.

C. S. Lewis, Chronicles of Narnia, including *The Lion, the Witch and the Wardrobe* (HarperCollins). Your kids don't have to know that this seven-volume series is a Christian allegory in fantasy form.

T. H. White, *The Sword in the Stone* (HarperCollins). A King Arthur fantasy with an orphan boy and Merlin the Magician. It became a Disney animated film that many kids love.

Jane Yolen, *Wizard's Hall* (Magic Carpet). Another preadolescent wizard like Harry Potter, but Yolen is a great storyteller.

Bruce Coville book that I think you'll like. Then you pick one more."

- "I'll pay for any reasonable book, but if you want another Baby-Sitters Little Sister book, you buy it yourself."
- "I don't care if the kid next door has read twenty Sweet Valley High books, it's time for you to read something with a little more challenge in it. Your cousin Kate recommended . . ."
- "I was at the library today, and Mrs. Frost said that some-

body who reads Christopher Pike all the time, as you do, might also like this book . . ."

Some Childhood Classics

The proficient reader finally is able to read original versions of the childhood classics that previously he's only seen on TV or in scaled-down formats. Here are some that still appeal (with a little parental encouragement), available from many publishers:

Louisa May Alcott: *Little Women*
Frances Hodgson Burnett: *The Secret Garden*
Lewis Carroll: *Alice's Adventures in Wonderland*
James Fenimore Cooper: *The Last of the Mohicans*
Walter Farley: *The Black Stallion*
Esther Forbes: *Johnny Tremain*
Rudyard Kipling: *The Jungle Book* and *Just So Stories*
Astrid Lindgren: *Pippi Longstocking*
Lucy Maud Montgomery: *Anne of Green Gables*
Marjorie Rawlings: *The Yearling*
Antoine de Saint-Exupéry: *The Little Prince*
Anna Sewell: *Black Beauty*
Johanna Spyri: *Heidi*
Robert Louis Stevenson: *Treasure Island*
Mark Twain: *The Adventures of Tom Sawyer* and *The Adventures of Huckleberry Finn*
Jules Verne: *Journey to the Center of the Earth*
Laura Ingalls Wilder: *Little House on the Prairie*

Most kids will get out of a particular reading rut after a few months all by themselves. With a little encouragement and nudging from you, the move to other, more varied books will come sooner.

What makes a good book for the proficient reader? Pretty much the same qualities as those that make a good book for an adult—respect for the reader and the subject of the book, the artistry or clarity of the writing, the capacity to entertain and inform, the honesty of the author's vision. Not all good books get the sophisticated covers and packaging that make them look appealing on the library shelf.

Here teachers, librarians, and bookstore proprietors can be a big help to you. They can suggest books that have been reviewed favorably but that your child might not choose himself. *The Diary of Anne Frank* will not jump off the shelf with a snazzy cover, and, like many good books, it's more expensive than a cheap, series novel. But it's a fine book and deserves reading.

Your child has no easy way of knowing this. He's more likely to judge a book by its cover, which was done by an artist who may have only skimmed through the book. Or he'll read the back-cover blurb, written by an editor at the publishing house. Or he'll listen to the recommendations of Johnny from down the street. None of these will say much about the actual quality of a book.

Part of your job, as a parent, is to encourage your child to read more than that which is immediately appealing. If you can get advice from teachers or librarians or bookstore owners, that's wonderful. If you come across recommendations in the newspaper or the other media, those also will be helpful. But often you won't have much to go on when you're at the library or bookstore. Let me suggest the Page 40 Test for those times. This quick test works for both adult and children's fiction—and can be done by you and your child together.

- Open the book to page 40. By page 40, the author has got the story going, the editor has relaxed his blue pencil, and you'll get a real sense of the bottom-line quality of the book.
- Read the page carefully. Listen to it. Is the prose lively and interesting? Is the dialogue realistic? Are you inclined to read on?
- Or is the prose leaden and dull? Is the dialogue the kind you'd expect on a soap opera but would never hear in real life? Is the book obviously moralizing or patronizing? Do you really want to read on?

Two minutes spent on page 40 could save you and your child many hours reading a lousy book.

EXPAND THEIR UNIVERSE

When young children begin to read, they start with picture books and then move on to longer stories. In both cases, the genre is fiction. Teachers and librarians estimate that only 4 percent of what young children read comes from the "information books" or nonfiction section. Yet adult readers buy more nonfiction than they do novels.

These last elementary school years are when the crossover begins especially for boys. Fortunately, the big book superstores now carry a wide range of nonfiction books for kids, many of them beautifully illustrated. The *Titanic* books are a current craze, and the big Dorling Kindersley Eyewitness series with over seventy books that cover subjects from *Africa* to *Weather*. There are also many biographies for younger readers, ranging from award winners on Abe Lincoln and Martin Luther King Jr. to more popular photo-bios on Ricky Martin and Felicity.

Best Magazines for Kids Aged 8–12

American Girl. Provides glimpses of girlhood at different times in American history and includes stories and articles about today's American girls.

Boy's Life and *The Guider.* The Boy Scout magazine and its Girl Guide equivalent. Both well done.

Cricket. The Literary Magazine for Children. Sort of *Harper's* for the young set, but it also publishes stories by young writers.

Mad. It's funny, irreverent, and obnoxious—just as it was when you read it.

Nickelodeon Magazine. An interactive and informative humor magazine.

Sports Illustrated for Kids. So well done that its adult counterpart could learn a few things. Kid focused. Great photography.

Zillions. A junior version of *Consumer Reports,* but more attractive than the adult number.

The key, of course, is to tie your suggestions to your child's interests. There is no sense pushing a book on bicycles to a girl who's wild about horses. But it makes very good sense to take a son in Little League to the bookstore for a book on the history of the game; or the girl who makes model airplanes out to buy the Scientific American's *Great Model Airplane Book.* Libraries are especially useful for nonfiction books. Smaller bookstores rarely have enough children's nonfiction to zero in on your child's interests (save perhaps baseball and horses), but they can order any book you discover elsewhere—from something on scuba diving to any number of books on stamp collecting. Book superstores like Borders and Barnes and Noble often have good selections.

How good are the nonfiction books your child might want to buy or borrow? Evaluating them isn't as simple as the Page 40 Test. You have to look through the whole book and try to answer some questions.

- Who's it for? Is the book really written for kids? How hard is it to read? How complicated are the sentences? How difficult is the vocabulary?
- Is it for reading or reference? Don't buy a reference book such as *Mammals of America* and expect it to be read. But no kid could resist a grabber like *Strange But True Sports Stories*.
- Are the illustrations appropriate? Older kids frequently prefer line drawings to beautiful color prints. For some books, say, one on bike repair, good illustrations are vital.
- Is the writing clear and interesting? Try reading a paragraph to get a feel for the author's style.

Magazines and newspapers also should be part of your child's expanded universe. Many newspapers have a children's page on Saturday or Sunday that tries to promote children's reading and knowledge of current issues. And the range of children's magazines is enormous—from the still-funny *Mad Magazine* to *Seventeen* and *Nintendo Power.* If some of them grab your child's interest, subscribe to keep the magazine coming.

LET THEM EXPLORE

The proficient reader will read everything, including books that might make you uncomfortable. Eleven- and twelve-year-olds, especially, look for gritty titles that measure up to what they see on television and in movies.

Trust your child. It's unlikely that he will ever bring home one of those steamy pseudo-Victorian porn novels you find at the corner store. But your ten-year-old son might want to read a title like M. E. Kerr's *Dinky Hocker Shoots Smack!* or your eleven-year-old daughter might bring home Lutz Van Dijk's *Damned Strong Love.* Don't panic. Children are naturally curious about everything from sex to volcanoes to street gangs. If you make a big deal about the homosexuality in *Damned Strong Love,* you'll not only distort what the book really is about but you'll give undue attention to material that probably isn't that interesting to an elementary school reader. I'd worry far more about what's available on your television or via your neighbor's satellite dish. One survey in New York suggested that a quarter of the children in eighth grade had already seen an X-rated movie. Far better that they should read about sex presented with some honesty in a young adult novel.

READING AND WRITING

Especially in senior elementary school, reading and writing should be interconnected. If you've done your job, your child is already on his way to becoming a lifelong reader. But our society demands that successful individuals also be skilled writers. Without pushing too hard, you can tie reading and writing together at home for your child.

- Write letters. To Grandma, to the author of a book your child enjoyed (send it to the publisher), to the newspaper, to the president. If that expensive squirt gun stopped working, send a letter of complaint to the manufacturer. Writing, like reading, will empower your child.

- Write stories. Your child is probably writing stories at school. Why not do one at home, together? Naturally your child will end up as the central character. Just add the real-life settings around you and let your imagination go.

- Write scripts. If your family has a video camera, try a family-written, family-acted drama. Write and polish the script before you start.

- Write feelings. As your child becomes more of his own private person, he might want to keep a journal or diary. Why not encourage it? But remember that you're not allowed to read it unless you're invited.

Don't spend a great deal of time worrying about spelling, grammar, and punctuation. First we write, then we go back and fix. If you have a home computer, a spell checker will correct many mistakes with hardly any effort. But no computer will ever get your child to write if every word has to be spelled perfectly and every comma put in just the right place. Research has shown that the average student makes three to four errors per hundred words from sixth to twelfth grade. The rate stays the same but the errors become more sophisticated. For that progress to happen, your child should feel secure and confident about writing, and have an audience to admire the work.

That audience is you. Be full of praise. Don't push too hard for corrections. Not every letter should be sent; not every story deserves to be printed. So always start with a few responses such as "That's wonderful, James. I never knew you had such an imagination." Then you might suggest: "Do you want to fix the spelling and print the story as a book?" Or "Maybe before we mail this to the mayor, we should look up a couple of the words and print it again."

Soon your child will become a teenager and enter a world that our society has cut off both from childhood and adult life. Your daughter will be full of secrets, your son full of swaggering intensity. For now, your child is in a golden age. Enjoy it while it lasts.

TEN MUST-HAVE BOOKS FOR YOUR PROFICIENT READER'S BOOKSHELF

Louisa May Alcott, *Little Women*. Not an easy read, unless you get an abridged version, but the classic story of Meg, Jo, Beth, and Amy March captures four very memorable young women. A recent movie also brings the book to life.

Anne Frank, *The Diary of Anne Frank* (Pocket). The real-life diary of a thirteen-year-old Jewish girl hiding from the Nazis has justly become a classic. A must-read for your child; a good read-again for you.

Madeleine L'Engle, *A Wrinkle in Time* (Dell). A classic fantasy novel, frequently boxed with two sequels, that can introduce the whole genre of fantasy fiction to young readers. Philip Pullman's *The Golden Compass* is more recent and just as good.

Lois Lowry, *The Giver* (Houghton Mifflin). Either a realistic fantasy or a novel of magical reality, *The Giver* is a much-acclaimed book about history, personal pain, and identity.

David Macaulay, *The Way Things Work* (Houghton Mifflin). A witty and informative exploration of everyday science that sets a new standard in children's "information books." Fascinating for both kids and adults—and now available in an effective CD-ROM format (Dorling Kindersley).

Patricia MacLachlan, *Sarah, Plain and Tall* (HarperCollins). A lovely historical novel of family life on the prairie in the late 1800s. Keep the tissues handy if you read it aloud.

Lucy Maud Montgomery, *Anne of Green Gables* (Bantam). The story of spunky Anne and her family is much loved by many preteen girls, even more so since the movie and TV series.

Katherine Paterson, *The Great Gilly Hopkins* (Harper). Tough Gilly Hopkins has been moved from one foster home to another, until she finds her place in a home full of eccentrics. Many readers also love Paterson's *Bridge to Terabithia*.

J. K. Rowling, *Harry Potter and the Sorcerer's Stone* (Scholastic) is just the first book in a fantasy series about an apprentice wizard. The series is a real delight for both parents and kids. Great characters and wonderful British whimsy.

Jerry Spinelli, *Maniac Magee* (Little, Brown). This novel took all the awards in 1991. It's a funny, exciting, and moving modern legend that will appeal, especially, to sports-minded boys.

The Teenage Reader

The teenage years are tough on parents. Suddenly we're cut off from our children's lives. We no longer really know their friends. We wonder what they're doing on Friday night at 2:00 A.M., and we worry without the power or information to act on our worries.

But these years are also tough on the teenagers themselves. Suddenly your children discover the opposite sex, shaving cream or lipstick, alcohol and/or drugs, Beastie Boys or Ricky Martin, pimples and the power of a driver's license. Your children can now form their own opinions and argue hotly with yours. They are so desperately trying to define their own identity that they expend a massive amount of effort rejecting yours.

All of this begins to explain why the early teenage years are the second most dangerous time for readers. If your children have weathered the fourth-grade slump successfully, then eighth, ninth, and tenth grade become the years that determine whether reading will remain a big part of their lives.

It would be safe to say that almost two-thirds of American children in middle school read widely for pleasure. After the ninth-grade slump, that figure has dropped to about 20 percent of the student population. In this chapter, I want to look at the reasons we're losing so many readers in high school and what you, as a parent, can do to make sure your child isn't one of the casualties.

ILLITERACY AND ALITERACY

The danger in adolescence is not that our children will lose their reading skills but that they will stop using them. A fair portion of our young people—competent readers through elementary school—suddenly declare that they have no time to read, or that they are too busy working, or that they read enough at school and no longer want to on their own. Their attitude toward reading goes from enthusiasm to indifference. This is what sociologist Daniel Boorstin calls "aliteracy." The term describes situations in which a child can read well enough but can't be bothered actually to do so.

I'll use one of my sophomore English students as an example.

"So what was the last book you read outside school, Richard?"

"Can't remember. We read something last year . . ." He searches his memory for *To Kill a Mockingbird* but can't come up with the title.

"I meant outside school."

"Not much," he says, embarrassed. "I saw a couple of videos this week and went to the movies." Richard looks up for approval.

"Open any books?"

"School books?"

"Real books," I say.

Richard looks down at his hands.

Five Top Young-Adult Authors

Former newspaperman Robert Cormier is among the most senior American young-adult writers. His *The Chocolate War* has become a school classic. His other works explore interesting moral questions, but recent works like *Fade* are more for adults.

Lois Duncan grew up in Florida but her teenage suspense novels are set all over the United States. Many of her works, such as *Killing Mr. Griffin,* have suspenseful plots yet offer a thoughtful approach to ethical and social issues.

Virginia Hamilton is a prolific writer from Ohio who often writes with honesty about the problems of young African Americans. Novels such as *Sweet Whispers, Brother Rush* have been called "daring and innovative" by critics.

Richard Peck, born in Decatur, Illinois, was a professor at Hunter College in New York when he began writing for young people. His work is popular with teachers and appeals to young adolescents for its treatment of difficult subjects, especially the novel *Are You in the House Alone?*

Paul Zindel's *The Pigman* was one of the defining works in the young-adult genre. Since then Zindel has won a Pulitzer Prize for his touching play, *The Effect of Gamma Rays on Man-in-the-Moon Marigolds,* and written many other weird and wonderful works for teens.

"Read a newspaper?"

He shakes his head.

"Any magazines?"

"Well, yeah." Richard smiles, relieved. "Tom had this magazine on Guns 'N' Roses, like, so I read this thing about Slash. It was awesome."

Is Richard illiterate? Definitely not. He has no problem with phonics, word-attack skills, definitions by context, vocabulary to a ninth-grade level, oral fluency, or reading rate. He just doesn't read.

Richard's problem, that of aliteracy, has everyone stumped. Newspaper publishers eyeballing the graphs of falling daily newspaper readership among young people have tried everything from pumping up the jolts in the writing of daily columnists to bringing in new tabloid "news" papers that focus primarily on rock stars and nightclubs. Book publishers have tried to hold on to teenage readers by offering junior versions of adult fare such as Harlequin Romances or by promoting writers such as Stephen King, whose strongest appeal is to adolescents. For some teenagers, these efforts are working, but for Richard and many others, books and reading are being discarded as childhood ends.

Our teenagers didn't create this situation themselves. Many of them are victims of a campaign to commercialize all of childhood. Sometime in the 1950s, teenagers in North America became a target market—a consumer group with both money to spend and specific product demands. No other demographic group, save the truly wealthy, has as much disposable cash. Ten percent of all the young people in North America will work during adolescence for one company—McDonald's. Two-thirds of all high school juniors and seniors will work, and 20 percent of them will work more than fifteen hours a week.

Many teenagers have been told that they don't have to worry about mortgages, health care, food on the table, family vacations, hard times, or even the cost of their own educations. Only a small portion of them will contribute earnings to their households. The rest will spend their money on specially marketed, high-profit items ranging from designer running shoes to cosmetics. No wonder our suggestible adolescents, who are pummeled by messages for Nikes, Maybelline, and Camaros, spend their money on what they're made to want instead of what they really need.

Adolescents may not see how much they need to read. Cut off from the responsibilities of adult society, they tend to ignore newspapers, many magazines, and serious literature about adult life. Told they are no longer children, they often begin to feel that their earlier reading was just childish.

To make the situation worse, there is no body of literature that appeals specifically to older teens. Every young person wants to read about kids who are somewhat older. Your third-grade daughter wants to read *Tales of a Fourth Grade Nothing*, but your sixth-grade daughter wouldn't bother. Your thirteen-year-old son will read Robert Lipsyte's *The Contender* to see what it's like to be seventeen, but your eighteen-year-old son wouldn't dream of it. Significantly, there is no body of literature about university students for high school students to read. No one has bothered to assemble such a genre, so our high school students must turn to adult books when they aren't yet adults.

Or they turn away from reading altogether.

Ten Top Sci-Fi Books

I've listed each writer's most famous title, but all these
authors have a long list of good books.

Isaac Asimov, *Foundation* (Ballantine).
Ray Bradbury, *Fahrenheit 451* (Pocket Books).
David Brin, *Startide Rising* (Bantam).
Philip Jose Farmer, *Dayworld* (Ace).
William Gibson, *Neuromancer* (Ace).
Robert A. Heinlein, *Stranger in a Strange Land* (Ace).
Frank Herbert, *Dune* (Ace).
Spider Robinson, *Stardance* (Dial).
Fred Saberhagen, Berserker series (Tor).
Robert A. Wilson, *Schrodinger's Cat* (Dell).

DON'T GIVE UP

Reading remains vital, both to our society as a whole and to our
children as individuals. The 20 percent of our teenagers who
survive the ninth-grade slump are the ones who will develop the
sophisticated reading skills they need for work, community college, college, and graduate school. The others are losing ground
in the highly competitive world our young people must enter.
As parents, we naturally want to provide the encouragement
that will keep our teens reading for their own pleasure—and
their own futures.

The key is the three Rs, somewhat modified for your child at
this age.

Ten Worthwhile Fantasy Novels

Many of these books are part of a series, so look for authors more than titles.

Piers Anthony, *On a Pale Horse* (Ballantine).
Robert Aspirin, *Another Fine Myth* (Berkeley).
Orson Scott Card, *Seventh Son* (Tor).
Raymond E. Feist, *Magician: Apprentice* (Bantam).
Robert Jordan, The Wheel of Time series, now eight books (Tor).
Ursula K. Le Guin, *The Wizard of Earthsea* (Puffin).
Anne McCaffrey, *A Diversity of Dragons* (Harper).
Terry Pratchett, *The Colour of Magic* (Penguin/ROC).
Philip Pullman, *The Golden Compass* (Del Rey).
Robert Silverberg, *Lord Valentine's Castle* (HarperCollins).

• Keep reading with your teenager on some kind of regular basis. You might feel awkward reading out loud to a hulking teenage boy, but there's no reason you can't pick up your son's sophomore English course novel, read the back-cover blurb or a page of the text, and talk about it. I know a single parent who shares every book she reads with her daughter—and asks for the same in return. The mother has read more young-adult novels than I have, and enjoyed most of them. I know a family who keeps their teenage son reading by making a point of talking about books at dinner—not movies or TV or schoolwork—but books. Jewish families have long made oral reading a part of their cultural and family tradition at holidays. You can create your own reading traditions—a special reading of Dickens at Christmas, or a family gathering at which everyone writes or reads a poem about a special event. At our house, we take time to read out loud from the newspaper—everything from Ann Landers to horoscopes to outrageous editorials. Many families enjoy reading aloud a magazine quiz or questions from a trivia book as evening entertainment. Reading will stay important to your teenager so long as it stays important to everyone.

• Keep buying books for your teenager. I've said it before: Books are too special to be rolled into the weekly allowance or their purchase left to chance. Why not provide a special book allowance—and then read a portion of the purchased book yourself so you can talk with your son? Why not use the reading lists in this book to provide reading material for your teenage daughter? Tell your child she can have two books for free from the lists. Kids love the idea of getting something for nothing, and she'll probably have her interest piqued enough to give the books a try. Our family always takes a trip to the bookstore and library for a book binge before we leave for holidays. And then we trade the best "reads" when we're on vacation, sharing the good books with each other. Our neighbors know that if they borrow a video at the library, there's a good chance their teenage daughter will also take out a book. The way in which you share reading with teenagers in your family's life depends on how you live. Just be sure that books aren't left out.

• Rule the TV so reading can happen. Statistically, teenagers watch less television than anyone else, but that's only because so many of their waking hours are taken up with school, jobs, and friends. However, the remaining hours still can be spent plopped in front of the tube: music videos after school, *Gilligan's Island* through dinner, *Wheel of Fortune* at seven, the nightly movie until news time, *Saturday Night Live* reruns until exhaus-

Young-Adult Books in High School

A number of young-adult books have made their way onto the high school curriculum because they deal honestly with the problems young people face and because they actually get read. Here are some teacher favorites:

Judy Blume: *Tiger Eyes*
Alice Childress: *A Hero Ain't Nothin' But a Sandwich*
Robert Cormier: *The Chocolate War, I Am the Cheese*
Paula Fox: *The Moonlight Man*
Bette Greene: *The Summer of My German Soldier*
Robert Lipsyte: *The Contender*
Lois Lowry: *The Giver*
Katherine Paterson: *Jacob Have I Loved*
Robert Newton Peck: *A Day No Pigs Would Die*

tion . . . with the screen still going for cartoons in the morning—unless you maintain rules that shut the machine down.

Your teenage child, of course, will tell you she can read, do homework, and think about existential philosophy—all with headphones on, a Game Boy on the desk, and the TV screen five feet from her face. She's wrong. While today's children really can shut out the TV better than we could, very few can combine a passive attitude such as viewing with active attitudes for reading or writing. The research is conclusive: Any teenager who watches more than three hours of television a day is more likely to have problems in school, problems at home, and problems as a reader. Do your teenager a favor: Turn off the TV after two or three hours.

WHAT'S HAPPENING
IN HIGH SCHOOL

Reading itself is not specifically taught in high school; it's simply expected. Every subject, from English to calculus, depends on reading—often with textbooks written at university levels of difficulty. If your child isn't reading well enough to cope, the first report card will show it. Turn to Chapters 12 and 13 for some solutions.

Most teenagers do read adequately to handle high school work. They just don't read enough. I've seen very few students who can't do the assigned reading in novels or textbooks. What the students don't do is outside reading: novels for themselves, newspapers and magazines on current events, nonfiction on anything more substantial than rock music.

Younger teens will tell you that they're too busy to read, or that they have more important things to do. Older teens will tell you they don't have time to read after juggling school, part-time jobs, homework, and a social life. Recreational reading, when it happens, is pieced into a busy schedule—a few pages on the bus, a few more in study hall, a few minutes before sleep. Interestingly, some readers—the 20 percent—still manage to find more than ten hours a week to read because reading has become a habit. The aliterate teen will tell you she has no time at all.

High schools try to keep some outside reading alive through book reports or research projects, but their success is spotty. In some schools, the move to semestered (half-year) courses has made it more difficult to teach longer works. The typical high school English course still has an assortment of short stories, poetry, a bit of Shakespeare, perhaps one other play, an essay or two, and a novel—but rarely more than one novel. There just isn't time to cover any more in a twenty-week course. As a result, your child may come home bent over with required work for presentations or reports, but she's unlikely to appear with piles of books to read.

For high school students to survive the demands of the senior grades—and to keep some time for their own reading—they have to learn to read efficiently for school. Good schools take time to discuss reading and study skills in freshman English, history, or guidance programs. If your child's school does not, you might want to discuss with her the three kinds of reading an adult has to master.

THREE KINDS OF READING

When younger children read, they read in only one way. They have a single reading speed, usually 120 to 200 words per minute. They have a single approach to the text—to read all the words on the page and to get from them as much as possible. This reading works perfectly well 80 percent of the time, like a bike with only one gear. It's only going up hills or racing to destinations that requires a ten-speed derailleur. So, too, with reading.

Reading for Pleasure

Reading for pleasure is the way children read all the time and adults read most of the time. It's perfect for enjoying novels, the newspaper, and magazines. Every adult has a comfortable general reading speed. If you stop to measure, you'll likely find that you're reading this book a little more slowly than you would a novel, but your average speed will still run about 200 words per minute.

Reading speed tends to increase with education, from about 140 words per minute for a grade-school grad to about 240 words per minute for a university graduate. So long as you read fast enough not to get bogged down (about 100 words per minute is enough for this) and not so fast that you have to work at it (say 700 words per minute, or 30 seconds a page), reading for pleasure feels comfortable.

The only problem with reading for pleasure is that it won't do some of the work that reading has to do in adult life. That's why teenagers need to learn two other kinds of reading.

Reading for Study

Reading for study is slow. It's laborious. It's a necessary drag. Your daughter can't read a biology textbook as fast as she reads a novel. Your son can't read the fine print on a credit card agreement as fast as he reads *Popular Mechanics*. Reading for study involves different techniques and a different attitude.

An adult reader makes a decision to read for study. This is reading for work, for seeking information, for examining arguments and ideas. We apply this kind of reading to difficult material, whether it's the imagery of poetry, the ideas in a physics textbook, or the clauses in a contract. We do it with pencil in hand, a serious attitude in mind, and a sufficient amount of time set aside. Then we begin.

1. *Overview.* Look over the whole piece, get some sense of the structure and approach of the author, *then* go back and read a section at a time. It is sometimes very helpful to read the "about the author" section and the preface to understand the general slant of the book.

2. *Slow down.* Reading for study runs from twenty to eighty words per minute. If your eyes start traveling too quickly, start moving your lips as you read. Take the reading in small sections, then look away from the text and think: What is the author trying to get across? What is important in what I just read?

3. *Reread.* If you don't understand a sentence, go back and read it again. And again. Understanding is paramount; speed is trivial.

4. *Read for details.* The fine print and footnotes sometimes count more than the main text. That's where you'll learn that the research sample was too small or that department store credit card interest runs at a rate just shy of that of the local loan shark.

5. *Take notes.* Notes, comments, and responses scribbled into a notebook or in the margin ("Pavlov/bell/dog"; "Skinner is full of it") are far more valuable than simple underlining when reading for study. Marginal notes are a physical way to respond to the material—and responding encourages understanding. Underlining or highlighting merely produces a black and yellow page and the sense of having worked hard. Trade in your highlighters for pencils and respond to what you read.

6. *Get help when you need it.* Reading for study is sometimes done best with a dictionary beside you, or a calculator, or by calling for some advice on the phone. In casual reading, we can skip over difficult words or concepts, but not in reading for study.

Reading for Speed

Speed-reading is obviously the other extreme—where the reader skims rather than studies the material. Speed-reading involves both a change in reading rate and a change in attitude. There are certain methods a reader uses to make up for words

Tools Your Teen Can Do Without

Some items available to help teenagers in high school are of
questionable value:

Encyclopedia. A print encyclopedia rarely sees enough use to
be worth $600 to $1,000. Far more sensible to use the sets at
the library or buy a CD-ROM version for your computer.

Thesaurus. While some English teachers swear by these, I've
seen so many words misused because of "thesaurusitis" that
I'd like to see them banned. Build your vocabulary by
reading and using the dictionary, not by pulling words
you've never read off a list.

Colored highlighters. Substitute coloring for thought. Far better
to use a pencil to underline *and* comment in the margins.
Then you can erase it all when the course is finished.

Their own phone line; their own television set. Parents who give
teens their own phone lines or televisions, often for very
"logical" reasons, are abdicating a key responsibility. The
more private your teen becomes, the more isolated her life
will be from yours. Stay connected.

and phrases missed in the push to get reading speed up toward
1,000 words a minute. Here are the basics:

1. *Understand your own purpose.* No one speed-reads for fun.
You turn to speed-reading to find out something, or see if there's

Tools for Good Students

Dictionary. It's still the only way to really check spelling and whether you want "weather" or "whether."

Calculator. Essential for high school math courses and many science and technical courses.

Pocket planner. Teens don't need a leather daily planner, but they do need a handy calendar to record assignments and due dates. Some schools have taken to issuing one free to each student.

Pencil. Not just for underlining; students should respond to books in the margins. Also helpful for (a) note taking, (b) multiple-choice tests, and (c) rough drafts of assignments.

Computer. I know we're talking a thousand dollars here, but a computer really is worth the money if you can afford it. These days, spelling and grammar checkers can turn even bumbling writers into competent wordmeisters—a real plus for every subject. Then there are programs in math, business, science, engineering . . . the list is lengthy. Sometimes working but out-of-date computers can be bought for less than the cost of high-tech running shoes.

anything valuable in the books in front of you. A speed-reader always knows why she's reading and what she's looking for. Then she focuses her attention on exactly what she needs.

2. *Orient yourself.* A speed-reader always looks at the whole piece first to orient herself. Then she decides what portion to

read and sets her reading speed depending on her own needs. Indexes and tables of contents save reading time by allowing you to go right to the relevant pages.

3. *Use the big headings.* Chapter titles and subheads show how the work is organized. They also tell the reader what sections can be skipped altogether and how fast other sections should be read. Read more slowly if the topic is close to what you need: speed up when it seems unrelated.

4. *Keep up the pace.* Reading for speed means pushing your eyes to handle 800 to 1,000 words per minute. Rumor has it that John F. Kennedy could skim-read at 20,000 words per minute, but Kennedy legends ranging from reading to sexual prowess are likely overstated. Still, any competent reader can double her reading speed with a little willpower and a fingertip.

5. *Use a finger pointer.* Running your finger down the page will keep your speed at a constant rate. You can buy machines to do the same thing, or cut a piece of cardboard with a rectangle in the middle to focus your attention, but simply running your finger down a column of type—and keeping up with it—will have the same effect.

6. *Take in more words at a glance.* When you read, your eyes stop at several points along a line of type. Like this:

beginning/readers/stop/at/every/word;

more sophisticated readers/ read in clusters/

of three to five words.

Each eye stop is called a fixation. The fewer fixations per line, the faster you'll read.

7. *Avoid going backward.* When we read normally, our eyes "regress," or reread chunks of print that we didn't understand fully. Speed-reading advocates suggest that skipped words don't matter that much. Your brain will reconstruct what your eyes

> ## Not All Reading Is Fun
>
> One of the terrible shocks about reading in high school and college is how much of it is *work* and how little of it is *fun*. Alas, this may just be preparation for adult life. I asked various friends to take one week and count the number of pages that came across their desk. Here are the results.
>
> - Lawyer: 500 pages: letters, reports, and the like (plus reading to research cases)
> - Two teachers: 350 pages—marking and mailbox (not including course material), 30 computer screens
> - Engineer: 300 pages "looked at": 100 pages of diagrams, probably 200 computer screens
> - Chemist: 4 technical articles, 2 business magazines, 20 reports, 80 data sheets, 20 pages of notes, 50 computer screens
> - Computer company executive: 400 pages, 350+ screens e-mail, 200 other computer screens

didn't quite see. By stopping eye regression, you can easily increase your reading speed by 25 percent or more.

By working on these techniques and practicing on gradually more difficult material, many adults have managed to double their regular reading speed. Whether this is important to you depends on your school or your work, but every adult needs to learn to read for speed when required. Otherwise, we will spend some portions of our lives almost buried under print.

BUILDING CRITICAL
JUDGMENT

Teenagers are capable of wonderful flip-flops. They are incredibly enthusiastic one day—about Mötley Crüe, or Mrs. Jones the English teacher, or Maya Angelou—and incredibly cynical the next—about Mötley Crüe, Mrs. Jones, and Maya Angelou. This mix of childish exuberance and growing sophistication is part of adolescent charm.

But we want more from our children than this. We know, as adults, that they will be called upon to make reasoned, critical judgments. They'll be voting, buying houses, looking for promotions at work, someday having children of their own—and all these require more judgment than enthusiasm.

That's what adult reading is all about. A book provides ideas and opinions that can and should be talked about. At home and at school, that talk should be promoted. Only through talk can your teenager understand some very important aspects of what she reads:

- Print carries the author's ideas—it is not holy writ.
- Authors can lie or misrepresent or be mistaken in print, just as people can be in conversation.
- Authors have their own political and personal agendas, which must be respected or discounted in understanding what they write.

Small children have an inordinate respect for what they read. How many times have you heard, "But that's not what it says in the book, Mom!" For little kids, any book carries tremendous authority. The cynical attitude of many teenagers is a rebel-

Nothing Wrong with a Little Schlock

Recently I was on a television panel discussing the current fascination of teenagers with the horror genre. The other panelists took delight in trashing "cheap series novels" with their "artificial plots" and "total absence of any literary value." And all that may well be true, but the same things were being said about Dickens in the 1870s.

Somehow the argument turned around so I ended up having to defend the right of kids to read Stephen King and Christopher Pike. This brought attacks from the other panelists and dire predictions about the way in which such reading would twist the minds of today's young people.

Needless to say, I took a real drubbing in the debate. But afterward, when the cameras were turned off, a teenage girl came up from the audience and went over to the most aggressive woman on the other side. The teenager's rhetorical questions were brilliant: "Just how stupid do you think we are? Don't you think we can tell a story from real life?" *Touché*.

lion against that authority. This rebellion can reach such outrageous proportions as "I don't believe anything I read."

What's needed in adolescence and adulthood is a critical stance, but not cynical abandonment. We want our children to understand that William Buckley supports right-wing Republican policy just as the *New York Times* often promotes the Democrats. We want them to see that the current slew of articles about Leonardo DiCaprio is part of a movie publicity package—

and probably much less important to their lives than our te-
dious, but essential, political debates.

And we want all this at the same time as our children are
least interested in what we, their parents, have to say.

So make demands of your child's high school. If everything
you see from your son's history course or your daughter's English course seems to be short answer or multiple choice, talk to
the teachers and the principal. According to Jean Piaget, the
Swiss psychologist, and other researchers, our children can't
fully reason until the age of thirteen or fourteen. That gives our
high schools only four years to develop children's sophisticated
reasoning skills. Multiple-choice tests and simple factual recall
questions won't build the skills your children need.

Demand more. High school students should be reading in-
tensively at school and widely at home—as part of the program.
High school programs should be calling for research, argument,
debate, and a great deal of writing to match all the reading. And
teachers in the school always should challenge your children, regardless of their abilities, to stretch themselves intellectually.

Then be sure to follow through at home. Teenagers don't
have to be questioned about their every sentence, but they can
be asked to explain or defend their ideas. The correct response
to "This book is stupid" isn't "Shut up and read it anyway"; it's
"Why do you think so?" The correct response to "I don't understand this dumb history textbook" isn't "Go back and try it
again"; it's "What do you think the author might be trying to
say?" If you're there at the kitchen table with your teen, the talk
can begin. You've reached a point in your child's school life
where you certainly won't have all the answers, but you'll know
far better what the questions should be.

What Are the Classics?

Former Secretary of Education William Bennett surveyed 325 journalists, teachers, and business leaders to come up with a list of the classics. Here's his try at the top twenty-five:

Shakespeare, *Macbeth, Hamlet*
The Bible
Mark Twain, *Huckleberry Finn*
Homer, *The Odyssey, The Iliad*
Charles Dickens, *Great Expectations*
Plato, *The Republic*
John Steinbeck, *The Grapes of Wrath*
Nathaniel Hawthorne, *The Scarlet Letter*
Sophocles, *Oedipus Rex*
Herman Melville, *Moby Dick*
George Orwell, *1984*
Henry David Thoreau, *Walden*
Robert Frost, poems
Walt Whitman, *Leaves of Grass*
F. Scott Fitzgerald, *The Great Gatsby*
Chaucer, *The Canterbury Tales*
Karl Marx, *Communist Manifesto*
Aristotle, *Poetics*
Emily Dickinson, poems
Fyodor Dostoyevsky, *Crime and Punishment*
William Faulkner, *The Sound and the Fury*
J. D. Salinger, *The Catcher in the Rye*
A. de Tocqueville, *Democracy in America*
Jane Austen, *Pride and Prejudice*
Ralph Waldo Emerson, essays

WHAT TEENAGERS DO READ

Teenagers who do read read unpredictably. A senior student of mine last year brought in her own books to read when she had a spare period. One week I made some notes on Alison's reading: a Constance Beresford-Howe novel on Monday, a handful of Robert Munsch picture books on Tuesday, Kahlil Gibran on Wednesday, *Cosmopolitan* on Thursday, and back to the Beresford-Howe novel on Friday. This same girl tried to convince me to put *Alice's Adventures in Wonderland* on the teen "must-have" list because she'd found so much in it the second time through.

Alison, like most teenagers, is not the finished person she would like to think she is. Teenagers are still being formed—or forming themselves. They haven't let go of their own childhood, yet they are busy exploring the adult world and trying to find their place in it. As a result, avid teen readers are looking for information everywhere: novels, poetry, letters, philosophy, religion, biography, and history.

For your teenager, certain types of books serve as a transition from children's fiction to adult literature. Some of these may keep your child reading right through the ninth-grade slump until she's ready to handle adult books.

• Realistic young-adult fiction. Walk into any library and you'll see the rack: paperback novels, about 175 pages long, with teenage central characters confronting—and usually triumphing over—problems ranging from divorce to date rape. The pioneers in this field—Paul Zindel, S. E. Hinton, Robert Cormier—sought to give young people a literature that valued teenage experience and didn't shy away from the real difficulties kids face. This genre remains important, especially for teens up to age fourteen or fifteen.

- Fantasy. Fantasy is a mixture of the classic adventure novel and some Sir Walter Scott derring-do with the long saga of Arthurian legend, set in some indeterminate time where magic and heroic deeds somehow seem plausible. Once lumped in with science fiction, fantasy now has become its own genre, with writers ranging from Lloyd Alexander and Madeleine L'Engle for the younger set to Piers Anthony and Ursula Le Guin for the more mature teenager. The popularity of the Harry Potter books will only accentuate this trend.

- Science fiction. These days, fantasy is pushing sci-fi books off the bookstore shelves, but this genre remains popular with many teenagers, especially boys. Again, these books offer heroism, philosophy, adventure, and a simplified moral universe that is empowering material for young people.

- Romance. With effective marketing of junior Harlequins such as The Twins and Sweet Valley High, teenage girls are moving on naturally to real Harlequins, Silhouettes, and spicier cousins, such as Harlequin Mystique. Teen readers ignore the interchangeable characters and plots to get lost in the idealized romance they hope to find later in real life. More sophisticated readers will find books by Barbara Cartland and Danielle Steel form a crossover to mysteries and popular fiction. The growing field of historical romance offers idealized characters and plots in novels with solid historical settings.

- Horror. The rise of horror seemed to follow the decline of the western as a genre—and this may say something quite terrible about the current direction of our society. Nonetheless, Stephen King is probably the single most popular author among adolescents, and his creepy novels are likely to be a cut above the positively gory films your son or daughter might otherwise be watching. Testing out their capacity for fear through the books of King, Christopher Pike (for the younger set), and Peter

What Rock Musicians Read

Here's a much-condensed version of a CITY-TV/THE NEW MUSIC listing. Try this on your teenager:

- Bryan Adams:
  Emily Carr, *The Book of Small* (Stoddart)

- Rick Astley:
  Martin Amis, *Success*, *The Rachel Papers* (Penguin)

- Barney Bentall:
  Thomas Hardy, *The Mayor of Casterbridge* (Penguin)
  John Irving, *Hotel New Hampshire* (Dell)

- Duran Duran (as a group):
  Truman Capote, *In Cold Blood* (Signet)
  Clive Barker, *Weaveworld* (HarperCollins)
  Mervyn Peake, *Titus Groan* (Methuen)

- Gowan:
  Hermann Hesse, *Siddhartha* and *Steppenwolf* (Bantam)

- Deborah Harry:
  Peter Straub, *Ghost Story* (Cape)
  Hubert Selby, *Last Exit to Brooklyn* (Grove)

- Jon Bon Jovi:
  Charles Bukowski, *Hollywood: A Novel* (Black Sparrow)

- M. C. Hammer:
  The Bible

- Simon Le Bon of Duran Duran:
  Gabriel García Márquez, *One Hundred Years of Solitude* (HarperCollins)
  Hunter S. Thompson, *Fear and Loathing in Las Vegas* (Warner)

- Jane Siberry:
  Agatha Christie murder mysteries.

- Paul Stanley of Kiss:
  Ayn Rand, *Atlas Shrugged* (Signet/NAL)
  Kurt Vonnegut, *Breakfast of Champions* (Dell)

- Sting:
  Robert Bly, *Iron John* (Addison Wesley)
  Anne Rice, *The Vampire Chronicles* (Ballantine)

- Suzanne Vega:
  Simone de Beauvoir, *The Second Sex* (Vintage)

Straub (for the brighter readers) is as much a part of adolescence as testing out the capacity for dreaming through romance fiction.

- Classics. There are still teenagers who enjoy reading great works of literature, especially if this taste is quietly encouraged at home and at school. Some older teens spend several months reading "The Russians" (usually Dostoyevsky more than Tolstoy or Gogol), or Franz Kafka, or Jean-Paul Sartre, or F. Scott Fitzgerald. Some will read classic horror writers such as H. P. Lovecraft, or classic sci-fi such as Ray Bradbury. Others will get excited about a particular writer's work if there's a current movie or a fad at school to spur motivation.

• Nonfiction. A fair number of teenagers will read only biographies of rock stars, or books on automobile racing, or magazine after magazine on computers. Chapter 12 goes into more detail on reading tied to particular interests.

• Magazines. In the last fifteen years, the number of U.S. magazines has doubled to over 6,000 different titles. Teenagers and adults all love them—and have many to choose from.

• And all the rest. Some teenagers read more widely and with greater sophistication than their parents. If that is true in your family, or if you've fallen out of the habit of reading for pleasure, the next chapter is for you.

TEN GOOD BETS FOR YOUR TEEN'S BOOKSHELF

A caution: By this age, your child's interests and tastes may be so specific that purchasing books on other subjects might be met with grunts or sneers. But if you don't broaden your teen's reading, who will? Here's a ten-book starter list:

Douglas Adams, *A Hitchhiker's Guide to the Galaxy* (Pan), and the three sequels. Monty Python meets science fiction; based on the radio series but very well written. Strong appeal for bright teens.

V. C. Andrews, *Flowers in the Attic* (Pocket Books), and many other titles. These are low-rent, family-terror titles, but awesomely popular with girls from the seventh to the ninth grade.

Robert Cormier, *The Chocolate War* (Dell). This author's most famous book is about conflict and loss at a New England private school. His new book, *Tenderness* (Dell), is a real page-turner.

S. E. Hinton, *The Outsiders* (Dell). Written when the author was just seventeen, this novel provides a picture of gang conflict about as accurate as that in *West Side Story*. Nonetheless, young teens love it. Personally, I think Hinton's *Rumble Fish* is a much better book.

Stephen King, *The Dead Zone* (Signet). How can any kid grow up without reading at least one Stephen King chiller? This one is less gruesome than others.

Harry Mazer, *Snow Bound* (Dell). Adventure and self-realization in a snowstorm, for readers age eleven and up. Mazer is one of our top young-adult writers, and this book shows all his skill.

Katherine Paterson, *Jacob Have I Loved* (Harper). Paterson's beautiful prose offers us twin sisters, their difficult relationship, and the gorgeous Chesapeake Bay area in World War II. A thoughtful, sensitive book.

J. D. Salinger, *The Catcher in the Rye* (Bantam). A classic coming-of-age novel that still appeals to bright teens. Attempts to ban this now-innocuous book just add to its appeal.

J. R. R. Tolkien, *The Hobbit* or *Lord of the Rings* (Ballantine). Now your kids can read these on their own.

Paul Zindel, *The Pigman* (Dell), and others. Zindel won a Pulitzer Prize for his play *The Effect of Gamma Rays on Man-in-the-Moon Marigolds*, but he's won the hearts of millions of teens with his young-adult novels. Realistic and poignant.

Chapter 11

The Adult Reader

Throughout this book, I've been looking at reading as a life-long process, as something we learn and develop from infancy through school and into adulthood. It would be foolish, then, to suggest that learning to read is somehow complete by the end of high school or college. It's not. As adults, we continue to learn to read in ways that can enrich both our appreciation of books and our own lives.

The tremendous advantage we have as adult readers is experience. I remember as a child in Buffalo trying to tackle some of the great works of literature with the intellectual tools I had available at the time. In sixth grade, a number of us decided to read *Macbeth* out loud because somebody had said it was an important play. So at age eleven, my friends Irwin, Marshall, Robbie, Anita, and I read the words in *Macbeth* with all the dramatic passion we could muster. When we finally finished the play, none of us could understand what all the fuss was about. How could this play have survived for 350 years and be so revered by all these adults? For us, it was just a bunch of weird, old-fashioned words with a story about a greedy man, his crazy wife, and the good guys finally winning at the end. Quite simply, we didn't get it.

I didn't tackle *Macbeth* again until my junior year in high school, with another five years of worldly experience under my belt. This time I "got" a little more of it. Using my sketchy knowledge of Freudian psychology, I decided the play was really about sexual frustration. The fact that my own life was largely about sexual frustration was impossible to admit at the time, but I could certainly see the problem writ large in Shakespeare. As an adolescent, I managed to get my first handle on the play, but it was only a beginning.

I came back to *Macbeth* again as a teacher. At age thirty-four, I had a bit more under my belt: another seventeen years of living, two children growing up, experience producing and directing two school musicals. Unlike my eleventh-grade students, I was no longer interested in the sexual problems of the Macbeths. The scene that riveted me was the one in which Macduff is told of the death of his children. That scene literally brought tears to my eyes.

Nor will I pretend that my readings of *Macbeth* are complete these days, in midlife, as I see aspects of politics that I'd never noticed before. What will my reading of *Macbeth* find when I am sixty or seventy? I suspect it will be characters and themes I can't begin to uncover at this stage in my life.

Does this mean that I am a *better* reader now than I was at age fifteen or twenty-five or thirty-five? Probably not. I am a different reader than I was, reaching out to the book or the play in a different way.

So our children must keep reading great literature in high school, and we must keep reaching back to that literature as adults. Again and again in my adult life, I come back to words that I read in high school and college but only dimly understood at the time: lines of poetry from Thomas Hardy, John Donne, and T. S. Eliot; speeches from Shakespeare and George Bernard

On Leisure Reading

Percentage of Americans who read more than one hour a day: 71

Percentage of Americans who read books: 33

How much time these readers spend reading books, on average: 47 minutes a day

Number of minutes the average person in Torun, Poland, spent reading books, per day, in 1972: 16.4

Number of minutes the average person in Jackson, Michigan, spent reading books, per day, in 1972: 3.7

Among the world's adult population, amount of time spent daily on reading: 35 minutes

On reading books: 5 minutes

How accurate are all these statistics? Three studies of U.S. college students indicate that their weekly reading for pleasure totals 7.2, 2.7, or 1.1 hours, depending on the researcher. Obviously we have a few measurement irregularities.

Shaw, and Arthur Miller's *Death of a Salesman;* chunks of prose from Joseph Conrad or Charles Dickens or Dostoyevsky. I find in these bits and pieces the solace I need at a given moment, the wisdom I need to move forward. I am a member of a generation that was inundated by the popular—from early television to the Beatles—but the words that have stood by me are those that have already passed a more substantial test of time. Sometimes I

"If you read a story that really involves you, your body will tell you that you are living through the experience. You will recognize feelings that have physical signs—increased heart rate, sweaty palms, or calm, relaxed breathing and so on, depending on your mood. These effects are the same you would feel in similar real-life experiences—fear, anger, interest, joy, shame or sadness. Amazingly, you can actually 'live' experience without moving anything but your eyes across a page."

—Joseph Gold, *Read for Your Life*
(Fitzhenry and Whiteside, 1990)

look at our young people, headphones plugged into their ears, Ricky Martin plugged into their minds, and I can only hope that they are finding a way to get something more substantial upon which to build a life.

THE RESONANCE OF WORDS

In the first chapters of this book, I described the ways that young children get beyond print to the dream or ideas of a book. As adults, I think we use books in an additional way—to get beyond print to words and images that bring a delicious resonance.

A book or story that is meaningful for adults resonates within; it touches something in our bones. A passage can make us respond with "I've thought that" or "I've felt that." Print connects our humanity at its deepest level with the ideas, hopes, and dreams of another.

Read with me:

It is a winter's night in 1936 in Halifax, Nova Scotia. A small boy is being read to. He is warm from a hot bath, wearing striped flannel pyjamas and a thick woollen dressing gown with a tasselled cord. He has dropped off his slippers to slide his bare feet between the cushions of the sofa.

Outside, a salty wind blows snow against the panes of the windows. It sifts under the front door and through the three ventilation holes in the storm windows, creating tiny drifts. Foghorns are grumping far in the distance. The coal fire in the basket grate burns intense and silent. His mother reads . . .

So Robert MacNeil transports us in the opening paragraphs of *Wordstruck*. I am moved by the sheer beauty of the writing: the foghorns grumping, the tasseled cord on the boy's dressing gown, the repeated *s* sounds in the salty wind words of the second paragraph. And I resonate with the images MacNeil provides. I grew up in Buffalo, but I've since felt the salty wind of Halifax. It was my father, not my mother, who read to me in my crumpled pajamas, but I know that memory—that feeling—and it is part of my response to MacNeil's printed words. Other details, too, are rich for me in remembrance: Those old storm windows with the three ventilation holes where my friends and I would run telephone wires, or whisper conversations when they weren't allowed in the house. The feeling of a hot bath and the tingling of the skin when I emerged, warmed despite the chill room. These images from my own life are conjured up as I read MacNeil's prose.

As adults, we can savor the words, the images, and our own memories. We automatically slow down our reading when we come to a section that especially grips us so we can relish the prose. While we may zip through a description of Boston harbor at 400 words per minute or more, we will slow down our reading to less than half that speed to enjoy the words that resonate within us. When we read, unlike the experience of television, we have control over the images that are presented to us. This control gives us the power to linger over the words and to enjoy the images and memories they create in our minds.

FINDING TIME

The joys of adult reading are available to us only if we make the time to read. Simply finding quiet time is becoming more and more difficult as our leisure hours shrink. According to one measure, the number of free hours available to North Americans peaked in 1973 at twenty-six hours a week and has shrunk by a third since then. Simultaneously, the demands placed on our leisure—by everything from television to sports to dining out—have multiplied. The result is obvious: We read less.

And we read differently. Witold Rybczynski in his brilliant book *Waiting for the Weekend* talks about the way reading has changed as our leisure time shrinks and fragments. To read a novel, for instance, we should devote a certain amount of time every day. We cannot begin A. S. Byatt's *Possession* on Sunday morning, put the book down for a week, and hope to pick up where we left off. A big novel has too many characters, too many plots and subplots, too many themes and ideas for our memory to hold that long.

Maybe that is the reason we've seen such an increase in short literary forms: the short-story collection, the formula novel, the magazine article. Reading a short story, for instance, is a complete experience that takes the twenty minutes most of us have before bed. Many mass-produced novels, such as Harlequin romances, are only 50,000 words long and can be completed with about three hours of reading. Magazines require even less time. The breakthrough of *People* magazine wasn't based on great design or new material. It was based on very short articles. Now there's hardly a magazine on the racks that doesn't have several sections or columns that used to be called "snippets," tiny, 200-word fragments that compress stories into snappy prose that grabs our attention, but not our time. Even the venerable *Harper's*, an intellectual magazine for almost 150 years, has a "Readings" section for short articles that takes up a third of the magazine.

This kind of reading simply isn't enough. In order to enter fully into the story, to feel with the characters, to join the imaginative world of the author, we must give a book time. A big

---

How Adults Pick Books

Here's what readers in one survey mentioned when asked how they became aware of the book they were currently reading, in order:

1. Through conversation with friends, family
2. Interested in author
3. Browsing or display in bookstore
4. Browsing or display in library
5. Book club promotion
6. Read a book review or article
7. Saw it as a movie or TV show
8. Heard about it on radio or TV
9. Saw newspaper or magazine advertising

novel, such as John Irving's *A Prayer for Owen Meany*, will have over 300,000 words in its 430 pages and require some eighteen hours to complete. In the book trade, this is considered a summer book because that's when people head off to vacation homes and the beach, apparently with enough time to read it. Certainly reading a big novel on vacation is a joy, but why should that be the only time for it?

We find more than twenty-three hours a week to watch television. We have found an additional nine hours to add to our work week since the 1950s. We regularly find four hours a week to travel to and from work. Surely there is time in our lives to read more and to read with greater regularity. But we must be aggressive to seize that time.

• After reading with your child, take the rest of that hour to read for yourself.

• At breakfast, or just before leaving for work, set aside fifteen minutes for reading a book with your coffee.

• Make reading time a special time. As one person suggested to me, "The children aren't allowed to bother me so long as I'm reading—at least, not until I turn a page."

• Set aside a reading time on Sunday afternoon. I have a friend who manages to watch football on TV with the sound off, play Mozart on the stereo, *and* read a novel. He maintains that in this way he combines all the joys of life at one sitting.

• Transform some TV time into reading time. There might well be half an hour between dinner and the 9:00 TV movie for a good read.

• Organize a time for reading as you might organize a time for daily exercise. I love to open a book at 5:00 P.M., sitting outside, knowing I have half an hour before I have to worry about dinner.

Remember that reading was first—and should still be—a social experience. Nothing will get a person as excited about a book as a strong recommendation from someone else. A book you read and enjoyed should be lent out and talked about. Part of the joy of reading is in sharing—"Have you come to the part where . . . ?" "Isn't it great when . . . ?" I was so excited by *Waiting for the Weekend* that I spent most of a dinner party talking about it, then I lent it to a friend, then spent another dinner talking to him about it. The thriller *Hannibal* by Thomas Harris may not be great literature, but it's been read by everyone in my family because enthusiasm for a good read is contagious. Perhaps

---

"Reader's Bill of Rights"

The French author Daniel Pennac has written persuasively about the joys of adult reading. In his book *Better Than Life*, he attacks teachers, academics, and librarians for putting too much emphasis on interpretation and not enough on pleasure in reading. Among his tools to give pleasure back to readers are a bill of rights, including

- the right not to read
- the right to skip pages
- the right not to finish a book

Reading, after all, is about our control over the world, not the internalized voice of Miss Tudd in sixth grade, who checked to see if our eyes were glued to the page. We need more pleasure in our adult reading and less guilt.

you can join a group of friends to exchange book enthusiasms—and books as well. Some libraries, bookstores, and communities have regular reading groups where the members read a chosen novel each month and then discuss the book and its ideas. These groups are excellent ways to spur your own reading.

Reading is too important to be left for a few weeks of vacation, or the Christmas holidays, or limited to the daily newspaper and *Time* magazine. We must give ourselves time—serious, quiet time—to read and respond to books. A reader for life, by definition, finds time to fit reading into an adult day.

Chapter 12

Exciting the
Bored Reader

It can happen to the nicest kids. Your son Jonah, a good enough reader through fifth grade, suddenly declares that reading is boring. When you offer to read a book with him, the response written on his face says "Do I have to?" Or your daughter Jennifer, who brought home piles of books right through fifth grade, is now reading only one novel a month in junior high, and that's just because a book report is due for her English teacher. When you offer to read with Jennifer in the evening, she gives you that withering almost-adolescent look and declares, "Mom, I *know* how to read."

Both Jennifer and Jonah do know how to read. All the technical skills are there: the sight vocabulary and instant phonic analysis and reasonable reading speed. They would score just fine on any standardized reading test. But neither of the kids *is* reading, and that's ultimately going to hurt them. One researcher has declared that unless children and adults read twenty-two minutes a day, their reading skills will go into decline. I'm skeptical about magic numbers such as "twenty-two minutes a day," but I do know that kids who stop reading start to fall behind their classmates. They lose ground in vocabulary, in comprehension, in advanced thinking skills, even in the ability to write. If Jennifer and Jonah stay stalled with the skills of their grade level, they'll be significantly behind many of their peers in two years' time—and in real trouble within four years.

I'm using Jennifer and Jonah as examples of "bored readers," kids who are not illiterate but aliterate. Jennifer and Jonah have the skills, but they are developing an indifference to print. Unlike the reluctant readers I'll discuss in Chapter 13, Jennifer and Jonah have no intellectual or medical problems to explain their reading attitude. They are not among that 5 to 10 percent of the school population with reading difficulties that require testing, analysis, and remediation. Jennifer and Jonah are just bored with books.

In Jennifer's case, we have a young adolescent whose life is suddenly taken over by the prospect of boys, the secrets and rumors that run through junior high school, an emotional life that seems to take all her energy, and the growing demands of the school curriculum. Compared to the real life she's discovering, Jennifer finds kids' books too tame and teenage novels too safe. She could probably read adult potboilers, but her school library doesn't have any, her junior library card won't let her check them out, and her parents wouldn't approve anyway. So she reads only what she has to for school, borrows the occasional book from a friend without telling her parents, and spends many hours plopped in front of the TV or with the stereo blaring in her bedroom or booming through headphones. Jennifer likely will start reading again some years after this phase, which educator David Booth calls the teenage "fallow period." But in the meantime her reading and intellectual skills will be stagnant.

Jonah's case is more serious because his boredom will hold back progress in reading at a more crucial stage. While Jennifer's

Books for Kids Who "Hate" to Read

Members of the California Reading Association asked
reluctant readers in seventh to twelfth grades to recommend
books to their peers. Here are the titles not listed elsewhere
in this book.

- Maya Angelou, *I Know Why the Caged Bird Sings* (Bantam)
- Richard Bach, *Jonathan Livingstone Seagull* (Avon)
- E. R. Braithwaite, *To Sir with Love* (Jove)
- Margaret Craven, *I Heard the Owl Call My Name* (Dell)
- Lois Duncan, *I Know What You Did Last Summer* (Pocket)
- Jean Craighead George, *My Side of the Mountain* (Dutton)
- Fred Gipson, *Old Yeller* (Harper)
- Harry Mazer, *The Last Mission* (Dell)
- Frances Miller, *Aren't You the One Who . . . ?* (Fawcett)
- John Neufeld, *Edgar Allen* (Signet)
- Robert Newton Peck, *A Day No Pigs Would Die* (Dell)
- Wilson Rawls, *Summer of the Monkeys* (Dell) and *Where the Red Fern Grows* (Dell)
- Anne Snyder, *My Name Is Davy—I'm an Alcoholic* (NAL)

eighth-grade reading skills probably are sufficient for her to
function right through high school, Jonah's fifth-grade skills will
doom him, unless they improve, to semiliteracy. He'll end up at
the bottom stream in high school, and eventually he'll be stuck
in an adult life without books—unless something is done
quickly.

GET INVOLVED, AGAIN

For many bored readers, the solution is quite simple—renewed involvement by parents using the three Rs. Parents must renew a commitment to read with their child every day, even if it starts out simply with books assigned by the school. Parents must reach into their wallets for money to provide books or magazines for their child, perhaps augmented with a biweekly library trip. And parents must make sure there's time for reading to happen, by turning off the TV, or cutting back the ballet lessons, or putting limits on time kids spend on the phone. Routines must change.

The problem with this simple prescription is that routines are very hard to change. Your kids will resist your involvement, seeing it as an intrusion; they'll call your offer to buy books a bribe; they'll say that any new rules around the house are "unfair," or "fascist," or worse.

Make the changes anyway.

I'm not one to call for raw displays of parental power, but there's much to be said for parental *resolve*. The reasons behind the changes should be presented seriously, and the changes should be enforced despite initial whining and complaints. Often school provides a good excuse for initiating change. One opening: "Your dad and I were talking to your teacher last week, and she's concerned that you're not reading as much as you used to . . ." Another approach is to use this book: "Your mom and I have been reading a book lately about the importance of reading. We've both become concerned that you don't read as much as you used to, and we're afraid that it's going to hurt you in the long run. So we've decided to change one or two things around here . . ."

A third approach is to talk about your child's welfare: "You

Those "Series" Books

There's mixed opinion in the book and library trades about novels that come out in a series, such as Sweet Valley High or Goosebumps, as opposed to individual titles issued in "trade." Some specialized children's bookstores and some libraries won't even put series books on the shelves. On the other hand, many chain bookstores stock so many series books that there's no room left for even excellent trade novels.

Critics maintain that the series books stifle author creativity, promote formula writing, and sometimes push objectionable values or depict too much blood and gore. Defenders point out that series books have an appeal like weekly television shows, that they offer what kids really want to read, and that few mass murderers get their instructions by reading Goosebumps books.

There's probably a middle ground that would give kids access to The Baby-Sitters Club or Christopher Pike without cutting into sales of Katherine Paterson's *Bridge to Terabithia*. And some series books might turn on a bored reader in your family.

know that reading is important, maybe the most important thing that's worked on in school. We've decided to promote it a little more at home, starting tomorrow . . ."

Then keep to your new routines. If the new rules call for a quiet time between seven and eight, don't make yourselves an exception. Leave the dishes in the sink, take the phone off the hook, disconnect the TV, take the batteries out of the Walkman—and read. If the new rules say you'll read together at 9:00

Best and Worst
of the Series Books

- Walter Dean Myer's 18 Pine Street series. Serious, well-written stories, many good enough to stand alone.
- Steve Jackson and Ian Livingston's Fighting Fantasy series. These are fantasy books that kids "play" while they read, skipping from section to section to create many different plots. They are slightly better than the action-oriented Choose Your Own Adventure novels.
- Ann Martin's The Baby-Sitters Club. The prose is often clunky, but the values are solid and the books remain very, very popular.

and then . . .

- Francine Pascal's Sweet Valley High series. The original junior Harlequins, and about that good in terms of quality. The competing Sweet Dreams series isn't even this good.
- Linda Cooney's Freshmen series turns college into a print sitcom. Like, gag me.
- Supermodels of the World is probably the most repugnant series of all. The message: Pretty equals popular. It's hard to imagine something like this actually being published.

P.M., then do it exactly at 9:00 until the routine gets established. If the new rules say there'll be a bookstore trip once a month, start right away, telling your son he can choose one book on his own and that you're going to choose one more from the suggestions in this book.

It is, quite literally, never too late to help the bored reader.

One of the consultants for this book tells the story of a teacher who inadvertently ended up helping his son stop being a bored reader. The father, a senior elementary science teacher, kept challenging his son's junior high to do a better job spurring his son's reading—test more, challenge more, require more, do more to make the child a better reader. None of this was successful, and the son's reading remained sporadic and forced.

Then the teachers of his school board went on strike, and father and son were stuck at home, bored. The father decided that his own son's education wouldn't be sacrificed, and he started bringing home books from the library and bookstore, two a day. He and his son read the books, sometimes together, sometimes separately, and spent time talking about them. When the strike was over a month later, the son had a changed attitude toward reading and books, and had become a much more competent reader.

The father, of course, is still convinced that his child's school wasn't doing its job. But the truth is that the father wasn't doing his job until the strike spurred him to do so. Suddenly the son was given quiet time, an interested parent, and a chance to talk about what he read—and he became a reader. Inadvertently, the father was following the three Rs, and the results speak for themselves.

PLUG INTO INTERESTS

While some of us will read anything that passes in front of our eyes, from cereal boxes to medical textbooks, the bored reader is much pickier. The bored reader will not look at the newspaper just because it's on the kitchen table, or pick up a magazine in the bathroom just because there's time, or begin a novel unless there's some reason to do so. The bored reader is choosy. The bored reader wants reading that ties into his interests. And the bored reader needs a push.

If you've been reading with your child every day, you already know what he likes and dislikes in terms of reading. But if you haven't been doing this, you will have to go back and rediscover your child's interests. As parents, we are often too close or too far away from our own children. We are too close when we know our children's favorite breakfast cereal but never hear about their dreams or fears or what makes them cry at night. We are too far when we lecture them about coming in after 1:00 A.M. when they're really worried about birth control, AIDS, and the stories their ex-boyfriends might or might not be telling around school. If your child is a bored reader, you'll have to take a middle position to find books which will appeal.

Let's start with four questions:

1. What are three things your child is interested in?
2. What three activities are your child and his friends involved in?
3. What three adult activities would your child like to do someday?
4. What were the last three books/stories/magazines that your child seemed to enjoy?

If you can already answer all four questions, you have a dozen bits of information with which to select books from the library or the bookstore. But if you're like most parents, the answers we can give to even these simple questions are spotty. I couldn't come up with a full dozen answers for my own children. Most kids have trouble coming up with answers even about themselves. Nonetheless, any answers offer a place to start.

Perhaps Jonah is interested in soccer and baseball, does

skateboard tricks with his friends after school, wants to be an as-
tronaut, and loves *Mad* magazine. A book like Martyn Godfrey's
Can You Teach Me to Pick My Nose? would be perfect. It's funny,
a quick read, and about skateboarding. A trip to the library could
yield a few nonfiction books on space flight and astronomy, two
joke books, and a collection of Far Side cartoons. Here's enough
reading to keep both of you involved for two or three weeks and

Crazy About Sports

For some athletic kids, there comes a time in the middle
grades when they want to read only about sports. With
some urging on your part, this stage will pass, but in the
meantime . . .

• How-to books. Your library is full of books on how to
improve your child's game, many of them well illustrated.
• Biographies. Every kid wants to read about the stars in his
sport. Some of these are written for kids; if your child wants
to tackle an adult biography, be around to help.
• History of the game. Baseball, football, and hockey
fanatics are often highly specialized historians. These books
will help.
• Sports novels. Many writers have turned their hand to
novels set in the environment of a particular sport. In
baseball, for instance, there are novels by Dean Hughes,
Johanna Hurwitz, Carla Heymsfeld, Jonah Kalb, Martyn
Godfrey, Gordon Korman, and over a dozen by Matt
Christopher. Check with your librarian for such titles—they
are requested pretty regularly.

to reestablish your involvement and your enjoyment of reading together. Once you know what works, you can use a reference book such as the *Bloomsbury Good Reading Guide* or a library CD-ROM program to find other, similar books for your child. Or you can broaden the pick to include books you'll enjoy more or topics that weren't so obvious on the first run.

Unfortunately, there are some problems with plugging entirely into a child's interests. For one thing, eventually you'll run out of books. I've heard many parents say, "My son will only read books about baseball" or "My daughter spends all her time reading about horses. She's read every Black Stallion book five times." I would caution that books about baseball, or horses, or space flight are only the beginning of wider reading. Children are much more complex than a simple list of interests and activities. As a parent, you should promote books that appeal to deeper aspects of your child's personality—as many books will—and make sure more such books are around the house. My youngest son enjoys soccer, Nintendo, and bicycling, but none of these interests explains his fondness for Bruce Coville's *My Teacher Is an Alien*. Children have complex personalities. Once they begin reading again, they will find that many different kinds of books are of interest.

Teenagers sometimes are reluctant to reveal what really matters to them. If you ask Jennifer for a list of her interests and activities, she'll give you one of those bored looks and announce, "I'm not interested in anything." Of course, the truth is that she spent the previous day worried about everything from hairstyles to existential identity, from Mötley Crüe to birth control. You probably will have more success with teenagers if you pick a young-adult novel you enjoy, say, Robert Cormier's *The Bumblebee Flies Anyway*, then simply announce that you like the book and want to read some of it with them. Sometimes the reading will hook, sometimes not, but discussion at the end of the reading will reveal clearly whether to go ahead or to try a different book.

USING FRIENDS

An important way to build enthusiasm for books and reading is to find a social context for what's read. Your child probably has a group of three or four close friends and perhaps a dozen kids he sometimes hangs around with. Chances are that some of those kids enjoy books. With a little effort—a question to a couple of the kids when they raid your refrigerator, a phone call to their parents—you can find out what's popular with your child's group. Then use that information to provide reading material for your son or daughter.

If your daughter's girlfriends are all reading Ann Martin books, you won't go far wrong if you buy or borrow a couple for her. If the kid next door is hot on Lloyd Alexander sci-fi, use that enthusiasm when you sit down to open the book.

Here's a recent exchange between my youngest son and me, just to give you some idea of the patter involved.

"I was talking to James's mom the other day, and she said that James had just finished reading a great book."

"Yeah?" Alex said.

"It's called *The Indian in the Cupboard*, kind of a mystery, or maybe a fantasy, where this tiny little Indian shows up in a kid's cupboard."

"Yeah?"

"Anyway, I talked to James and he says it's a great book and he couldn't put it down. So I went out and bought you a copy."

The real-life conclusion to this dialogue came when Alex

Great Movies Tie to Great Books for Teens

The Color Purple. The novel is by Alice Walker (Pocket); the film stars Whoopi Goldberg.

Field of Dreams. The popular baseball film with Kevin Costner is based on W. P. Kinsella's *Shoeless Joe* (Ballantine).

Little Women. Louisa May Alcott's nineteenth-century novel made a great 1994 movie with Winona Ryder.

The Lord of the Rings. The animated film is by Ralph Bakshi. It's based on J. R. R. Tolkien's trilogy (Unwin).

Misery. The Stephen King novel (Signet) about a kidnapped novelist became a Stephen King film. Quite witty and not nearly as gruesome as *The Shining.*

Cider House Rules (Ballantine). John Irving wrote his own script for this Oscar-winning version of his long and complex novel.

The Silence of the Lambs. Gruesome novel by Thomas Harris (St. Martin's); gruesome film by Jonathan Demme. Not for the fainthearted.

Star Wars. The Lucasfilm saga has given birth to many spin-off novels at various reading levels. Not great literature, but good reads.

And many more . . . The film industry has figured out that both kids' books and classic literature can lead to good film scripts. From Lois Lowry's *Anastasia Krupnik* and E. B. White's *Stuart Little* to James Joyce's *The Dead* and Shakespeare's *A Midsummer Night's Dream*, there are a dozen films each season that are spun off from books. Your trick as a parent is to spin the other way—from watching to reading.

announced that he had already read the book in school a year ago. So I suppose I could have returned the book to the bookstore and used the five dollars to buy something else, but I was already halfway into chapter 2 and I was hooked. Who says kids' books are for kids?

USING TELEVISION

For much of this book, I've talked about the importance of setting rules on television watching and never letting kids view more than three hours a day. But there is an upside to TV that can't be ignored—the tube is a motivator with real force.

Television tie-ins for books provide an immediate social context for what otherwise might be the lonely act of reading. Many shows for young children, from *Romper Room* to *Reading Rainbow*, have a book segment in which a picture book is read. If your child seems interested in the segment, a simple question such as, "Would you be interested in getting that book from the library?" will give you many titles to seek out on your biweekly visit.

Of course, readers at the picture book stage are rarely bored. Our problem readers are older, age ten and up, and the TV tie-ins for them are more likely to be full-length videos or established series. ABC's after-school movies frequently are based on novels for teenagers about problems important to that age group. The current slew of TV movies based on Lucy Maud Montgomery's *Anne of Green Gables* books will make those characters highly visual for readers who have trouble "seeing" through print. ABC-TV's afterschool specials are frequently based on young-adult novels.

The most important action for the parent here is the follow-through. Many books worth reading are suggested by television and videos, but those books will be read only if you follow through with a trip to the bookstore or library. And those books might be read cover to cover only if you give up your time, once a day, to read or discuss the book with your child.

NOT JUST NOVELS

Many parents despair that their kids are bored with reading in seventh or eighth grade because they have stopped reading the reams of fiction that younger children plow through. Yet sometimes the reading has simply changed form. While I think imaginative reading—novels, short stories, fables—always should be part of the reading smorgasbord, I can understand that some children might use early adolescence as a time to start feasting on magazines and nonfiction for a while.

There's nothing wrong with that.

As a parent, you should be encouraging reading and trying to broaden your child's reading interests. But there's no point in disparaging what he actually does read, whether it's a biography

Two Winners for Kids Who Won't Read Anything

Librarians know that when all else fails, every young person will enjoy two books:

Guinness Books of Records (Guinness Publishing), for sixth grade and up. Then try some of the other "list" books or trivia books available.

Driver's Examination Handbook. The actual name of this publication varies from state to state. It's available free from your local department of transportation. Guaranteed to catch the interest of young teenage boys.

of Axl Rose or a weight-lifting magazine from the variety store. Your "bored reader" is at least reading. If you join in by reading a chapter or an article, you'll have a window on the parts of the universe your child is currently exploring. And you'll have something to talk about.

The young boy who reads about motorcycles might be persuaded to read Matt Christopher's *Dirt Bike Racer.* The teenage girl who's reading *Cosmopolitan* magazine might be interested in looking at the quirky novels of California writer Francesca Lia Block. Even if you can't use magazines and nonfiction as an edge to promote fiction, your child is still reading. So long as that's taking place, I refuse to declare *Soap Opera Digest* or *Muscle-mania* unfit for human intellectual consumption. It sure beats nothin'.

MOTIVATORS AND GIMMICKS

I said at the outset of this chapter that the bored reader needs special motivation—and so far I've suggested you, your time, your child's friends, and the television set. From my point of view, these are the motivators that work consistently to produce long-term changes in behavior that will build a lifelong reader.

It is here that I differ with many teachers and librarians who use gimmicks to promote reading. A gimmick is any scheme with short-term rewards for short-term reading improvement. When I began teaching, I used them myself: reading contests with charts on the wall, even free pizza for the five kids who read the most books. Yet none of these contests ever turned a nonreader into a reader. None of them ever resulted in mea- sured reading skill gains that lasted. Even worse, these gimmicks reduced reading to a task, to a kind of work that had to be ac- complished to reach some outside reward. This was backward. Reading should be the reward itself.

Let me be clear: I don't think universal silent reading in school is a gimmick, or giving your child a book allowance, or taking regular trips to the bookstore and library. I don't oppose summer reading clubs at libraries that make reading a social ex- perience, or school book clubs and book fairs, or any of the other wonderful ideas that you'll find in many schools and libraries. But I feel no child should be pushed to read by dangling a pizza slice, or a gold star, as some external reward for finishing a book.

Getting the bored reader interested in books again requires time, commitment, rules, enthusiasm, and sometimes the pur- chase of a few books—the same basics when reading began early on. The good news is that improvement can come very quickly, even in a few weeks, if your involvement as a parent is clear.

Dealing with the
Reluctant Reader

These days, the phrase "reluctant reader" is used by teachers more often than the old term "slow reader," but neither term accurately describes kids with serious reading problems. If your child is a reluctant reader, his problem is not one of reluctance. In fact, your child may be working much harder at learning to read than many of his classmates. His problem is that the act of reading is much more difficult for him than it is for most children.

Both the reluctant reader and the bored reader are likely to turn away from books and fail to keep pace with their classmates. The difference is in the reason why. The bored reader is able to read perfectly well but lacks the motivation to tackle print. The reluctant reader, on the other hand, has so much difficulty reading that he finds even the attempt embarrassing—or so frustrating that the reading itself lacks any enjoyment. While children frequently become bored readers around the fourth and the ninth grade, the reluctant reader suffers from his problem from early childhood and often throughout life.

The previous chapter talked about bored readers and what a

parent can do to spur them on. This chapter will focus on the much more heartrending problem of the reluctant reader—the one child in twenty who has serious and continuing difficulties with reading. Let's begin with two portraits of two different kinds of reluctant readers.

Mandi A. was born prematurely and developed all her skills slowly. She didn't walk until eighteen months, didn't begin to talk until after her second birthday. By third grade, Mandi was behind her classmates in every subject area. Her printing and handwriting were virtually unreadable. She lost interest in stories read aloud within minutes and had little ability to read by herself. Mandi's second-grade teacher suspected problems, but it wasn't until third grade that Mandi's parents agreed to testing by the board of education's psychometrist, a specialist in psychological testing. A three-hour-long intelligence test showed that Mandi's mental abilities were in the low-normal range. Halfway through fourth grade, Mandi was placed in a special class for children with learning disabilities. In this environment, her reading skills improved, but even now that she is in high school, Mandi's reading remains painfully slow and full of errors in decoding words.

Brandon T. was a bright and active little boy who enjoyed school up until third grade. His math skills developed quickly, and he enjoyed gym and geography, but reading was always a problem. Brandon liked to listen to stories but seemed to have difficulty concentrating on pages of print. Medical tests showed that both his vision and hearing were normal, but his reading skills developed very slowly. By fifth grade he was significantly behind the rest of his class. A remedial reading teacher began working with Brandon once a week, reviewing phonics, but this had little effect. Brandon's oral reading remained stilted and full of errors. By sixth grade, Brandon's teacher recommended he be held back a grade, but Brandon's parents refused and asked for a full assessment by the board's psychometrist.

Neither Mandi nor Brandon had problems with motivation or attitude when they began learning to read. They both *wanted* to read well. Neither of them was going through a family crisis that interfered with their progress in school and reading. Neither was ignored by parents, overlooked by teachers, or left to grow up without books.

Mandi's case is one of "general learning disability" (GLD)—a low level of functioning in many areas that can affect everything from physical coordination to higher-level thinking. While Mandi still has the capacity to learn a great deal, her rate of learning and skill development will be quite slow. Mandi will either be in special classes right through school, or, if she is "mainstreamed" in with regular students, she will need assistance from a special teacher on a regular basis. Mandi may learn to decode words quite well, but her skills might be limited to "word call," the capacity to read the words without understanding what they mean. Teachers working with Mandi will try to expand her comprehension by enriching her life experience, tying that into books, and working patiently to build her reading skills. If her parents offer similar encouragement at home, Mandi's comprehension skills could develop sufficiently to make reading an important part of her life.

Brandon's problem is more unusual. He's part of that tiny portion of the population that is correctly labeled "dyslexic." To use school language, Brandon has a "specific learning disability" (SLD) in the reading area. He functions quite well in all intellectual and skill areas—except reading.

Children with an SLD are frequently kept in the regular

Join with Other Parents

Your child's school principal or local district of education
probably knows of parent groups meeting in your area.
Failing this, contact a national organization and ask about
support groups where you live:

Association for Children with Learning Disabilities (ACLD)
4156 Library Road
Pittsburgh, PA 15234

Council for Exceptional Children
1920 Association Drive
Reston, VA 22091

Parents' Campaign for Handicapped Children and Youth
Box 1492
Washington, D.C. 20013

For other organizations, see the Department of Health,
Education and Welfare, *Directory of National Information
Sources on Handicapping Conditions and Related Services*
(OHDS 80–22007) at your library.

classroom and provided with a special teacher to help them in
their area of difficulty. In Brandon's case, no amount of remedial
phonics or vocabulary will make much difference. He has to
learn to cope with his disability. In senior elementary and high
school, a teacher's aide working with the resource teacher will

read out loud to Brandon to compensate for his problem. In high school, Brandon will use audiotapes to help with English reading requirements and tutors to help with other subjects. For English and history, Brandon will do all his written work on a computer with a spell checker. Brandon's reading skills will likely remain weak, but they can be sufficient to take him through college with extra time and special one-on-one assistance.

A Checklist: Early Warning Signs of a Reluctant Reader

- ☐ Is your child unable to concentrate or listen to a story for more than a few minutes?
- ☐ Is he unwilling to read aloud even on a one-to-one basis?
- ☐ Does he ask assistance of others for decoding easy words?
- ☐ Does he have difficulty blending phonic pieces to decode long words?
- ☐ Does he guess wildly at difficult words—or skip over them?
- ☐ When reading, does he fail to correct misread words that create nonsense?
- ☐ When reading out loud, does his voice seem flat and disconnected from meaning?
- ☐ Is his silent reading speed slower than average?
- ☐ Does he tend to move his lips when silent reading?

If you answer yes to three or more of these questions, consult your child's teacher and/or seek further assessment by a professional.

Beware the Gimmicks

Parents of children who have trouble reading often are quite desperate to find something that will miraculously "cure" their child and make him a reader. Over the years, this has led to some quite dubious—and sometimes quite expensive—approaches to remedial reading.

Controlled readers: Machines to force the eye to move at a constant speed—though the eyes of good readers don't.

i.t.a.: James Pitman's initial teaching alphabet was a forty-four-character alphabet that was phonetically perfect, but the transition to reading real English just didn't work.

Color-coded text: A complex system of colored print, so children not only had to learn letters, but the color code on how the letters were supposed to sound.

Behavioral reinforcement: Based on Skinner's psychological theories, it rewards reading with candy or pizza.

Irlen lenses: For $900 a California psychologist will outfit your child with blue or pink lenses that, she says, help reading; impartial authorities doubt it.

Phonics kits: Since D. H. Stott's first kit of cardboard pieces in the 1950s, these have mushroomed for everyone from infants to adults; "Hooked on Phonics" is nothing more than SRA cards and some audiotapes—hardly a cure-all for reluctant readers.

WHAT PARENTS CAN DO

If you suspect that your child may be a reluctant reader, it is important to act. Don't let relatives or friends minimize the problem, or suggest it's "just a stage," or use that tried-but-often-untrue line "He'll grow out of it." No parent wants to panic, but you have every right to seek information and to take action that promotes the welfare of your child.

- Step one: The doctors. You might have an indication that your child is having difficulty in reading or in other areas well before he begins school. If so, ask your family doctor to check your child's vision and hearing. A cursory examination in the doctor's office may not be sufficient to diagnose some vision and hearing problems. If either you or your doctor suspect further problems, arrange for additional testing with an ophthalmologist (eye doctor) and a hearing specialist. Phonemic awareness is based on concepts that must be heard. If your child can't hear the difference between *m* and *n*, he can hardly be expected to read *came* differently from *cane*.
- Step two: Speak to your child's teacher. Remember that your goal is to ask questions and exchange information. Has the teacher noticed anything about your son that might give a clue to the problem? Does the teacher know of any special interests, or emotional problems, or other factors that might help both of you provide additional support for your child? Have you any observations from home that might make sense of what's happening in school?

You can't automatically assume that the problems will be simple. Children aren't simply "lazy" or "dumb," nor are teachers simply "boring" or "incompetent." With reluctant readers, the problems are frequently complex, involving biology, genetics, motivation, psychology, intelligence, teaching methods, inter-personal relations at school, and pressures at home. A good teacher can help you understand how some of these might be affecting your child, but only if you are prepared to listen.

Some parents, unfortunately, are quick to point a finger at teachers and schools, forgetting that four other fingers are point-ing back at themselves. If your child seems to be developing a reading problem, be prepared to ask difficult questions of your-selves, as parents, and then act on the answers. Are you expect-ing too much of your child? Are you providing the home support your child needs? Is your family undergoing a disrup-tion that might be upsetting your child's concentration in school? Are you reading daily with your child? Are you provid-ing a model of the importance of reading by reading yourself?

• Step three: Testing by school professionals. If you or the teacher feel your child might have a more serious learning prob-lem, it's time to call in the professionals. Most boards or districts employ a number of psychologists, audiologists, speech patholo-gists, and other specialists. These people can help determine whether your child requires further help.

Usually a school assessment is begun at this time. It looks at your child's school history, his achievement, and his behavior in different classes. If testing hasn't been done before, your child

---

What Really Works

One-on-one tutoring: Whether it's Reading Recovery or a simple volunteer program, nothing works better than individual attention.

will take some basic, standardized test, such as the Iowa Test of Basic Skills or the California Achievement Test. In many states an assessment of this kind can be brought about by requests from either parents or the school. Your local school district probably has a pamphlet explaining the procedure for your area.

The next level is a full assessment by a psychometrist (an M.A.-level psychologist who specializes in psychological testing) or psychologist (a Ph.D.-level specialist who does both testing and diagnosis). Such an assessment involves two to three hours of one-on-one testing and interviewing with your child. A full I.Q. test, such as the Wechsler Intelligence Scale for Children (WISC), will be administered; a wide range of information can be obtained from that test. Your child may have tremendous ability in some areas and real deficits in others. The school psychologist can help you interpret all the results and develop a plan that draws on your child's areas of strength and helps improve the areas of weakness.

Unfortunately, the backlog for this kind of elaborate testing is sometimes months long. It is possible, through your doctor or local mental health organization, to arrange for your own testing. But be prepared for fees of up to $500 which are rarely covered by employer medical plans.

• Step four: Changing the program. All the testing in the world is useless unless it results in a change in your child's classroom program. The information you've received by this point should result in changes at school, in the classroom, and at home to deal with your child's special needs.

Your child may be served best by moving to a new or special school after the testing is completed. For some problems, especially hearing and vision impairment, there really is little choice.

Coming to terms with a disability is difficult for everybody. Moving to a new school or special program doesn't make it any easier, but it is sometimes the best option to ensure a proper education.

Your child may be able to stay in his neighborhood school and perhaps his own classroom, where school professionals will map out a special program for him. This program may involve some time away from regular class (often called "withdrawal"), some special assistance in the school (usually from a "learning resource teacher"), and some changes in curriculum (different reading materials, access to a computer, changes in assignments).

All these changes involve you. You'll be asked to okay any moves that are made for your child, and you'll be asked to help out at home in certain ways. At times you'll feel confused and anxious about all this—as if you were at the mercy of all these high-powered professionals. Often it is helpful to speak to other parents who have been through this before. Contact your local branch of the Learning Disabilities Association for their support.

Be sure to investigate any new program yourself. Reread Chapter 4 on how to evaluate a school. Ask yourself how *you* would feel in such a school or program. The professionals likely have your child's best interests at heart, but you are still the parent. Don't be bowled over by a conference table of M.A.'s and Ph.D.'s if you have serious doubts about their recommendations for your child.

WHAT CAUSES READING PROBLEMS?

The only simple answer to the question is this: We don't know for sure. When you consider the complexity of reading as a skill,

Readability and Reading Difficulty

For beginning or reluctant readers, reading difficulty is vitally important. Nothing is more frustrating than a book that is too hard to read.

• "Readability" is a technical measure of reading difficulty. To calculate readability, a teacher will pull three 100-word passages from a book, count syllables and number of sentences, compare vocabulary against standardized lists, then use a chart or formula to calculate the reading level. This figure, say 5.5, means that the average reader halfway through fifth grade would be able to read the text with reasonable comprehension. Ask your child's teacher for a Fry graph and you can calculate readability yourself.
• "Reading difficulty" involves still more factors that affect reading: size of type, space between lines, whether margins are justified (straight) or ragged, whether there are headings or subheadings, how unfamiliar words are brought in, how sentences are constructed, and whether there are pictures or illustrations.

it's amazing that such a high percentage of the population becomes readers. But for those 5 percent of our children who have real difficulty with reading, the question *why* is serious indeed. Here's a rundown of the current thinking on the issue:

• Medical approaches. Children who had a difficult birth, who were born very prematurely, or who have problems in intellectual development often may have trouble reading. Recent work reported in the *New Scientist* suggests that dyslexia can be

---

Matching Books with Reluctant Readers

To avoid frustration, a book for a child with reading difficulties should have a readability level roughly equal to the child's tested reading ability. Thus, an eighth-grade boy, whose reading ability tests at level 4.3, will have little trouble with *Rumble Fish*, which averages level 4.5, but a lot of trouble reading Nathaniel Hawthorne's *A Scarlet Letter*. That's the reason it's important for teachers to know the reading ability of their students and the readability of the books used, not just for reading, but in every subject.

---

predicted by using brain scans taken shortly after birth. Dr. Dennis Molfese of Southern Illinois University studied almost 200 children over eight years. Though the correlation between early scans and later dyslexia wasn't perfect, it was strong enough that other scientists are certain to be exploring this area. Molfese, incidentally, favors the phonemic theory that dyslexia comes partially from hearing problems.

• Psychological factors. Some children seem to use reading—or the failure to read—as a means of self-punishment, or a way to get back at their parents. This kind of behavior frequently appears on a short-term basis after parents separate or divorce. But even apparently happy families can harbor deep-seated problems that become visible only in the child's problems in school. The treatment of choice is family counseling with a psychologist or psychiatrist.

• Brain hemisphere dominance. At least one researcher,

noting the connection between poor reading and erratic right-and left-handedness, maintains that reading problems stem from the failure of some brains to establish dominance of either the right or left hemispheres. The suggested treatment includes a set of physical exercises to develop coordination and "handedness." The effectiveness of all this remains rather questionable.

• Skill deficits. This approach—big in the 1950s and '60s—suggests that reading is made up of a number of definable sub-skills (such as phonic blending or consonant recognition), not all of which are mastered by poor readers. Treatment involves careful testing, then drill exercises to improve any weak areas.

• Behavioral reinforcement. Some followers of behavioral psychology see reading difficulties as a problem of motivation. They have suggested techniques that range from electric buzzers to stop subvocalizing (moving the lips when reading) to providing candies to readers who attain a certain reading speed. While short-term results seem good, long-term improvement in reading has not been proven.

• Organizational problems. A very popular approach twenty years ago was to assume that poor readers have trouble organizing their thought patterns. Practitioners felt they helped children read better by developing their logic and organization. They used everything from the Mastermind board game to flowchart idea organizers. The jury is still out on whether there's a spillover from such activities into reading comprehension.

• Mechanical approaches. This theory, largely discredited now, held that poor readers read slowly because they had too many eye regressions (going back to reread parts of the text). Treatment had students read with a tachistoscope machine, which kept their eyes moving forward so they couldn't look back at misunderstood words. Recent research indicates that

Best Series for Reluctant Readers

Unfortunately, the best books for reluctant readers are hard to find in bookstores because they come from educational publishers. Still, your school should have a supply on hand for you to use at home with your child.

- *Action* and *Double Action* (Scholastic). Realistic stories, photo illustrations, reading difficulty levels from second to fifth grade. Scholastic's *Sprint Library* books are even shorter and easier.
- *Bestellers, Sportellers, Spectre, Fastbacks, etc.* (Fearon). Paperback-size short novels and stories, reading level approximately fourth and fifth grade.
- *Encounter Series* (EMC Paradigm). Problem-centered, high-action stories, line drawings, reading levels from third to mid-fourth grade.
- *Sundown Books* (New Readers Press). Short novels with teenage characters overcoming problems; reading level: third and fourth grade.

Best to avoid: Abridged versions of "classic" novels. Classics are difficult enough to abridge, much less make readable for kids who have reading problems.

this popular 1960s' idea was dead wrong. Good readers have *more* eye regressions than poor ones; they just do it all faster.

• Learning styles. Proponents of this relatively recent theory suggest that each person has a specific learning style. The lecture approach may work for me; hands-on may work for you. Failure to receive instruction in the proper form will be a stumbling block for some students in reading and virtually every other subject. Good teachers, these days, try to vary instruction techniques to suit a wide range of students.

• *Caveat emptor* is not a learning theory. It's Latin for "let the buyer beware." Over the thirty years I've spent studying and teaching reading, I've seen theories and procedures come and go. There are no magic cures for serious reading difficulties—not blue filters, or special glasses, or machines, or eye exercises. You can spend thousands of dollars for after-school tutoring—and achieve some real advances—but only because reading will suddenly have become very important around your house. You can make reading just as important, much more cheaply, by following the three Rs in this book.

WHAT WE DO KNOW

While theories on reading problems continue to be developed and debated, two points seem clear:

• One-to-one support helps poor readers read better.
• More reading makes for better reading.

Ordinary children can be taught fairly adequately in a classroom setting with twenty-five other students, but reluctant readers frequently need one-on-one help. There are various ways this can be accomplished at school. At home, the commitment must be yours. Someone must sit down with your reluctant reader and, at an early age, reinforce the phonics and word-attack skills while reading your child's favorite books. Someone must listen, later on, as your child begins to read for himself. Someone must be there, later still, to applaud silent reading and to talk about the ideas in what's read. Older brothers and sisters, grandparents, and sometimes baby-sitters can do all this. But the person to organize a home reading time—and the most important person to follow through with it—is you.

A good school will try to match your effort with similar one-on-one support. Tutors, or education assistants, are trained to help special students on an individualized basis. Reading buddies are older students or volunteers who try to do the same, but less formally. Both tutors and reading buddies will read out loud with your child, help with written assignments, and sometimes write up stories from your child's own experience—a kind of highly personalized reading program. With this kind of assistance, your child will likely find a success in school that had eluded him before his problems were understood.

The final proven component of any remedial reading program should come as no surprise. It's reading. Nothing improves reading ability like the act of reading. One study compared the results of a dozen remedial programs, from phonic drills to comprehension cards to behavioral reinforcement systems. The study concluded that the best gains were made when reluctant readers were allowed to choose books they *could* read and then actually did read. It makes sense. If you wanted your child to learn to swim, you could discuss arm movements, look at charts, and consider the theories of buoyancy. Or you could get in the water and help your child to float. The best way to learn to swim requires getting into the pool. The best way to improve reading requires getting started in the right kind of book.

BOOKS FOR THE
RELUCTANT READER

There are two basic principles in finding books for a reluctant reader. First, they must be within the range of the child's reading ability. Many of the books suggested on my "must-have" lists in Chapters 5 to 10 will work well with reluctant readers, especially if you help with the reading.

Second, because motivation is so important, the books must be "age-appropriate." Your thirteen-year-old son might be reading at a third-grade level, but that doesn't mean he would willingly read third-grade books. Special novels, such as those in Scholastic's *Action* series, are a much better choice. These are books written for a teenage audience, but with vocabulary and sentence length controlled so they can be read by students with third- or fourth-grade skills.

We know, too, that reluctant readers are easily discouraged by books that are technically too difficult. If you can't be present to provide reading support, the reading level of the book must be within the range of your child's abilities. You can't insult your child with "baby books," but at the same time you can't demand that he read *Moby Dick* all by himself. Check with your child's teacher or the school librarian—and with your child—to find books that will suit.

Some special factors can make it possible for a reluctant reader to read even a difficult text:

- Motivation. An interested or motivated reader can read up to four grades higher than tested.
- Pre-reading. A teacher can make a difficult text more accessible by teaching key vocabulary and ideas beforehand.
- Assisted reading. Having a parent or reading buddy to

assist with difficult words or concepts can make it possible to read three or more grades higher than tested.

• Independent reading. If your child is going to be reading a book without assistance, keep it at his tested reading level or below. Recreational reading should be easy, not work.

Many novels are now available on tape, including books for reluctant readers. I have mixed feelings on the idea of "reading along with the tape" for beginning and reluctant readers, because I don't think it encourages the proper attitude for independent reading. What's more, most commercial audio book tapes are abridged so it is almost impossible to follow along in the real book. However, most of my colleagues in the field feel that audiotapes are a reasonable substitute for an adult reader or a reading buddy. Certainly tapes are better than struggling through a difficult book without any help, especially if your child is trying to keep up with other students in a mainstream class.

YOUR CHILD CAN SUCCEED

Nothing is more frustrating than working with your own learning disabled child—and nothing is more rewarding than when progress is made. Parents will suffer a natural swing from hope to despair and back again that is literally exhausting. But your child's long-term success requires you to persevere. Here, an organization like the Learning Disabilities Association can help. A chance to meet with other parents once a month to share anger and irritation, achievement and breakthroughs will help you keep a proper balance at home.

It is never too late to reach a reluctant reader—but it

involves commitment and cooperation from everyone concerned. Some years ago, I worked with a young man named Don over a three-year period from tenth to twelfth grade. Don had been in various special education programs before reaching our high school. He had never developed strong reading skills or much interest in reading. He had good language skills—a real gift of gab, or blarney, if you like—but he couldn't and didn't read.

I tested him in tenth grade and the results were dismal: third-grade skills across the board. Then, in the middle of that year, Don decided that he wanted to become a priest. He was afraid that with his low-level skills, no Catholic order would take him in—so he found a motivation to read that had been missing before.

I put together a reading program at school that used simple novels and basal readers for skill building. Don enjoyed machinery, so at lunchtime I had him work with a tachistoscope to bring his reading speed up. And I called Don's mother, who didn't read well enough herself to help him much, but who was willing to listen to him read every night for twenty minutes or so.

By the end of that year, Don's tested reading skills were up to the fifth-grade level and he was on to novels like *Rumble Fish* by S. E. Hinton, and print material from the newspaper. By the end of the next year, Don's reading speed on the machine broke 200 words per minute, his Stanford test showed eighth-grade skills, and he was reading Paul Zindel's *The Pigman* and William Golding's *Lord of the Flies*.

The following year, Don made it into a seminary. With motivation, reading at home, and an individualized program at school, he compressed five years of normal school progress into two and a half years of real effort.

Your reluctant reader can do the same, at the right time, if you and the teachers are there to help.

TEN GOOD BETS FOR A
RELUCTANT TEENAGE
READER'S BOOKSHELF

Remember that any teen is more likely to be moved by enthusiasm of his or her peers than by what parents and teachers have to say. So if there's a local trend—from rock star biographies to Star Wars books—go with it. Otherwise, here's a list of young-adult fiction with gripping stories. Reading levels vary.

Judy Blume, *Tiger Eyes* (Dell). A teenage girl recovers from the murder of her father in a strong and gutsy book.

Caroline Cooney, *The Terrorist* (Scholastic) and other titles. All of Cooney's books are big on action and suspense.

Robert Cormier, *Tenderness* (Dell). A runaway teen, looking for love, finds trouble in the person of a pschopathic killer. "Awesome!" But with mature themes.

Christopher Paul Curtis, *The Watsons Go to Birmingham* (Bantam). Ten-year-old Kenny Watson tells about his African-American family in 1963 with the civil rights movement in the background. A book that's funny, but with serious undertones.

S. E. Hinton, *Rumble Fish* (Dell). The story of two brothers, one mixed up in a gang. A grade four or five reading level makes it an easy read for any teen. There's also an excellent movie by Frances Ford Coppola.

Paul Kropp, *Amy's Wish* (EMC). Hate to plug my own book, but this is the kids' favorite of twenty high-interest, low-vocabulary books I've written. The grade-four reading level is very consistent throughout.

Gary Paulsen, *Hatchet* (Alladin). A thirteen-year-old has to survive a plane crash in Canada with nothing but the clothes on his back and a hatchet to cut firewood.

Richard Peck, *Ghosts I Have Been* (Dell). An award-winning book about a girl with psychic powers. Second in a series of novels.

Jerry Spinelli, *Wringer* (HarperCollins). Peer pressure and pigeon slaughter make for a gripping novel.

Walter Dean Myers, *Fallen Angels* (Scholastic). While a 300-page book might seem an odd choice for reluctant readers, this one is a winner. A coming-of-age story set in the Vietnam War.

Nurturing the Gifted Reader

"Thank God I've only got one of these," said the father of a gifted teenager in one of my creative writing classes. Adam's parents are teachers and are both intelligent, but they have had to work hard for their achievements. Adam's older brother and sister are bright but not exceptional in ability. And then there's Adam.

Adam showed all the early signs of being gifted. He was walking at seven months, reading Dr. Seuss by two, breezing through *Time* by five. He began tackling high school math in fourth grade and college math by seventh grade. His cello playing began at age four and led to public performances as a soloist at age ten. Adam's accomplishments are impressive, sometimes even astounding. As a child, his party trick was to calculate dates forward, in his head, to tell you that March 15, 2013, will be a Friday.

But Adam's personal life is much more difficult. As a teenager, he has few friends and has never had a girlfriend. His quick and sometimes caustic sense of humor alienates his classmates and teachers. He spends more time communicating through his computer modem than he does talking to any living person. His teachers describe Adam as lonely, frequently de-

Raising a Gifted Baby

Dr. Burton White in *Educating the Infant and Toddler* talks about the ways successful parents raised babies who turned out to be bright, if not gifted. Here's what such parents were observed doing to build language skills from infancy:

- They identified the interests of their child and talked about them.
- They engaged in fifteen to twenty verbal interchanges an hour, most lasting between twenty and thirty seconds.
- They rarely "taught" or lectured their children.
- They spoke in full sentences, using words slightly above the child's apparent level of comprehension.
- They read picture books and stories from infancy, even though children rarely sustained attention until age two.

pressed, demanding to the point of being obnoxious, and below average in emotional stability.

Adam is quite gifted, of course, and has considerable potential to become a highly successful adult. But he is also a child at risk, always in danger of emotional upset, always facing the possibility that he will be marginalized by abuse of drugs, relationships, or his own intellectual intensity. His parents want to nurture his gifts, to help him reach and make use of his potential. To do that, they must obviously support his cello playing and his interest in computers. But they also must help Adam balance his life with reading that is far wider than the fantasy and sci-fi novels he polishes off each night.

Raising a gifted child can be as exhausting as raising a child who is learning disabled. No wonder both these "exceptionalities" are lumped together in school special education programs. Both demand a degree of parental involvement that just isn't necessary with normal children. Both require a special effort on your part to maintain a childhood that is balanced, challenging—but not frustrating—and emotionally satisfying. Books and reading can play an important part in helping you with all this.

IS YOUR CHILD GIFTED?

If your child is gifted, evidence of it will begin appearing early, even before school age. Look for these characteristics:

• Curiosity. All young children are curious, but gifted children are especially so. Every child wants to know that a particular funny-looking bug is a dragonfly. A gifted child wants to know why it is called a dragonfly if there never were any dragons, why it has four wings instead of two, and why it exists at all.

• Intensity. Gifted children are also marked by the intensity of their concentration on a task or idea. Virtually all young children enjoy playing with Lego blocks. But a gifted child will miss lunch to finish a special six-wheeled moon vehicle of her own design. Many bright young people will be interested in space or cars or Barbie dolls. A gifted child can get hung up on a topic for months, collecting books and pictures, building exhibits and doing experiments.

• Ability. Most gifted children start reading and talking at an early age. Some have very special talents and interests. These often appear without prompting by parents. A gifted musician needs her parents' help so she can get her hands on a violin. But after discovering the instrument, she'll want to play the violin herself and will do so for hours at a time.

By the time your child is in second or third grade, her school can provide some additional testing and observation to make the "gifted" label official. This is what the school will look for:

- General Intelligence. By giving your child a Wechsler intelligence test or similar instrument, a psychologist or psychometrist can measure her level of general intelligence. One common measure is I.Q., a term developed by the French psychologist Alfred Binet, who used standardized tests to measure a child's mental age, then divided the results by actual age and multiplied by 100 to arrive at an "intelligence quotient." A child who scores with normal twelve-year-olds at the age of ten, for instance, has an I.Q. of 120 ($12 \div 10 \times 100$). Such a child is bright but does not need a special program. About 3 percent of the population has an I.Q. of 130 and above. This level is usually required for a "gifted" designation in schools.

- Creativity. The problem with I.Q. tests is that they best measure certain kinds of thinking, sometimes called "linear" intelligence. Creativity tests, such as the Torrance Tests of Creative Thinking (Ginn), measure "divergent" thinking, which may apply to more creative activities. For instance, your child might be shown a picture of a stuffed toy and asked to suggest changes that would make the toy more fun to play with. The phrase "gifted" is used for a child with wide-ranging high intelligence. The phrase "talented" is more accurate for a child who has special ability in a single area, perhaps in art or music. In school programs, gifted and talented students usually are combined into a single group.

Magazines for the Gifted

Here are some favorites with gifted students:

Creative Kids. Publishes works by gifted children, for gifted children. Write:

> Creative Kids
> P.O. Box 637
> Holmes, PA 19043

Prism. Calls itself "the magazine for creative and talented young people." Different themes each issue. For a sample, write:

> Prism
> 2455 E. Sunrise Blvd.
> Ft. Lauderdale, FL 33304

Scientific American. Cutting-edge research; the first few paragraphs of articles are rewritten to be intelligible to everyone; the rest is still fascinating.

OMNI. A rather low-rent science magazine that appeals to gifted teens.

Time or *Newsweek.* These national news magazines are essential reading for involved gifted students who may do debating or public speaking.

• Observation. Experienced teachers have taught hundreds of children. Their day-to-day observations of your child's interests and abilities are an important indicator of whether your child would profit from a special gifted program.

• Personal and peer evaluation. A gifted child frequently knows that she is "different," as do the other children in the classroom. One study found that three out of four gifted students could have been identified by "self or peer nomination."

YOUR CHILD IS GIFTED—
NOW WHAT?

You always had a hunch your child was gifted. She began reading for herself long before school and began asking for definitions of words you had to look up when still in the primary grades. She pesters you frequently for new things to do, but once spent two months studying everything she could find about ancient Egypt. Your neighbors think her marks and her achievements are quite remarkable, but you know the truth. Gifted children are frequently tough to live with.

Boredom is the greatest problem. Your gifted child likely taught herself to read. Now she demands new books constantly. If she suddenly becomes interested in knights in armor, she'll want every book on the subject at your local library, then she'll want a trip to the big library downtown. And when she's run out of things to read, she'll start pestering you for other ideas: projects to start, places to write to, things to do. Dealing with all this can be exhausting and expensive, but it also can be wonderfully exciting if you have the time and energy to give to your child.

Social problems are frequently number two on the problem list because a gifted child may feel quite isolated. Her interests are too obscure, or too intense, or too mature for the kids next door. She wants to spend time with older kids or adults, who may not relish time with a very questioning child. As a parent, you want her to have a normal childhood, playing normal games with normal kids, but sometimes this just doesn't happen.

Maintaining a normal life for a gifted child requires a special effort. If your child is gifted in music and busy practicing piano two hours or more a day, you'll have to put a special push behind more ordinary activities. Gifted young pianists who do nothing but play the piano rarely make it beyond the first one or two international competitions. They have not developed the personal breadth to connect their playing with life and emotions. Your gifted child deserves more. She needs a whole universe of books to learn about the aspects of life she hasn't time to explore herself. She needs to take time out from her gift so she can play hockey, or learn to use a handsaw, or jump rope with her friends. She needs you to ensure that there is some balance in her life.

However intellectually dazzling a gifted child may be, she is still a child. A mathematical genius or a violin virtuoso may develop the intellect or skills of an adult by age eleven, but emotionally she is still eleven. Your gifted daughter may say she wants to read only Charles Dickens or William Thackeray—especially if this would please you—but she needs to read Daniel Pinkwater and Suzy Kline. Your gifted child may prefer to spend time with adults, but she needs the company of children, especially children her own age. Any attempt to short-change the basically slow pace of emotional growth can lead to an adult whose life is lived within an intellectual shell.

If there is a single general piece of advice for the parent of a gifted child, it's this: Don't push. Your child is already being pushed enough by her own unusual abilities. Your job is to nurture those gifts and help provide balance for her life.

AT SCHOOL: TOUGH CHOICES

Your best support in raising a gifted child should be your child's school. Teachers can confirm, counterbalance, and even console you as your child grows. Successful school programs should liberate your child from needless routine assignments and stimulate new interests to be explored. Exactly how these things happen at your child's school depends very much on the policies of your state, the facilities of your school board, and the choices you make as a parent.

Thirty years ago, the first choice in dealing with gifted children was acceleration—skipping a grade or two, usually through the elementary years. These days, acceleration is frowned upon. The reasons are simple. Skipping a grade assumes that all skill areas develop equally, and this is true only sometimes. Also, placing a child with older children often limits friendships and models of "age-appropriate behavior." By this, teachers mean that an eleven-year-old with limited interest in sex who has accelerated into high school will either have to withdraw from adolescent hormone-dominated social life, or try to fit in by manufacturing desires and interests that aren't really present. In sophisticated school systems, acceleration is recommended only for children who are emotionally mature, physically large, and perhaps a few months older than their classmates.

When gifted elementary school programs first appeared in the 1950s and '60s, they took the form of self-contained classes. Teachers with special education training were placed in

*School Programs for
the Gifted*

There are a number of school options and opportunities for gifted students. Here's a rundown:

- Enrichment in a regular classroom
- Part-time enrichment class
- Full-time ("self-contained") enrichment class
- Extra projects/independent study
- Itinerant teacher/resource teacher
- Special schools
- Acceleration (skipping a grade)
- Moderate acceleration (three grades in two years)
- Special, fast-paced courses
- Extracurricular programs
- Mentorship/internship programs
- Special summer courses or camps
- "Saturday" programs
- Academic fairs or challenges
- Correspondence courses/independent study
- Part-time college credits

classrooms with a somewhat smaller group of students than usual—say, fifteen to twenty kids—rather than the thirty in a regular classroom. The teacher would try to create a program to stimulate all these children as best he could. The children, clustered in their gifted ghetto, often used their intelligence to torment their peers, the teacher, or both. Student refugees from such classrooms have not been highly enthusiastic about the effectiveness of self-contained classes.

Evaluating a Gifted Program

Here are a dozen questions that deserve answers before you hand over your child to a school's gifted program:

- Are there stated goals or outcomes for the program?
- What screening process is used to select students for the program?
- How are parents informed and involved?
- Does the program make use of community resources?
- How are teachers chosen for the program?
- Is there a mix of group and individual work?
- What is the student-teacher ratio?
- Do students contribute to the direction of the program?
- Is there continuity from year to year?
- How is creativity encouraged?
- Is there extra funding for program activities?
- How does the program tie into regular classroom work?

The preferred approach these days involves modifying regular classroom programs for gifted students and supplying some special activity on a daily or weekly basis. This approach permits your child to spend most of her time with children of the same age, but to be stimulated by special work both in and out of class. A good teacher can free your child from the rote work that she masters quickly and can challenge her with the special, creative projects that she craves.

As a parent, you should be very closely involved with what's going on at school. Creating a special program is a great idea, but hard for a teacher to organize when teaching a class of twenty or thirty. You are within your rights to expect this for your child—

Use Your Community

Many communities have special programs suitable for gifted kids—if their parents sign them up.

- Local museums and art galleries. Most have some sort of outreach program to involve kids. In Chicago, for instance, the Art Institute offers classes in art media from acrylic to watercolor for children.
- Universities. Some universities offer special programs for high school students on weekends, or make their computer or sports facilities available to families for a small fee.
- Forts, pioneer villages, and other tourist attractions. Check for special Saturday/Sunday workshops, March break programs, or summer activities.
- Community language programs. Check with your local board of education or appropriate community center.
- The Ys. The YMCA and YWCA offer more than just swimming programs. Check out their after-school and art programs in your community.

especially if she has been designated as gifted. Speak clearly with the teacher and principal if you see signs that your child is becoming bored with school.

One sad truth about schooling in much of the United States is that it can differ so much from district to district. The local taxation base of inner-city school districts, even with federal Title 1 grants, often is not sufficient to allow for budgets that will support excellent gifted education programs. A neighboring suburban district, where parents are willing to pay the extra taxes to provide for high-quality education, may well offer a better program for your child. While I am reluctant to suggest that parents change homes simply to have access to better schools (in fact, often it's important to stay put and fight for improvements where you live), a move is sometimes the least expensive way of ensuring that your gifted child gets an education that meets her needs. There is no greater tragedy than that of a gifted child who is frustrated and whose potential goes unrealized because of poor schooling.

While the combination of special outside activities and a modified classroom program seems to work reasonably well through elementary school, students of high school age begin to balk at taking on an extra workload. It is here that a large high school with special "enriched" or advanced-placement classes can provide the intellectual challenge a gifted teenager demands. Failing this, you can look into special programs and summer camps for your teenager. Your school's guidance office should be able to provide a number of possibilities in your area.

AT HOME—READING
FOR BALANCE

One of the joys that many gifted children experience is their ability to read early and to appreciate very adult material. An ordinary seven-year-old will be just getting out of Dr. Seuss and into short "chapter books." A gifted seven-year-old might well enjoy Ray Bradbury or Douglas Adams, and probably will not need much help to read the books herself. As a parent, you'll enjoy being able to read such sophisticated fare to your child. You'll be able to listen to Sue Grafton mysteries on tape as you drive. You'll find yourself talking about Isaac Asimov, or tele-scopes, or bits of Greek mythology almost as if your child were an adult.

But you mustn't forget that your child is still a child. Your gifted child may well groan when you say you want to read *The Wind in the Willows*, or she may tell you that she's read it before, twice. But your reading of the book keeps a balance in her life. It tells her that it's okay to be the child she really is.

I've taught gifted teenagers for a number of years, and I'm always amazed at the number of these kids who go back at age seventeen or eighteen to read the childhood classics. These teenagers feel that they missed a stage growing up, and they re-capture it through *Abel's Island* or *Alice's Adventures in Wonder-land*. Reading can be "bibliotherapy." Books can be used to counterbalance the strains and demands of life. A sheltered child can see great difficulties heroically overcome. A quiet child can read about emotions loudly expressed. Reading is one way to make a gifted child more psychologically whole.

Because of the intensity of their interests, gifted children often want to focus their reading too much. If they get hooked on science fiction, or fantasy, or computer books, they may not want to read anything else for months or years. Your reading to-gether can provide a leaven. If your son is busy reading only fan-tasy novels, you should be reading Robert Cormier or Lois Duncan with him; if your daughter is on a Madeleine L'Engle kick, better that you read some Judy Blume to her. Balance is the key. Your child's teacher or school librarian can help you select the books you need once you've exhausted the choices in this book.

Chances are your gifted child will select her own books at the bookstore or library. Such children can be very pushy about

One Gifted Bookshelf

Courtesy of Jennifer H., now sixteen. The bookshelf over her bed includes, in no particular order:

E. B. White, *Charlotte's Web*
Anthony Burgess, *A Clockwork Orange*
Marilyn Halvorson, *Cowboys Don't Cry*
John Christopher, many titles
William Sleator, *Interstellar Pig*
Stephen King, *The Dead Zone*
J. R. R. Tolkien, *The Hobbit*
Ken Kesey, *One Flew over the Cuckoo's Nest*
John Wyndham, *The Chrysalids*
Nancy Drew books—five of them
Kevin Major, *Far From Shore*
Robert N. Peck, *A Day No Pigs Would Die*
The Berenstain Bears
Robert Cormier, everything
Frances Hodgson Burnett, *The Secret Garden*
The Mad Scientist's Club
Louisa May Alcott, *Little Men*
Janet Lunn, *The Root Cellar, Double Spell*
George Orwell, *1984, Animal Farm*
S. E. Hinton, *The Outsiders*
Douglas Adams, everything
Betsy Byars, *Summer of the Swans*
C. S. Lewis, the Narnia books
O. R. Melling, *The Druid's Tune*

getting exactly what they want. Just remember that you have the power of the wallet. You can use that power to make deals that will balance your child's reading.

Gifted children often prefer to read books written for kids who are three to four years older. By age ten or eleven, many are reading adult books—but adult books of a special kind. The gifted child's intellect makes adult science fiction, fantasy, and mystery very accessible and quite fascinating. But your child's more normal emotional development makes more subtle literature difficult to understand. That's why Piers Anthony and J. R. R. Tolkien will work with gifted children, but John Updike and Ernest Hemingway will not.

Reading with gifted children is a joy and a challenge. They love the music of words and the dream that lies behind them, but there's so much more they want to know. A gifted child will sit and be read to for an hour—and demand more. She'll understand every plot twist and demand explanations of words and concepts that an ordinary child would skip over. You'll have to take the time to explain, or admit that you don't understand.

Then you have to follow through. Gifted children flee boredom as other children avoid a bath. You've got to turn the reading into more reading or into other ideas. Why not rewrite the ending of the book? Why not create your own planet, or fallen empire, or perfect mystery? A clever parent can use reading to stimulate the gifted child's creativity and emotional growth.

READING TO NURTURE
THE GIFT

Reading can provide an emotional balance for your gifted child, but it also can be a means for her to explore and extend her gift.

Join with Other Parents

Parenting a gifted child can be trying and lonely. By joining together with other parents, you gain perspective, ideas, and enthusiasm that will make difficult parenting somewhat easier.

Many school districts—and some individual schools—organize regular meetings for parents of gifted children. Often there is a valuable information component, but such meetings also give you an opportunity to meet informally with other parents in the same situation.

A number of states also have statewide parent groups. For a list of these, see *Bringing Out the Best* (Minneapolis, Free Spirit Publishing).

Then there is the American Association for Gifted Children at Duke University, Box 90270, Durham, NC 27708–0270 (www.jayi.com/jayi/nagc).

A teenager gifted in science should have a subscription to *Scientific American*. A gifted young musician will want to read books on ancient instruments, copies of *The Strad*, and biographies of performers. Parents shouldn't have to push this kind of reading, but your gifted child certainly needs a chance to discover it.

Because of the sheer amount that a gifted child can read, almost no family can afford to buy all the books that might interest her. It's important, of course, for your child to own some books that relate to her special abilities, but many more books will have to be begged or borrowed.

The best source is a library. School libraries often are too general to provide many titles on baroque music or great mathematicians.

Public libraries can sometimes do better. Many public libraries also do interlibrary loans from branch to branch to bring in books not on their shelves. For the gifted child intently studying insects or the viola da gamba, such borrowing will be essential.

In some areas, college libraries can provide the other great source of books for your child. These libraries frequently keep millions of titles and have subscriptions to cutting-edge research journals and obscure magazines. You usually can arrange special borrowing privileges by accompanying your child to the library, explaining the situation to a library official, and sometimes paying a small fee.

Books related to your child's gift can't be allowed to take over her life. A computer genius still needs to read about much more than computers. But to understand the field that she will likely enter, your gifted child needs access to the field's current research and ideas. With the help of a library or two, you can make sure this reading is available to her.

YOU'RE NOT ALONE

Parents of gifted children sometimes need help. Just like the parents of children with learning disabilities, they may find it easier to cope when they can talk to others in similar situations. Your child's teacher in the gifted program is a good ally and source of advice. There may be an informal group of parents whose children are all in the gifted program, or more formal meetings may be arranged by your school district or the local gifted magnet school. Any of those groups can be helpful for you in seeking special programs, new challenges, or parenting ideas that will help your child.

Just don't try to be everything to your gifted child. You are not teacher, friend, librarian, science advisor, coach, and recital organizer. You are a parent. Seek out the help you need to be the best parent you can. Many gifted children can become very difficult teenagers, some of them in need of professional psychological help. Others need "mentoring," so their gift can be developed by older individuals familiar with the area in which they have special interest or talent. Other gifted children will turn to teachers at school for advice or activities, especially in adolescence. All these people can be helpful to your child and to you in those twin processes of growing up and parenting.

The stereotype of the young genius in glasses, shunned by her classmates, happy only in her home laboratory, is the stuff of Hollywood films. Your gifted child can lead an exciting, well-balanced life, using books to extend herself and explore a wide range of interests. Keep reading along with her to stay a part of this.

GOOD BETS FOR YOUR GIFTED CHILD'S BOOKSHELF

Gifted children usually read so much that it's impossible to restrict selections to a must-have list. But here is a bunch of highly arbitrary book ideas for that special kid, arranged by age level.

Age seven or thereabouts: David Macaulay, *Castle* or *Cathedral* (Houghton Mifflin). *Mad Magazine* special issues and books.

Age eight: David Macaulay, *The Way Things Work* (Palladin). John Fitzgerald, *The Great Brain* (Dell).

Age nine: *Calvin and Hobbes* cartoon books. Madeleine L'Engle, *A Wrinkle in Time* (Dell). Lois Duncan, *Killing Mr. Griffin* (Dell).

Age ten: J. R. R. Tolkien, *The Hobbit* (Ballantine). Katherine Paterson, *Jacob Have I Loved* (HarperCollins).

Age eleven: J. R. R. Tolkien, *The Lord of the Rings* (Unwin). *The Diary of Anne Frank* (Pocket). Various sci-fi fantasy. (See Chapter 9.)

Age twelve: J. D. Salinger, *Franny and Zooey*, *The Catcher in the Rye* (Little, Brown).

And all the books ordinary kids are reading—especially your child's friends.

Reading, Computers, and the Twenty-first Century

As we begin the twenty-first century, there's good news and bad news about the future of reading. Since the whole tenor of this book has been upbeat, let's begin with the positive:

- We're learning more about how kids learn to read. Through the national research centers in reading and various graduate programs around the world, we have many researchers tackling questions about reading instruction, reading problems, and the complex interactions of parenting and reading development. In the past, much of what we've done in the classroom has been based on old techniques and the limited experience of classroom teachers. Now we have researchers in psychology, optometry, and epidemiology looking at how kids learn—or don't learn—to read. The first fruits of this research can already be seen in the growing attention we now pay to phonemic awareness.

- Real readers are reading more than ever. The United States has never been a "nation of readers," at least not nearly as much as politicians would claim, but it has always had a

---

Good Web Sites on Reading and Kids' Books

- **www.bestbooksforkids.com** The Bank Street College of Education has lists of recommended books, updated regularly.
- **www.bookwire.com** Bookwire is a commercial site, but it has links to almost everything and interesting information of its own.
- **www.cbcbooks.org** The Children's Book Council, an association of U.S. kids' book publishers and sponsor of National Children's Book Week.
- **www.reading.org** The International Reading Association, for reading news, teacher information, and their recommended book lists.
- **www.rif.org** The Reading is Fundamental group organizes everything from book giveaways to Turn Off the TV Week.

---

significant percentage of people who liked to read. The good news is that those readers are reading more today than ever before. Younger readers are boosting magazine sales; older readers are boosting book sales. A burgeoning group of college-educated readers are supporting more sophisticated literature and, conveniently for Borders and Barnes & Noble, using the superstores to fill their homes with books. Thanks to the superstores and Internet retailers like Amazon.com, more readers are able to purchase books about obscure topics, books that wouldn't have been available at smaller bookstores twenty years ago. My own interest in croquet, for instance, is shared by only a tiny percentage of people in North America; but I now have a growing library of croquet books ordered via the Internet that arrive at my door less than a week after I confirm the order.

• We're teaching kids to read better than ever before—especially in the early grades. Not only is the latest generation of readers starting to read earlier than ever, they're developing formal reading skills at school through very sophisticated reading programs. At least five big, new reading programs made their debut at the end of the 1990s. All of these feature big books, wonderful picture books, fabulous teacher support materials, CD-ROMs and Internet materials to support reading for kids, and some kind of parent newsletter to acknowledge the important role you play in developing reading. We've come a long way since the days of Dick and Jane.

• Computers can sometimes enhance reading skills. While I see a number of problems in the future direction of computer games and programming, the current generation of computer software is still very reading-intensive. There are good, entertaining programs like the Arthur CD-ROM series that reinforce primary reading skills for young children. There are fascinating game programs like the Carmen Sandiego series that support more advanced reading skills for older children. And there are word processors and e-mail to encourage both reading and writing for people of every age. The age of letter writing is not past, it has just moved to an electronic form.

Many of the dangers people have predicted for reading have failed to materialize. Television didn't kill reading any more than it killed the movies. Television news hasn't eliminated the newspaper as an important means for people to get information. Nor have other electronic gadgets—from books onscreen via Project Gutenberg to the Sony Bookman—cut into book sales.

Videotapes haven't replaced books in our classrooms, nor have computer programs made much of a dent in schools, which are still dependent on teachers and books.

While any number of gurus have declared that the book is dead, they mostly develop their ideas . . . by reading books.

Unfortunately, not every indicator for this millennium bodes well for the future of reading. There are some trend lines that may interfere with our goal of developing full, adult literacy any time in the future. Here are three:

• Computers may short-circuit upper-level reading and thinking skills. As computers and the Internet have become less print-based and more cluttered with images, so the quality of material available has begun to decline. The development of Via Voce some years ago is just the first step in a process that will soon see us shouting at our computers rather than typing into them. The movement away from print instructions will not help our children develop literacy skills. Nor will the vast array of images and advertising on the World Wide Web do anything for their reading skills.

Ironically, the Internet was entirely print-based when it was developed in the 1980s. Initially, it was a tool for scholars at different universities to exchange cutting-edge research information. Even in the 1990s, the Internet was still a hand research tool for young people doing research reports. But increasingly the Internet has become a corporate advertising vehicle and a mindless tool for downloading untested information, pornographic pictures, and freebie music clips. None of this does much for literacy.

A nasty side effect of Web surfing and channel flipping is that today's young people are much less patient in seeking out information than we were. While I remember trekking to the library, going through spools of microfilm and stumbling along stacks of reference books to find information for school reports, the world is different for our children. A computer screen only holds about 150 words of text at most, about half a printed page, and can be skim-read in seconds. Students who are used to clicking from one skimmed page to the next, who say to teachers "I couldn't find anything" if the first twenty items of a Lycos search came up useless, haven't learned how to probe for more information. Or worse, they may assume that something "published" on the Web has some kind of authority. In short, computers and the Web can lead to a kind of intellectual laziness that does nothing for higher-level literacy skills.

• The literacy gap between the haves and have-nots is growing. Just as tax changes at the end of the last century made the rich richer and left the poor just scraping by, so family and technology changes are benefiting children of the upper and middle classes and leaving disadvantaged children behind. While many kids are supported at home by parents who read to them and have access to everything from educational videos to computer programs to boost reading schools, other children still enter school without ever having held a real book. Despite massive efforts ranging from Head Start to Title 1, school alone is not sufficient to bridge the gap. It is not hours in school, or mandatory summer school, or the nature of school programs that determines important literacy outcomes. It's the attitude that kids have toward reading and school—and that attitude develops at home.

Denny Taylor in *Family Literacy* states the sad truth: "Literacy transmission is highly dependent on the childhood experience of parents . . . and evolves only when the parent is intent on change." Too many parents are content to let the schools do it all—and too many schools are boastful enough to think that they, alone, can do the job.

• Unfortunately, computers don't teach kids reading. We've had computers in the classrooms for over fifteen years now, long enough for research to tell us what they can do and what they can't. The good news is that computers are useful tools for math and they tend to increase both the amount that kids write and the quality of that writing. The bad news is that the first ten years of computers in the classroom has failed to produce one unbiased study where computers actually improved tested reading scores.

The newer programs, of course, are more sophisticated than those in the past and research on them hasn't been done yet, but there's no reason to expect that they'll prove any more effective than previous mechanical and computerized means to improve reading. Reading is ultimately a people skill—it requires committed teachers, caring parents, and dedicated volunteers. Learning to love reading requires books in the classroom, books at home, and access to well-stocked libraries. A slick computer program just won't do the job.

Somebody should tell our legislators. They're putting billions of dollars into computers across North America under the mistaken belief that this will somehow boost all sorts of skills. Sorry, folks, but there's no evidence yet to expect that to happen in reading. Why not put some of that money into Reading Recovery, or smaller classes at the primary level, or more library books, or special help for disadvantaged kids? These programs have been shown to work and they involve real people—adults helping kids. Such effective literacy programming isn't high tech, but the reading payoff is huge.

ADULT ILLITERACY

We all like to think that ours is a literate country, that everyone is outfitted with the skills he or she needs to read a newspaper or fill out an income tax return. But the truth is much sadder than that:

- Sixty million Americans have problems with literacy that interfere with their jobs and their personal lives.
- Twenty-five million Americans cannot read the poison labels on a bottle.
- A million teenage children cannot read above the third-grade level.
- The United States ranks only 49 among 158 member nations of the U.N. in its level of literacy.
- Direct costs to business and taxpayers from illiteracy are in excess of $30 billion a year.

After hundreds of years of effort, the goal of universal literacy has still not been achieved. We manage to get children started reading and through most of the basics by third grade, then we collectively look the other way as the fourth-grade slump strands some readers with minimal skill levels, and we merely shake our heads as ninth-grade boredom maroons others in an aliterate world of television, videos, and Walkmans. It is not until these lost students reach the world of work that we (especially employers) say, "The kid just can't read."

Large-scale measurement of literacy really goes back fifty years to World War II, when incoming recruits had to be sorted on the basis of their abilities. One of the tests involved reading short passages of prose and then answering "comprehension" questions set in a multiple-choice format. The results from these

Literacy   and   Young   Adults

When the National Assessment of Educational Progress
(NAEP) studied the literacy abilities of young Americans
age twenty-one to twenty-five, the results were mixed.
The ensuing report, *Literacy Profiles of America's Young
Adults*, offers good news and bad news.

The good news: "Illiteracy is not a problem. . . ." The
report takes pride in the fact that 95 percent of the young
people can "understand" the printed word. The most
serious illiteracy does not afflict young people (though 85
percent of juveniles who end up in court are functionally
illiterate), but those who are middle-aged and older.

The bad news: "Literacy *is* a problem. . . ." Less than 20
percent of young Americans have literacy skills that
permit them to read and understand complex material.
Only 20 percent of the sample could fully understand a
set of everyday documents, graphs, and tables. Only 9
percent of the sample achieved the highest level
(375/500) on prose comprehension. The highest level, of
course, means the ability to read, respond, manipulate, and
synthesize what's been read. But shouldn't this be
expected of *all* our high school and college graduates?

tests provided a statistical breakdown of the reading abilities of
millions of men in the 1940s. Obviously, those scoring at the
low end were much more likely to end up on the front lines
than in officer training school, and reading skills have continued
to be used as a kind of social filtering system ever since.

The problem with this sort of measurement is that it handles
only one kind of literacy: reading and deciphering short passages.

It ignores what is sometimes called "functional literacy," the ability to read bus schedules or nutritional information on cereal boxes. And it overlooks "cultural literacy," a background of information that will enhance the reading of Dickens or an understanding of how Congress actually works. As members of the public, we have been so deluged with numbers and expectations about literacy that many of us ignore the real problem.

But there *is* a real problem. Within your family, or near you at work, or in your network of friends, there is at least one adult who is illiterate. I came across that statement during the 1990 International Year of Literacy and scoffed at it. The statistics may say that 20 percent of Americans are virtually illiterate, but surely I did not know any.

I was wrong. Some weeks later I wrote a note for our new housekeeper, a delightful woman who not only cleans the house but looks after everything from laundry to houseplants to gardening. My note was pretty simple: "Can we switch next week? Can you come Thursday instead of Tuesday? New vacuum cleaner bags are in the second-floor closet."

I'll admit the note was not highly logical, and my printing is a bit rough, but the message was simple. At least, I thought it was simple.

"Paul," my wife said that night, "I think we'd better *talk* to Mrs. B. when we want to change our schedule."

"Why's that?"

"She couldn't read your note," Gale explained. "First she tried to call her daughter—"

"What?"

"She tried to call her daughter to help her read it, but there was no answer, so she called me at work."

"You're kidding."

"And I didn't know what the note was about, so I asked her

Illiteracy Isn't Even-handed

Illiteracy, like crime, isn't everyone's problem. A wealthy suburban family doesn't have to worry much that *their* children will fall into the lowest percentile groups; but a single mother living in the inner city has every reason to worry for her children—and herself. As Jonathan Kozol points out in his book *Illiterate America:*

- While 16 percent of white adults are functionally illiterate, that figure grows to 44 percent for blacks and 56 percent for Hispanics.
- Functional illiteracy for black teenagers is getting *worse*, not better—47 percent were functionally illiterate in 1984. Today the figure is over 50 percent.
- Fifteen percent of the recent graduates of inner-city high schools read at less than the sixth-grade level.
- In Boston, where 40 percent of the adult population is illiterate, the largest literacy program reaches only 700 to 1,000 people.
- Combined literacy programs from all levels of government reach less than 4 percent of the illiterate population.

to read it over the phone. I thought that maybe you weren't very clear and it needed explaining. But it wasn't what you wrote. It's that Mrs. B. can't read. She got some of the words, but others she had to spell out to me. She was trying so hard, Paul. She wanted to be sure she got the message right."

Illiteracy isn't a problem that is out there somewhere. It is in your own house, or at your grandmother's, or around the corner.

Illiteracy isn't obvious. Those who are afflicted by it have developed coping skills to cover their inability to read. They manage to function in extraordinarily clever ways despite being cut off from the world of print. Yet illiteracy—the inability to read well enough to function in a print-oriented society—remains terribly widespread. We cannot simply pigeonhole illiteracy as a problem affecting the elderly, immigrants, or the poor. It cuts far more widely through the population. Its toll in human misery is enormous. And its cost to American business and society is estimated at more than $30 billion a year.

THERE ARE SOLUTIONS

Adult literacy programs are very different from the standard school approaches I described earlier in this book. For most adults, learning to read begins as a one-on-one experience with a volunteer tutor. As their skills increase, adult learners are grouped into small classes where they will likely find themselves writing a book about their own experiences, or creating a manual for new arrivals to America, or tutoring very young children in reading. Adult learners can make remarkable strides in reading very quickly because of their motivation and maturity. Often less than a year in a literacy program is sufficient to bring reading skills up to a "functional" level.

Unfortunately, the definition of what we might call "functional" keeps changing.

The literacy required by your child for the twenty-first century goes far beyond those elementary school skills I called "proficiency" in Chapter 9. True functional literacy today requires at least the skills of a teenage reader. A literate adult must have the ability to deal with difficult and complex documents, from

---

Community Literacy Programs

• Your local library. Many local libraries are centers for tutoring programs that pair up adult volunteers with adult learners who want to improve their reading. Such one-on-one private lessons offer an effective and confidential way to master reading skills.

• Local literacy councils. Many communities and some neighborhoods have a literacy council that offers classes, tutoring, and special programs. These councils have few paid employees but many dedicated volunteers who work with adult learners. Check the yellow pages under "Literacy Courses."

• Your school board. For adults who can read but want to read better, many schools offer night classes in Adult Basic Education and English for New Americans. These courses work best for those already literate but weak in English or those with third-grade reading skills who want to improve. Classes are small but, unlike the programs above, lessons are still done in class groupings.

---

credit card applications to income tax forms. A literate adult must have the capacity to apply his own purposes to the print, to find what's important in that twenty-page memo, or to know where to look in the phone book for the Department of Environment. A literate adult should have the ability to analyze what he reads, to question bogus surveys or outrageous claims in advertising. To maintain and develop these skills, an adult must keep on reading.

For the past thirty years, the biggest literacy issue has not been one of declining reading skills, it's been declining reading *attitude*. As leisure time has shrunk and television watching ballooned, the time available for reading has certainly grown smaller. That's understandable and regrettable, but it's only a symptom, not the problem. The real problem, as I see it, is that we are losing the active stance of the reader and replacing it with the passive stance of the viewer.

Bookstore owner Bryan Prince has an exercise that quickly demonstrates what I mean. The next time you sit down to read a

---

Literacy Help Nationwide

- National Literacy Hotline 800–228–8813
  The National Literacy Hotline provides information on community literacy programs for adults who might be interested either as students or as volunteer tutors.

- Laubach Literacy
  This is the largest, nationwide literacy organization. Laubach has trained thousands of volunteers and created Laubach Literacy Councils in many communities across the United States. Their philosophy is a good one: "Each one teach one." While their method uses traditional skill-centered workbooks, it does work. For more information, write:

  Laubach Literacy International
  1320 Jamesville Avenue
  P.O. Box 131
  Syracuse, NY 13210

book or lengthy article for half an hour, keep a pad and pencil beside your chair. Whenever you stop reading to think, or respond, or even go back and reread a section, put a tick mark on the paper. After thirty minutes, you'll find your pad literally covered with tick marks, because reading is really about responding to print.

Now try the same procedure when you watch a half-hour television show. Whenever you stop viewing to think or respond, put a tick mark on the pad. The results will be very different: a handful of ticks, most often marked during the commercial breaks. The reason for this is fairly simple: Television is a medium that controls our time. The more effective a television show or video happens to be, the more it seizes the viewer and draws him into the time span of the program. Even with a VCR controller in hand, we are most unlikely to stop, to take time out, to think, to review, or to question our own responses.

These activities are precisely what make reading so valuable. As readers, we are busy interacting with the words in front of us, but we ultimately have control over our own time. We read enjoyable sections of books two and a half times more slowly than we read boring sections. We frequently stop reading to question, or reread for clarity, or speed-read to get to what we really want. Our stance as readers is active.

Our stance as viewers is what Witold Rybczynski calls "staring." We are virtually at the mercy of the screen until permission arrives, via commercials, to turn our attention elsewhere.

Pete Hamill, a New York writer, wrote a provocative article for *Esquire* about television viewing and other kinds of "staring." He describes his visit to a twenty-two-year-old crack cocaine addict in a welfare hotel. He was interviewing her about drugs, prostitution, and her own sad tale of squalor while the woman's two children sat watching television. They ignored both Hamill and their mother, transfixed by the screen.

Hamill walked back to his office, disturbed by the interview, the kids, his own indifference to their situation, and a question. Why does a country like the United States, with only 2 percent of the world's population, consume 65 percent of the world's illicit drugs? "Why do so many millions of Americans of all ages, races, and classes choose to spend all or part of their lives stupefied?"

Hamill found an answer on the street: a homeless man in a doorway, begging, and the *look* on the man's face. "I suddenly remembered the inert postures of the children in that welfare hotel and I thought: *television*."

Hamill's moment of insight is based on no research, no statistics, and no longitudinal studies. But I believe he has seen something very important—the way the passive stance of television viewing is changing our society. No population in history has been entertained twenty-three hours a week. No population has been given the message for more than three hours a day that life should be easy and based on satisfying consumer needs. We are the first such experimental group, and the most obvious result so far is that most of us read less than people did in the past.

Perhaps some of television's power can be overcome by teaching our young people to understand how the visual media affect them, as the proponents of "media literacy" in the schools suggest. Certainly, our children need to understand the commercial forces that shape the images they see and the techniques that make those images so effective. But media literacy comes too late for most children, and it is not sufficient. By the time our young people reach an age when they can understand

Twenty-five Books That Change Lives

The International Reading Association asked its members to submit the titles of one children's book and one adult book that had "made a difference" in their lives. Here are the top twenty-five titles:

The Adventures of Huckleberry Finn by Mark Twain
Atlas Shrugged by Ayn Rand
The Autobiography of Benjamin Franklin
The Autobiography of Malcolm X
The Bible
The Catcher in the Rye by J. D. Salinger
Charlotte's Web by E. B. White
Democracy in America by Alexis de Tocqueville
The Diary of a Young Girl by Anne Frank
Gone with the Wind by Margaret Mitchell
The Gulag Archipelago by Aleksandr Solzhenitsyn
Hiroshima by John Hersey
How to Win Friends and Influence People by Dale Carnegie
I, Claudius by Robert Graves
Invisible Man by Ralph Ellison
The Little Prince by Antoine de Saint-Exupéry
The Lord of the Rings by J. R. R. Tolkien
1984 by George Orwell
Roots by Alex Haley
The Secret Garden by Frances Hodgson Burnett
Silent Spring by Rachel Carson
To Kill a Mockingbird by Harper Lee
Treasure Island by Robert Louis Stevenson
Walden by Henry David Thoreau
War and Peace by Leo Tolstoy

analytically what television is doing to them, they will already have watched 300,000 commercials via the tube. They will already have been sold everything from breakfast cereals to electronic toys through commercials so slick that one fifteen-second "message" frequently costs more than an entire thirty-minute program. At that point, after they have been rendered passive consumers, our media educators will explain how this has been done to them.

A CALL FOR REAL LITERACY

What our children need is not just media literacy but *real* literacy. They need to be able to read, to respond to what they read, and to write down their own ideas. Literacy is, after all, a tool for defining, expanding, and seizing power for the self—not for melding the self in some collective mass of consumers.

Literacy, as a goal, is connected to eighteenth-century rationalism, the needs of democracy, and the transfer of power from elites to ordinary people. The visual media, as they currently exist in North America, are concerned with presenting images, selling products, and maintaining or enhancing the power of the establishment. Unlike the governments in Europe, which place the needs of public and educational broadcasting first, our governments have encouraged television networks and movie distribution systems that have no higher aim than making money for their owners.

In an ideal world, thoughtful films and television programs would take their place beside books as means of communicating with citizens. Each medium would do what it does best. Books would inspire dreams and explore ideas in detail. Films and television would use the strength of the visual image to make emotional statements and raise awareness of problems.

But ours is not an ideal world; it is increasingly a commercial one. The cost of media production is so incredibly high that many voices and opinions are excluded automatically. While a publisher can bring out an entire book for $25,000, a half hour of prime-time television costs $250,000 or more. A Hollywood feature can hardly be made for less than $10 million and often costs upward of $40 million. Independent filmmakers who shoot on shoestring budgets have difficulty getting general theatrical distribution,

---

A Manifesto for Literacy

Here's my dream for a program that might create a fully literate country, given ten years' effort:

1. Every American has a right to be able to read—and to have access to reasonably priced books, magazines, and newspapers.
2. Every school should have a library—with a trained librarian—which would lend books to kids and their families.
3. Every school should have a yearly book budget for each student at least equivalent to the price of a fancy pair of running shoes.
4. Every town of reasonable size should have a public library—which would also be the town's literacy center for adults who have trouble reading.
5. Library/literacy centers should be open as long as the local video stores. That means seven days a week, twelve hours a day for much of the country.
6. Literacy means reading. Therefore, no book, magazine, or newspaper should be taxed.

which is virtually controlled by Hollywood studios. Low-budget television programs end up with small viewerships, frequently on limited-audience stations—PBS and cable access channels.

So the images that dominate our visual media are effectively limited to the ones that serve those already with power. It was never the intention of those who control Hollywood movies or network television to have it any other way. Nor have our governments made demands that the visual media fulfill a broader mandate—to educate or inform or otherwise empower the viewer. Our politicians seem quite content with voters who evaluate them on images rather than policies, who see themselves first as consumers and only secondarily as citizens.

Until the visual media change their nature or become far more accessible than they currently are, we must continue to promote books and traditional literacy. Any failure to protect reading dooms the weakest segments of our society to marginalized lives. A study from 1977 found that 55 percent of children in families earning under $10,000 a year were functionally illiterate. I suspect that the rate of reading problems among the poor and disadvantaged hasn't changed much since then—but it must if we are to maintain any role at all in a restructured world. All the media literacy skills in the world won't help your son read a technical manual or your daughter write a letter to her member of Congress.

FOR THE NEW MILLENNIUM

Much of this discussion has focused on the importance of books to children and to society. But I suspect that the future is not so much in the book or the printed page, but in print itself.

One of the problems with books is that they are expensive.

A hardcover book, historians say, has cost roughly the same as a good dinner out for some 300 years. The only real cost breakthrough in publishing came with the development of the paperback book, with its cheap glued spine and pulp pages. We now have new classes of books, such as trade paperbacks like the one in your hands, that fall halfway between hardcover and mass-market paperbacks. While there have been some attempts to cut the costs of producing a book—the "perfect" binding, computerized typesetting, simultaneous printing of hardcover and trade paperbacks—books remain quite expensive for large portions of the population. For this book to reach the parents of children in low-income families, it should be cheaper than a pack of cigarettes. But that's impossible with current technology.

While book prices have remained relatively stable, the prices for other kinds of information technology are rapidly shrinking. My family's first Philco television cost two months of my father's salary. Now a little black-and-white portable costs less than an average day's pay. The cost of renting a videotape at our local store has gone down from $5.99 to $0.99 over the past five years. The computer I worked on in high school, which took up two classrooms, can now be replicated in one microscopic dot on one section of a computer chip. Computer memory costs are declining by a factor of 1,000 every five years.

Yet I say that the future is still in print. Probably print on a computer screen, but definitely print.

My stepdaughter, a graduate student in psychology in Minneapolis, has to read a great deal—and much of that reading is from a computer screen. My older two sons, both in engineering, probably spend as much time studying screens as books. They're all still reading, but the print has moved off paper and onto phosphor or LCD displays.

In a charming and ironic way, the computer even has re-

The Cost of a Book: Where Your Twenty Dollars Goes

• Bookstore: $8.00. When the store purchases a book from the publisher or wholesaler, it receives a discount that runs from 38 to 48 percent.
• Printing and typesetting: $4.00. Costs vary widely depending on paper quality and the expense of the cover.
• Binding: $1.50. The "perfect" binding used for paperbacks and many hardcover books is basically just glue. The old sewn binding would triple this cost.
• Editorial work: 50 cents. A book usually has a substantive editor who calls for major changes and a copy editor to correct spelling and grammar.
• Publisher overhead: $2.60. Advertising, warehousing, copies to reviewers, salaries for staff.
• Mailing, shipping: $1.00.
• Author royalty: $1.60. The standard paperback rate is 8 percent; hardcover books pay 10 percent to the author. Most authors receive an "advance" against future royalties, frequently larger than what the book will actually earn.
• Profit: 80 cents. Three out of four books lose money for their publishers.

stored one nineteenth-century skill: letter writing. Most adults of my generation have written perhaps a few hundred letters in our lives. But more and more of us are plugged into computer networks that send and receive electronic mail at a staggering rate.

All of this still requires reading—often reading at great speed as information scrolls on the screen. It still requires the skills of analysis, response, and interaction that are the touch-stones of any real literacy. Computers, ironically, are not making skills in reading and writing any less necessary. They are making them more essential.

In the century ahead, I do not fear for literacy, which will certainly survive for the educated elite. My fear is that real literacy will be the preserve of only a few, while many others will lapse into a passivity that saps their economic and political strength. As parents, we can't allow this to happen. Reading—real literacy—should be a birthright for *all* our children.

Chapter 1

For a history of language, try Robert McCrum's *The Story of English* (revised edition, Penguin, 1999). A literary history of reading itself is in Alberto Manguel's wonderful *A History of Reading* (Viking Penguin, 1996).

The strongest proponent of reading out loud to children is a former newsman named Jim Trelease, whose *The Read-Aloud Handbook* (4th edition, Penguin, 1995) provides a bibliography of many excellent read-aloud books for young children. Basic principles of encouraging reading can be found in an inexpensive, 1990 booklet by Nancy Roser, *Helping Your Child Become a Reader* (International Reading Association, 800 Barksdale Road, P.O. Box 8139, Newark, DE 19714). Much work on the development of reading skills can be found in Jeanne Chall's *Stages of Reading Development* (McGraw-Hill, 1983). Caroline Snow's study of parents, families, and reading is called *Unfulfilled Expectations: Home and School Influences on Literacy* (Harvard University Press, 1990). The National Assessment of Educational Progress (NAEP) is ongoing and reports yearly.

Chapter 2

Two of the best books on reading theory are Jeanne Chall's *Stages of Reading Development* (McGraw-Hill, 1983) and Frank

Smith's *Understanding Reading* (Holt, Rinehart and Winston, 1978, 1982). The two conflicting theories on reading could be called instructional versus psycholinguistic rather than "phonics" versus "whole language." Chall still favors systematic instruction in *The Reading Crisis: Why Poor Children Fall Behind* (Harvard University Press, 1990), supported by a number of researchers, including George Spache in *Good Reading for Poor Readers* (Garrard, 1964, 1966, 1974). Frank Smith is joined with other important psycholinguists including the Goodmans: Kenneth Goodman, *The Psycholinguistic Nature of the Reading Process* (Wayne State, 1968), and Yetta Goodman, ed., *How Children Construct Literacy* (International Reading Association, 1990). Ken Goodman's latest book *In Defense of Good Teaching* (Stenhouse, 1998) looks at the "reading wars" from his side.

The strongest argument for simple phonics is still Rudolf Flesch's *Why Johnny Still Can't Read* (Harper & Row, 1981), the follow-up to his 1955 classic, *Why Can't Johnny Read?* Sylvia Ashton Warner's *Teacher* (Simon & Schuster, 1963) discusses her experiences teaching Maori children. Tololwa Mollel's *The Orphan Boy* is an Oxford University Press (1990) publication, with illustrations by Paul Morin.

Chapter 3

The issue of phonemic awareness and the importance of phonological discrimination was brought to the reading community's attention by Marilyn Adams in *Beginning to Read: Thinking and Learning about Print* (MIT Press, 1990), though the actual research was done by many people. The fourth-grade reading slump was identified by the late Dr. Jeanne Chall in a number of books and articles, especially *The Reading Crisis: Why Poor Children Fall Behind* (Harvard, 1991). The long-term effects of early reading problems are effectively spelled out in Keith Stanovich's "The Matthew Effect," *Reading Research Quarterly* 21 (1986): 360–406. The problem of teenage book boredom has long been a concern. Even G. Robert Carlsen's *Books and the Teenage Reader* (Bantam, 1967) included a discussion, but his book is out of print and little serious research seems to be ongoing in this area.

Determining the reading difficulty of texts is a whole academic industry. The simplest approach is the Fry Graph (first published by Dr. Edward Fry in *The Journal of Reading* in 1968 but frequently and freely reproduced elsewhere). Beverley Zakaluk and Jay Samuels's *Readability: Its Past, Present and Future* (International Reading Association, 1988) covers many other approaches to the topic.

Chapter 4

Jeanne Chall's *The Reading Crisis* offers a good discussion in chapter 7 of effective schooling. The most important book on the effective schools movement is James Slezak's *Odyssey to Excellence* (Merrit, 1984). The first chapter of Hedley Beare et al., *Creating an Excellent School* (Routledge, 1989), offers a good international overview of the same material.

The International Reading Association has a new book, *Families at School: A Handbook for Parents* (International Reading Association, 1999) with information about literacy programs at school and games to play at home.

Chapter 5

There is much good advice about reading with young children in the National Research Council's *Starting Out Right* (National

Academy Press, 1999). I'm less enthusiastic about Susan Hall et al. and *Straight Talk About Reading: How Parents Can Make a Difference in the Early Years* (Contemporary, 1998).

Marcia Baghban's study is *Our Daughter Learns to Read and Write* (International Reading Association, 1984). The importance of parental involvement in early reading is supported in many studies, including Jodi Grant and Carol Brown's "Precocious Readers: A Comparative Study of Early Reading, *Alberta Journal of Educational Research* 32(3) (1986): 223–233, and William F. White's "Perception of Home Environment and School Abilities as Predictors of Reading Power and School Achievements," *Perceptual and Motor Skills* 62(3) (1986): 819–822.

Two good scholarly books offer insight into how children's books enrich the lives of kids. Ellen Handler Spitz's *Inside Picture Books* (Yale University Press, 1999) does a close reading of both illustrations and text. Sheldon Cashdan's *The Witch Must Die: How Fairy Tales Shape Our Lives* (Basic, 1999) takes up where Bruno Bettelheim's *Uses of Enchantment* left off, looking for hidden meanings in the classic fairy tales.

Chapter 6

Marilyn Adams and her colleagues deserve credit for the research which brought attention to "phonemic awareness," though she prefers the phrase "phonological awareness" in *Beginning to Read: Thinking and Learning about Print* (MIT Press, 1990). Adams, Barbara Foorman, et al., have more recently done a book for teachers, *Phonemic Awareness in Young Children: A Classroom Curriculum* (Brookes, 1998). Wiley Blevins has created a cute paperback called *Phonemic Awareness Activities for Early Reading Success* (Scholastic, 1997). Earlier work by Marie

Clay in New Zealand showed that young children could handle letter recognition and word matching, and she coined the phrase "emergent literacy" to describe this period. See her *The Early Detection of Reading Difficulty* (Heinemann, 1985). Other research work by Teale and Sulzby *(Emergent Literacy: Writing and Reading*, Ablex, 1986), along with recent studies in California and Texas have reinforced the importance of this stage in reading development.

The Russian psychologist Lev Vygotsky showed how children learned through play, and gave us the phrase "zone of proximal development" to indicate just how much difficulty children can handle (see Hiebert and Raphael, *Early Literacy Instruction*, Harcourt, 1998). The International Reading Association (IRA) has been busy issuing position papers on the phonemics and phonics issues; these are interesting documents: *Phonemic Awareness and the Teaching of Reading* (IRA, 1998) and *The Role of Phonics in Reading Instruction* (IRA, 1997).

Chapter 7

For parents of beginning readers, there's much good advice and some excellent reading games in the *Reading Is Fundamental Guide* (Doubleday, 1987). The warning on ruling television is again based upon research by Caroline Snow. Frank Smith's *Reading Without Nonsense* (Teacher's College Press, 1986) offers solid theory. *Teacher* magazine devoted a whole issue to whole language: *Teacher*, August 1991.

The encyclopedic *New York Times Guide to the Best Books for Children* by Eden Ross Lipson (Random House, 1991) has synopses of 1,700 children's books. Donald R. Stoll's bibliography *Magazines for Children* (1990) is available from the International Reading Association.

Chapters 8 and 9

Again, Jeanne Chall's *Stages of Reading Development* (McGraw-Hill, 1983) is excellent in describing expectations by grade level. Michele Landsberg's *Guide to Children's Books* (Penguin, 1986) raises the issue of using boredom to further a child's reading and surveys many children's books as well. A book primarily for librarians by Joanne Oppenheim et al., *Choosing Books for Kids* (Ballantine, 1986), reviews 1,200 books for children under age twelve.

Chapter 10

Speed-reading is handled by many popular books; I like Robert Zorn's *Speed Reading* (HarperCollins, 1991), though he still thinks eye regression is a bad thing.

Chapter 11

Robert MacNeil's *Wordstruck* (Penguin, 1989) is worth reading just for the language. Mortimer Adler's *How to Read a Book* (Simon & Schuster, 1967, 1972) is now a classic. Joseph Gold's *Read for Your Life* (Fitzhenry and Whiteside, 1990) offers insight into the psychology of reading. His discussion of bibliotherapy is quite fascinating. Victor Nell's *Lost in a Book: The Psychology of Reading for Pleasure* (Yale, 1988) is intelligent but quirky in both its experiments and concepts. Witold Rybczynski's book *Waiting for the Weekend* (Viking, 1991) has much to say on reading and leisure time.

Chapter 12

Kenneth McLeish's *Bloomsbury Good Reading Guide* (Bloomsbury, 1988) suggests many teenage and adult books with an interesting approach: Look up an author you like and the *Good Reading Guide* will suggest a half-dozen other books you'll probably enjoy. M. H. Zool's *Good Reading Guide to Science Fiction and Fantasy* (Bloomsbury, 1989) does the same for those genres. Some CD-ROM programs do all this electronically.

Chapter 13

There is still much basic information in George D. Spache's *Diagnosing and Correcting Reading Disabilities* (Allyn & Bacon, 1976) on reading problems and testing procedures. Lee Cronbach's *Essentials of Psychological Testing* (Harper & Row, 1984) is the basic reference volume on testing. Readability in many languages is explained in *Readability: Its Past, Present and Future*, edited by Beverly Zakaluk and S. J. Samuels (International Reading Association, 1988). Learning styles can be found explained in Bernice McCarthy's *4-Mat System: Teaching to Learning Styles With Right/Left Mode Techniques* (Excel Inc., 1980). Teachers will be interested in the bibliography *Easy Reading* by Randall Ryder and Bonnie and Michael Graves (International Reading Association, 1989).

Chapter 14

A good overview of gifted education around the world is in Kurt Heller's *Identifying and Nurturing the Gifted: An International Perspective* (Hans Huber, 1986). Thomas Southern and Eric Jones have edited *The Academic Acceleration of Gifted Children*

(Columbia, 1991), which considers the pros and cons of various programs. For teachers, Jeanette Parker's *Instructional Strategies for Teaching the Gifted* (Allyn & Bacon, 1989) offers many clever, workable ideas. Mildred and Victor Goertzel's *Cradles of Eminence* (Little, Brown, 1962) offers life stories of 400 gifted persons. One of the best general books for parents is *Your Gifted Child* by Joan Smutney and Kathleen and Stephen Veenker (Oxford, 1989).

Chapter 15

Most of the books on computers and literacy or computer-assisted instruction (CAI) are outdated as soon as they get in print. Jean Marie Casey's *Early Literacy: the Empowerment of Technology* (Libraries Unlimited, 1997) is quite upbeat about the effects of computers. So is *Learning to Read in the Computer Age* by Anne Meyer et al. (Brookline, 1999). Reports from teachers in the trenches are less so. Gail Tillman's M.A. thesis (ERIC microfiche, 1995) does a good research survey, but is really remarkable for its honesty on what computers can and can't do for reading.

The strongest book on America's literacy problem is Jonathan Kozol's *Illiterate America* (NAL, 1985). More scholarly, but equally fascinating, is Denny Taylor's *Family Literacy* (Heinemann, 1983). Some of the statistics in this chapter are from the National Assessment of Educational Progress's *Literacy Profiles of America's Young Adults* (Educational Testing Service).

In addition to teaching reading for twenty years, Paul Kropp is the author of four novels for young adults and a highly recommended series of books for reluctant readers. He was born in Buffalo, New York, received his B.A. from Columbia University, and earned his teaching credentials and M.A. degree in Canada. Paul Kropp speaks regularly to parents, teachers, and librarians about reading and is featured in a series of "One-Minute Reading Solutions" spot announcements currently appearing on educational television.